Dr A.M OBOTE PALM PRINTS

Jack Stevens Alecho-oita

'African Historical Presence: Reminiscences on Dr Apollo Milton Obote of Uganda'

Publisher: Alawi Books Ltd

'African Historical Presence: Reminiscences of Dr Apollo Milton Obote of Uganda' - Copyright © Alawi Books.

All rights reserved. This book or any portion thereof may not be reproduced or used in any manner whatsoever without the express written permission of the publisher except for the use of brief quotations in a book review.

Book - ISBN 978-0-9929462-4-1

Publisher:
Alawi Books ltd
125 Second Avenue
Manor Park
London E12 6EN

Website at:
www.tboah.com

Contacts:
email: info@tboah.com
tel: [+44] 07983412790

Ordering information:

'African Historical Presence: Reminiscences of Dr Apollo Milton Obote of Uganda' is available as a hard copy from Amazon Books website:..www.amazon.co.uk

Cover design, Layout and Illustrations: Jack Stevens Alecho-oita

Published by Alawi Books Ltd.
125 Second Avenue, Manor Park, London, E12 6EN.
Copyright©Alawi Books Ltd. 2014.

Dedication

This book is dedicated to all who, through their political beliefs, have variously struggled to improve the quality of life of the different nationalities of Uganda. This que is taken from my father Israel Ochwo Alecho (RIP) and mother Besimesi Nyafwono Alecho, who were variously involved. Without overstating, it's in the memory of Dr A.M. Obote whose steadfast support to our family, after the passing away of my father, enabled me my 3 brothers, and 2 sisters to stay afloat and succeed in improving our quality of life. Alongside was our guardian, Augustine Ochieng-Alecho (RIP) who sacrificed his all to make sure we did not live in want; and Mr. Balaki Keba Kirya (RIP) who was standing there at different corners to signpost us to safety.

CONTENTS

Dedication 3
CONTENTS 4
Glossary 6
FOREWORD 7
EXECUTIVE SUMMARY 14
PART I: 1960- THE WEIGHTS ON MILTON OBOTE'S SHOULDERS. 19
    Man With A Warning Shadow 23
    Uganda's Prime Minister Obote 25
    Uganda's New Leader Sees Unity As First Aim 29
    Mr. Obote's Success As Master Of The Party Management 32
    What Is Kabaka Yekka? 35
    Uganda Independence Conference: 38
    Milton Obote's 1962 Uganda Independence Speech 42
    Uganda's Prime Minister Moves To The Front Rank 44
    East Africa Talks On The Six -Uganda Distaste For Associate Role . 47
    Mr. Obote's Soft Spot For "Imperialist" 49
    Uganda And The Federation 53
    Dangerous Mixture 55
    Pressure In Kenya 56
    Premier Stresses End To "Slavery" 58
    Obote's Address "Progress Through Co-Operation" Conference 60
    Dr. Obote On "Africa's Greatest Danger" 63
    Post-Independence Problems In Africa 69
PART II: 1966 - WEIGHTS ON DR OBOTE'S NAPE 74
    Private And Confidential 77
    Dr. Obote Takes Full Powers In Uganda - Five Ministers Arrested . 79
    Our Commonwealth Staff Writes:- 80
    Declaration By The Government 81
    1st Cabinet Ministers Under The Republican Constitution 83
    Foreign Plot Charge By Obote 84
    Dr Obote Suspends Constitution 86
    Declaration By The Government 88
    Dr. Obote Accuses President 89
    Uganda's New President 90
    Kabaka Escapes When Palace Is Attacked By Obote Troops. 93
    Dr. Obote Resourceful Rebel 104
    Press Release: 106

The President Appoints..108
PART III: 1971 - THE WEIGHT ON Dr OBOTE'S RIGHT SHOULDER....113
    Dr. Obote Says He Will Return To Power Without An Invasion. ...116
    Uganda - A Nasty Story 119
    Uganda: Amin's Denial Of Any Invasion Plans 121
    Tanzanian Comment On Threat Of Invasion..........................124
    1979 Statement On The Uganda Situation By A. Milton Obote 126
    The Situation In Uganda..142
PART IV: 1981 - THE WEIGHT ON DR OBOTE'S LEFT SHOULDER 146
    "Dp Strongholds Harbour Thugs" 151
    Obote Seeks Popular Support...156
    Rebels Report Killing 158
    ....In The Last Two Weeks; 159
    The Future Of Uganda 161
    Dear Mr. Hammarberge, ...164
    The Ministry Of Defence Announced 168
    Mercenary Coup Plan Frozen By Cash Shortage......................172
    Guerrillas Flee From Wrath Of Bush Women. 176
    And A Libyan Hand Over Uganda...180
    Terrorists Block Aid For Uganda Refugees............................182
    Dr. Runchie's Plea As Ugandans Are Butchered. 185
    Obote Wins Support Of Opponents 189
    Barracks And Prison Hit In Uganda Rebel Raid.....................192
    Uganda: Out Of Control 193
    "100 Killed" At Martyrs' Shrine In Uganda 194
    Uganda Killers "Are Disguised As Soldiers"............................197
    Rebels Claim Successes Against Uganda Army 200
    213 Soldiers 'Killed'..202
    British Policy In Uganda - 207
Part V: DR A.M. OBOTE'S SUMMATIONS. 250
    A. 1963 – Organisation Of African Unity (OAU) Inuagral Speech .250
    B. The Role Of The UPC In Uganda's Independence.................259
Epilogue 295
    My Last Words 295
Subject Index..298
Author's Profile 306

Glossary

DP – Democratic Party

UAU – Uganda African Union

UHCP – Uganda Hereditary Chieftainship Party

UPC – Uganda Peoples Congress

UPU – Uganda Peoples Union

UNC – Uganda National Congress

LegCo – Legislative Council

OAU - Organisation of African Unity

FOREWORD

It is no easy matter to context the role of the individual let alone, a historical personage in history.

Professor H. Butterfield once noted: There is something in the nature of historical events which twists the course of history in a direction that no man (historical player) ever intended it.

The Indian political economist Amit Bhaduri, in his essays on Indian political economy – 2009, at p.1 – also noted that:

> "...History is not merely unpredictable. It has almost a magical quality that takes at times bewilderingly strange turns..."

In the words of T.S. Eliot, "...*History has cunning passages...*" Along such passages, we might hope to travel in one direction, only to end travelling in the opposite direction and the irreversibility of time would prevent us from returning even to our initial position to correct the mistake.

Apollo Milton Obote's run in history is best visualized in the perspective of the historical context in which he lived and the unfolding of its histories.

Professor Geoffrey Till, a maritime historian, presents us with sobering observations. He notes that,

> "...The chief utility of history for analysis ... lies in its ability, not to point out lessons, but to isolate things that need thinking about. History provides insights and questions, not answers..."

Furthermore – that there is no denying that history warns, rather unsportingly, that major surprises occur. And because humans are active historical players, their beliefs about the future can function either as self-fulfilling or self-negating prophesies. The future is not out there; fixed, just waiting for the passage of time to see it unfold. Instead, the future remains to be made, to be constructed by people, including people in conflict, who strive to make a future they prefer. In his life of battles – this was, I dare submit, Milton Obote's subtle understanding of the flow of history in his homeland and Africa.

Variously, to a number of people, Obote, was Apollo, was Milton, was A.M. Obote, was Dr Obote, was Dr A.M. Obote, and today; the late Dr A.M. Obote. In this publication the hand '**Palm**' symbol or emblem of The Party - Uganda Peoples Congress is that of Obote. The Uganda Peoples Congress [UPC], hereafter, 'The Party', was a founding political party for the political independence of Uganda from British rule. The hand '**Palm**' is a symbol of 'The Party' and is always displayed alongside 'The Party's flag of Black, Red, and Blue. 'The Party' shares this symbolic identity with the Indian National Congress with which it developed friendly relations since its inception and formation.

To-date, since Milton Obote's appearance on the Ugandan political stage and the subsequent founding of 'The Party', I have not come across any counter claim or claims to this symbol or emblem of The Party by any other political party or leadership.

I am suggesting that Milton Obote's symbolic '**Palm**' as much as it became a symbol of 'The Party' touched many, changed many and affected many, in different ways, publicly and privately. In these facets some individuals have used the effect of the '**Palm**' positively – to do good things in general - and in some cases in particular; similarly in the negative to do bad things generally such as those that rub a whole nation the wrong way, and attempt to harm the party by falsely generating against it a myriad of accusations. All these we can live with because that is what human beings are prone to do. However, my discomfort is with those who 'sit on the right hand of the father' in judgement of others *ala 'personal merit'*, adulators *ala 'Sese Seko Kuku Ngbendu Wa Za Banga'* type, pretend to so pontificate and become unduly judgmental on everything UPC or Obote; the party symbol. This is largely the reason for scripting '**Dr Apollo Milton Obote's Palm Prints**'. However, the publication will not focus on negativities, but share related events and issues to immortalize the '**Palm**'.

Below, I use the metaphor of vehicle motoring gears to highlight the drive behind this publication and the historical context and meaning of the 'Palm Prints'.

First Gear: The excerpts assembled for this book are solely for purposes of the objective to highlight the import of the 'Palm' in the local and international context.

Second Gear: Is driven by revulsion of the absurd claims by those who have scripted some biographies of A.M. Obote under the rubric of claimed definitive knowledge. Dr. Obote was a public person, viewed differently by different people who have made various analyses. More so there are those who have authoritative information which they either were unable to share or have meant to run down and demonise Obote. Others are by self-appointed gurus making claims of *'owning and shaping Obote'* as to who he eventually became, which claims they present to the world at large. Bolted on these are self-appointed defenders of Obote from his critics who in effect may be, ala *'men of substances with final vocabulary,' 'thiefing'* from the radiance of his 'Palm Prints'. The records of these positions are sprinkled in various phases as demarcated in this publication. These different perspectives drove all sorts of wedges between pro-Obote and anti-Obote groupings. Often gaps widened when roles reversed, or positions changed, or when Obote changed 'gears', i.e. when his position changed. The one example, among many, was the episode on the re-engineering or reshaping of independence to meet the nationalist demands after independence that led to the famous fallout with Prof Ali Mazrui, then teaching political science at Makerere University, and newspaper publisher, Rajat Neogy, and their then publication Transition.

Third Gear: Is driven by those hurt by the vilifications of A. M. Obote; yet cannot publicly debunk or disassociate themselves from the vicious attacks because they cannot publicly share the story of their private benefit from Milton Obote's 'Palm', which he extended out-of-sight or knowledge of the vilifiers. Here I cite a Ganda lady friend 'DM'; I quote:

> '...we also became people...'

'DM' elaborated

> '...it was Mr. Obote's own hand ... [that] bought the taxicab that my father used, to ensure our domestic wellbeing and ... my eventual coming to the United Kingdom for education...'

Years later, I had the opportunity of meeting 'DM's' father on his visit to London in 2012 at a Ganda Sunday Pentecostal Church Service at Waterloo. While being introduced and while shaking his hand I muttered in Ganda language something like '... *nsuse nyo okulamusa* ...' which translates to read '... *am extremely privileged to meet and greet you* ...' From my voice intonation and pronunciation, he must have sensed that I was not of Ganda nationality, but I had a good go at it with all the humility deserving. Here is one Ganda family that made good from Obote's 'palm'.

Another example is that of a Ganda family who had lost their loved one in 1962. With Abu Mayanja and his connections in tow, Obote privately met and helped this family with financial and burial expenses. In their presence, in the heat of the emotions and commiserations, Obote, said that;

> '...he [the deceased, that is] must have been a good Muganda...'

My meek observation is that Obote's choice of word given he was a non-Ganda was unfortunate.

Much later after his political fallout with Obote (to be addressed in a different publication), Abu Mayanja was to paraphrase and re-engineer the famous and oft repeated statement; to quote,

> "...*Obote says a good Muganda is a dead one*..."

This was generally believed, given the then public knowledge of the political closeness between Abu Mayanja and Obote. With the hindsight of a sound-bite-age, '...*a good Muganda is a dead one*...' was devastating and effective in trashing the relationship between the Ganda and Obote in particular and with non-Ganda generally, in the habitat of Uganda.

The family affected or offended did not or could not drag private grief into the public arena by denouncing a fellow Ganda, especially given the power distance between them and Abu Mayanja. Obote never contradicted that imputation by Abu Mayanja, who never identified the offended family or offered them a public apology. This Ganda family lived with the hurt caused to Obote. Given the power distance between them and Obote, bridged and destroyed by Abu Mayanja, they could do nothing. The Ganda as a people nurse this injury oft repeated despite being unfounded or based on false premises.

My Ganda friends born long after this betrayal by Abu Mayanja, use this phrase in jest unconscious of the fact that a Ganda family was injured and suffered more in their silence than Obote.

Fourth Gear: Is driven by those who did not wish Milton Obote well and by public display of merriment to his political misfortunes unknowingly hurt their loved ones or those closest to them. Here, I recall 'T' a friend of mine from Kigezi, Western Uganda, who was married to a girl in the same neighbourhood.

In 1986, after the second overthrow of Milton Obote's elected government, and 'T's friend, Gen Amos Kaguta Museveni, had ascended to the apex of political power in Uganda; my friend 'T' and his family went home to their Kigezi homes to celebrate this event. On reaching the gate of his father-in-law's courtyard, the old man came to welcome them. However, the father-in-law stopped 'T' from entering the courtyard. The old man politely informed 'T' of his reasons in words phrased as follows:

> '...if I let you come in I do not know where you will sit as the furniture is Obote's....' and '...the food is Obote's...''.. This very courtyard and the house were built by Obote...' '...all the children in this home including your wife were educated by Obote....'; adding that '...You go away and come back to collect your wife and children when going back to Kampala...'

'T' joined his ancestors in 1990 as a result of alcohol poisoning.

The Overdrive: Is driven by the late Israel Ochwo Alecho, who was recalled by his ancestors in 1961. He was a personal and political friend of Milton Obote at the advent of building 'The Party', in Bukedi District, Eastern Uganda. A.M. Obote saw to it personally and supported by Messrs. Balaki Keba Kirya, Shafique Arrain, and Anil Clerk; that the widow, Mrs. Besimesi Nyafwono Ochwo-Alecho, and six children, namely the undersigned, Constance Tolofina Awino, Justine Stephen Alecho, Christine Tolofina Awino, Jeroham Stephen Alecho, Jesse Stephen Alecho would not and did not live in want in their life time. Of the named here, Balaki, Shafique, Anil, Christine, and Jeroham were also later recalled by the ancestors.

The ancestors know best why I have used this motor-engineering analogy and how it found its way in this book (May be, it's the engineer in me). Maybe it is a method of asserting the complex historical emergence of Obote on the Ugandan political scene, which in turn, attracted some international attention; both positive and negative, as evidenced in the newspaper excerpts and sampled reports highlighted in this book.

Milton Obote is now with his ancestors and all sorts of newspaper reports and private recorded exchanges from 1960 on or about his person too gather or have gathered dust in different archives in various places on this planet earth or are in the computer and cloud data banks of our times.

Given all the above, the nationalities of Uganda were bequeathed their country and habitats in trust for successive generations to come. Over the years they have never ceased to struggle or to relentlessly work hard to ensure that their progeny acquire tools for better decision making in the politics of their country and Africa. To this end, in my opinion, Milton Obote rose through the ranks to become an opinion maker, then opinion leader, and to live up to the expectation of the nationalities in the habitat that is today called Uganda. More so, I believe, Milton Obote vindicated himself and gave a good account to the nationalities for the tools he acquired for better decision-making, in more than one way.

I wish to humbly submit that this publication, recording the historical impact of Dr A.M. Obote's 'Palm Prints', is an effort towards accounting for the tools I have acquired to enable better decision making for our homeland. The Uganda political progeny and other readers too should benefit from the presented snapshots on Milton Obote and be able to continue with the good practices to make better decisions for African humanity both inside and outside our country.

Jack S Alecho-oita
London, United Kingdom
2014.

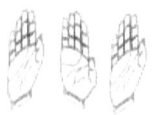

EXECUTIVE SUMMARY

The samples of newspaper reports and various records presented in this publication capture the sentiments about Milton Obote at each point in time. The writers or recorders expressed in writing what they felt they observed or knew at the time.

From 1960, the samples capture the formative years of Uganda attaining its political independence from Great Britain. Uganda fell under the category of a 'Protectorate', implying that the British found a fledgling collection of states and disparate political administrations that needed or could do with its protection as a world power. A.M. Obote laid out his case on the question of political independence for the country which the nationalities of Uganda enjoyed. He had an eye on both the British and the Ugandan political elite who would have to walk, the talk. I have depicted this as *'weight'* which was thrust on the neck of the person of A.M. Obote, to carry or to be strangled by it.

From 1966 – the *'weight'* on Obote's right shoulder became heavier threatening to crush him. A.M. Obote met the challenge head-on despite facing certain death '*...by a thousand cuts...*' None expected him to survive as evidenced by the collated documents from observers with more than an interest in his political and physical demise and his own testimonies during the period. In the effort to build a democratic Uganda, he failed to carry favour with the country's political classes and imperial interests outside Uganda. At some point in 1996 in London, the UK, when I was discussing this observation with 'Sir Neph' (Akena Adoko – Obote's first cousin) as he was referred to, he retorted

' *my friend, Milton felt that he had no problem with anybody but that it was up to the conscience of others if they felt they*

> had a problem with him. As far as Milton was concerned, he had the mandate of the voters...'

This was the actual divide between him and his erstwhile political opponents.

Here, I ruminate that the British who were aware of the difficulties he faced, did not lend a hand or signpost him as to the potential options, given their long experience in governance especially of the 'Protectorate'. The collated documents contain signature tunes or swan songs as to why A.M. Obote should fail and not why he should succeed. I came to this view after a private meeting in 1994, with a highly placed UK security officer who educated me on how the British deal with situations. He said; I quote:

> "...first we take note of you carefully
> "...second we observe what you are doing and assess the direction...
> "...third we conclude that we knew you would do it that way..."

He did not tell me what action they take though. In all probability this was a warning to me, I would imagine, after a close observation of my romantic antics with matters of politics. Arguably, it was also an insight into how the British dealt with democratic nationalist leaders in their former colonies like A.M. Obote. Obote at the time carried the burden of reshaping the dysfunctional political edifice they as a colonial power, had left in place at independence.

From 1971 – the **'weight'** A.M. Obote carried on his nape caused him to stumble. Obote was falsely buoyed by a combination of his confidence in his ability to weather and navigate through local and international political storms and the unassailability of the UPC on the Ugandan political landscape. This gave him the false confidence that the gathering storm of military overthrows of nationalist-centred/driven governments elsewhere in Africa would pass him by. My later years of political activism and association with Ugandan political luminaries and keen observers of its culture have made me review my feelings about what may have led to the stumble.

In 1979, in Kitgum to be exact, when then President Godfrey Binaisa was officially receiving and thanking the Save Uganda Movement's Kitgum Militia, I was seated with Dr Obyara Anyoti, then member of the Interim Parliament (the National Consultative Conference); later Minister of Information. We observed a retinue of cultural dances from both the Acholi and Lango peoples who hail from Northern Uganda. Dr Obyara-Anyoti turned to me and pointed out saying that just observe the Lango dance ritual and sequence

> '...you will see that they first of all sing and sing and sing ....after these are silent, ...then the drummers, the flute and sonnet players enter the arena to beat and beat and beat the drums followed by flutes and horns, etc., sequentially and in that order ... after those are silent ....THEN the dancers enter the arena to dance following the rhythm of all that had been sung and drummed and fluted...'

For a moment, I did not follow what Dr Anyoti Obyara was intimating or asserting but then he added:

> '...that is how the Lango people make decisions...'

I went silent, shocked and confused for some moments. I never did respond as to what was swirling in my mind. I can now share that, I thought that, this scenario probably explained how A.M. Obote, a national leader of Lango origin, processed his thoughts and made decisions!! May be the English saying '...*you can take a villager out of the village but cannot take the village out of a villager....*' captures this too. I am not saying A.M. Obote should have been *'dry-cleaned'* of Lango-ness or '...*the village taken out of him...*' as this most likely would have added to the difficulties in dealing with the weights on his nape.

From 1981 – the **'weight'** on Obote's left shoulder took its turn. This shoulder was now 54 years old and with a 20-year share of political buffeting. The now much older A.M. Obote dusted himself up and occupied the political stage for the political fight of his life. His clear and steadfast intention variously expressed in private and public sessions '...*to work for the common man and common woman...*' was undiminished. The fighting talk: '...*show me you commanders...*' and '*....people voted for me...*'; the embracing posture, '...*UPC everywhere...all of us UPC...*'; and the private admonishments, '...*this is the most democratic constitution in the world...*', '*....never say my people, you cannot own people...*','...*that sounds like tribalism to me, be careful...*'

I came to this 'weight-on-shoulder' analogy and the consequences of the political weights on A.M. Obote's shoulders in 1990 when I visited him in Lusaka, Zambia, where his old pal of the Mulungushi Club had offered him second round political solace and shelter. In a private meeting, he told me of his concern about his left shoulder which needed attention but did not explain to me the cause – say no more.

However, Dr Opiote, his personal and long-term physician, while escorting me back to my hotel surmised to me this nagging issue of his 'left shoulder' thus;

'...*your uncle spends a lot of writing hours in the privacy of his bedroom and while in bed...*'

Say no more.

This conversation with Dr Opiote, reminded me of a meal I had had years before in a Bombay Hotel, in India, with the Uganda High Commissioner to India then. I asked the waiter as to what meat was being served, as the menu only stated 'meat'. He duly went for the confirmation from the Chef who told him that it was cow meat. I then retorted:

"...*how come that you put cow meat on the menu since the cow is 'sacred'....*"

The waiter shot back, this time without recourse to the Chef;

'...*we had no choice but to kill it...*'

A.M. Obote had no more shoulder left to heave political weights on; and it was now the left shoulder he was crushing. As he was lying down on his left shoulder, I doubt if he was even conscious of the fact that this was the only shoulder left and he was thus party to crushing it. In any case, he had no choice left but to crush it. Throughout his political career in the service of the people of our country and Africa, Milton Obote was self-sacrificial.

A.M. Obote's political throws can be found in the documents assessing his tenure in the period and more so in the last document before the Epilogue, which in my view captures the weights he carried on his head/whole body. A.M. Obote's various writings are also sampled and those included in the highlighted phases are reflective of his various and separate tenures on the political stage.

I wish to restate or to assert 'ad nauseam' that, the mix of sampled records is exactly that: samples of records. This mix was collated, just as the samples were collectable and therefore cannot be said to be authoritative, but they are at least representative of what A.M. Obote was to the various interested parties who observed, interacted or communicated with him. Doubtless, they may contribute to appreciating Obote's 'Palm Prints'.

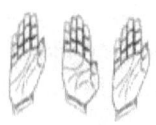

PART I

1960- THE WEIGHTS ON MILTON OBOTE'S SHOULDERS.

The collection of reminiscences and historical records here published are snippets of the challenges Milton Obote grappled with in the local and international political environment, in delivering political independence to Uganda, managing the multiple and diverse competing socio-economic and political needs and interests in the country until his exit from the political stage or theatre.

The published newspaper articles, private records shared here, and Obotes's own statements highlight the challenges faced by the first among equals in the Uganda political scene. Undoubtedly, Obote was never alone.

The challenges were like weight that Obote had to carry.

On his right shoulder were weights that the former colonials and his political opponents put. These waited to see him fail or worked to ensure that he failed.

Then on his neck were weights put by associates who fancied the position he occupied and waited for their chance.

On his left shoulder were weights hipped on him by the pressure from well-wishers and fanatics who wanted him to succeed at all cost.

Around Obote's neck were weights deposited by the Ugandan people who hung on every word from him directly or the words of observers who came from all sorts of places and had all sorts of reasons of their own.

Since these listeners or readers were not sophisticated

citizens they could not as such have been expected to be able to decipher subtle vilifications or to read intents or motives of the observers. They therefore were always unable to read or see coming dislocations and fallouts from the political upheavals that resulted from the negative words of observers. I dare add that, those who knew what they were writing about hid their intents quite well. And those who had the opportunity to help/guide Milton Obote to navigate the choppy/muddy political waters rather used their palms to close their eyes and block their ears.

The views held by my betters variously assert that the higher up the ladder of power one is, the higher is the *'benefit of the doubt'* one is given to deliver on the promises made. This confers good and honest intention on the part of the person in handling things or issues. It allows for slippages of time, mistake making, changing of mind, etc. It appears that from close reading of the texts of the various documents collated for the era 1960-1966, A.M. Obote did not or was not given the benefit of the doubt. I have however not come across any text that refers to 'A.M. Obote telling lies or lying'.

A.M. Obote took possession of the state and attendant instruments from foreign rule that lasted 60 years, with rudiments of induction - 6 months to be exact. The then new political leadership of the country had to take stock of the experience of the 60-year colonial rule within this short time.

Many argued that the British Governor baby-sat A.M. Obote and associated political luminaries, and therefore they should not have failed, except for their ineptness and/or the electorate choosing '...*unsuitable leaders*...' I read an authoritative write-up that referred to these categories of African leaders as '...*people who did not have a clear understanding of things*...' I have tried to unpack what this meant at the time, have shared the content of this text with other political readers, and am yet to have an informed opinion. What is at least clear is that the colonial rulers must have had a register of well-groomed opinion-makers who had a clear meeting of the minds with the colonial masters, and the A.M. Obote-types were not on that register. In a formal roll call at Whitehall, they would be marked – NOT PRESENT. Even if the A.M. Obote-type answered PRESENT SIR, the returns would show they were ticked as being NOT PRESENT. The tick I refer to here are those generated from the reports of embedded Fleet Street journalists, the briefs of intelligence agents, and the analyses of allied academics that informed the decisions made by the colonial authorities at Whitehall.

The Governor surely could not stick his neck out and risk a backlash from negative assessors in his backyard, that their assessments were wrong. The Governor had a career to save and livelihood to keep and A.M Obote failing would be '...*good for business.... we told you so...*'

Let me share the experience of a 'Mr. Wanda', an Airforce Officer, 1973-79, in the Amin regime who was working with the external opposition to oust Amin from power. 'Mr. Wanda' came over to Nairobi, Kenya, in 1975 to brief 'Owako' on the Save Uganda Movement [SUM] cell within the Airforce. 'Owako' who was commiserating with 'Mr. Wanda' on the challenges of working deep in the enemy territory asked him how he was fairing, to which 'Mr. Wanda' answered;

'...*we have learnt how to walk in muddy waters...*'

Well 'Owako' said no more.

It now dawns on me that this statement was an accurate depiction of the situation of all our people who were working from within the enemy ranks. It is now clear to me too that this is what must have been the experience of A.M. Obote in the 1960-66 era of his political life.

On the other hand, the collection of write-ups covering the period post-1960 may be best viewed as depicting Obote's early days of walking in muddy waters. Well, the weights he carried on his shoulders while walking in muddy waters must have surely given him a sinking feeling, yet he soldiered on. The expectations of the common man and woman in the country on him left him with little choice. Millions of them saw and regarded him as their own voice in their endless battles to keep soul and body together.

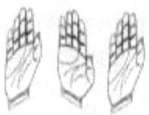

1. A NEW COMMONWEALTH, publication, December 1960 carried:

PROFILE

MAN WITH A WARNING SHADOW

Mr. Milton Obote

Head butting forward, teeth clamped on a curly briar pipe, eyes crinkled against the smoke, Apollo Milton Obote, leader of the Uganda People's Congress, waits for the question. "...*DOES YOUR PARTY BELIEVE THAT ELECTION SHOULD COME FIRST BEFORE ANY CONSTITUTIONAL DEVELOPMENT IS IMPLEMENTED?*..." asks a pressman. Mr. Obote's eyes twinkle. In contrast to his aggressive pose, his reply is a mild, almost chatty, appeal to reasonableness.

> "...*Of course the Uganda People's Congress would welcome an over-all agreement,...*" he says. "...*This would mean a united nationalist movement in Uganda. We are always ready to negotiate with anybody on the subject. But failure to reach an over-all agreement must not be allowed to stultify all political progress. We are due to have an elected legislature early next year. Nothing must be allowed to delay that...*"

Thus, Uganda's leading politician states his case in the battle against traditional tribal interests. A member of the Nilotic, non-monarchical Langi tribe of Northern Uganda, he is the bogey man of the Bantu Kingdoms. The hereditary rulers of the central and western Uganda see in him the shadow of Nkrumah and the shape of things to come.

Mr. Obote's rise has been rapid and, by Uganda's standards, solidly based. After an education at Busoga College, Mwiri and at Makerere University College, he went to Nairobi as an oil company employee. There he became an associate of Tom Mboya and learned a lot about political in-fighting. In 1957 he returned to Uganda, took over the Lango Branch of the Uganda National Congress and was returned to the Legislative Council as Lango representative in the 1958 elections.

In 1959, after a bitter dispute with the U.N.C. Chairman, Joseph Kiwanuka, Milton Obote led his supporters and a rebel group of the U.N.C. executive to form a splinter party which later merged with the Uganda people's Union to form the Uganda People's Congress, holding 12 of the 13 elected seats in the Legislative Council. Mr. Obote was elected President of the U.P.C.

As a member of the Wild Committee, he had much to do with framing the Constitutional proposal to give Uganda an almost wholly elected legislature in 1961. On current form, he looks like being leader of the African majority in the House and one of the most influential political figures at this stage in Uganda's progress towards independence.

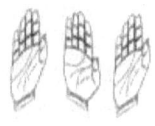

2. MARTIN LOWENKOPF in another publication AFRICA REPORT'S April, 1962.recorded this profile:-

UGANDA'S PRIME MINISTER OBOTE

APOLO MILTON OBOTE is an astute professional politician who has moved sure-footedly from anonymity to the Prime Ministership of Uganda in less than five years.

Abu Mayanja with whom he was closely associated for a number of years, has described Obote as an earnest humanist of Anglican origins,

> "...who reads books on political science for relaxation and makes his point convincingly without ever raising his voice... "...Although he is one of the most skilled parliamentary debaters in East Africa, his manner is reserved even with closest friends and he clearly keeps his more profound thoughts to himself... As the West Africans often say about East Africans, "he speaks from the front of his head..."

The Road to Makerere

Obote brought to the political arena advantages except his own acumen. He is Nilo-Hamitic, the less prosperous minority "race" in Uganda, and comes from a tribe in the North which has little in common with any other in Uganda. When he was born in 1925 into a family of a poor sub-county chief in the Lango District, his prospects did not appear very bright. His father was ambitious for him, however, and managed to send him through the Lira Protestant Mission School in Lango, Gulu Junior Secondary School, Busoga College Mwiri and finally to Makerere University College in Kampala.

Young Obote reportedly wanted to be an Agricultural Scientist, but his parents persuaded him to prepare for teaching.

He ended up by being neither, and his first job was with the Mowlem engineering firm.

The horizons for a politically minded, non-Muganda were limited in Uganda in the late 1940's, so he migrated temporarily to Kenya in 1950, two years after leaving Makerere. In Nairobi, he continued to work for a time with Mowlem, then transferred to the Standard Vacuum Oil Company and eventually worked also for the Railway services and a sugar factory. More important, he became a founder member of the Kenya African Union, under the leadership of Jomo Kenyatta. Later, he became a close friend of Tom Mboya.

Obote returned to Uganda in 1956 and was married the same year. It was not until 1957, however, that he began a serious political career there. Sheer luck played an important part in his first success. He was invited back to Lango in 1957 to take over the branch leadership of the Uganda National Congress, following the imprisonment of his friend, the popular local chairman, Y. Engur.

In 1958, his career took a sharp new turn when Lango's member of the Legislative Council resigned. Sponsored by his uncle, then the Rwot Adwong (an honorary head chief) and leader of the dominant clan and supported by a number of chiefs and the U.N.C. organisation, Obote won the appointment. In Uganda's first direct elections in 1958, he was returned to the Legislative Council with the largest margin in any district. From that time, Obote's star rose steadily.

Buganda's refusal to take part in the 1958 election put the non-Buganda members of the Legislative Council in the limelight. The Buganda boycott also brought about major changes in the truncated U.N.C. central organisation. After a party split early in 1959, the flamboyant party chairman, Joseph Kiwanuka, chose Obote for what Kiwanuka considered a figure-head post of party president. When Abu Mayanja, a founder of the U.N.C. returned to Uganda from his law studies in England shortly thereafter, he and Obote set out to revitalise the party. Finding Kiwanuka's one-man show intolerable, they read him out of the party and started afresh.

New Political Ties

The Mayanja-Obote partnership seemed an ideal one; Mayanja provided dramatic flair and legal skills, Obote a calm perseverance and eloquence which made him the leader of the African representatives in the Legislative Council. In 1960, however, Mayanja accepted post of the Minister of Education in the Kabaka's (Buganda) Government. Obote was left in sole control of what had become, by then, the non-Buganda faction of Congress. Obote shortly thereafter took his followers into a coalition with the newly formed Uganda People's Union, a non-Buganda party led by several members of the Legislative Council and became President of the resultant Uganda People's Congress.

As a member of the Wild Committee, he had much to do with framing the constitutional proposal which gave Uganda an almost wholly elected Legislature in 1961. In the subsequent elections, his party won 495000 popular votes against 415000 for the Democratic Party but did not get a majority of seats in the Council. A boycott of the elections in Buganda enabled the predominantly Catholic Democratic Party to win all Buganda seats with a very light popular vote.

At the London Constitutional Conference in September 1961, at which Uganda's independence was set for October 9, 1962, the Buganda delegation and Obote's U.P.C. forged a tactical alliance which has so far remained intact despite dire predictions to the contrary. But Mr. Obote cannot really breathe easily until and unless he can tread his way to a solution of the Lost Counties issue that both Baganda and Banyoro will accept. This is his most immediate political task if Uganda is to have an orderly transition to independence in October.

Assuming that national unity can be preserved, what kind of leadership can Obote be expected to offer on larger issues? In spite of his participation in the Pan African Freedom Movement of East, Central, and Southern Africa (PAFMECSA), and his party's acceptance of assistance from Tanganyika African National Union, Obote will probably not endorse an East African Federation in the near future. This will be one of the costs of the alliance with the Baganda, who are antipathetic to any political association that would reduce their eminence and threaten their relative autonomy. In economic matters, too, Obote will probably have to follow relatively conservative lines to hold together the U.P.C.-Buganda alliance. He has already offered foreign capital a warm welcome in Uganda and has assured potential investors against expropriation.

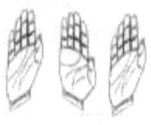

3. On 27.4.62 in the LONDON GUARDIAN, Clyde Sanger's view were recorded thus:-

UGANDA'S NEW LEADER SEES UNITY AS FIRST AIM

Although Mr. Apollo Milton Obote whose party is leading in the Uganda elections is not well known outside East Africa he is bound to be widely hailed as "another Julius Nyerere." Whether he will want to outgrow such description swiftly is another matter.

The problems Mr. Nyerere has faced in Tanganyika and those Mr. Obote must now face in Uganda have, of course, much in common. Before independence Mr. Nyerere told his people to treat the situation as one of a "national emergency" until development had raised the per capita income far above the present of 18 a year.

In his turn Mr. Obote has called for "a massive revolt against poverty," although the widely established peasant crops, Cotton and Coffee, have made his 6.5 million people seem comparatively prosperous. The Uganda herdsman puffing at his pipe, the lilies grown at the cottage door, the fashion-conscious Uganda women, all tempt the visitor to believe the problem of poverty is not so pressing here.

Stress On Unity

Certainly, Mr. Obote sees as his first task not so much the eradication of poverty as the fostering of tribal unity. Unity is the first word in his Uganda Peoples Congress Party's slogan-- relegating independence almost to an afterthought and unity was the theme of his thoughtful election campaign.

If he can sweep away the fears of the domination that the million Baganda both hold and inspire in the country he will have removed the curse of the century, when Buganda-both for themselves and later, for the British newcomers set about conquering the Kingdoms to the west and east. Mr. Obote was well placed by birth to achieve this.

Mr. Obote was born in 1926 in Lango, a northern district protected by the swampy lake Kyoga from interference by the Baganda. When he entered the Legislative Council five years ago, he was faced with the scorn of the Baganda reserved for the Nilo-Hamitics and other less developed people.

Now, however, he is in a position of being able to stand outside the quarrels of Buganda and her neighbours and to lecture gently to both of sides. In his forward to the impressively detailed party election manifesto Mr. Obote used phrases reminiscent of Abraham Lincoln's first inaugural address in writing of unity.

Electoral Alliance

Mr. Obote built an electoral alliance with the Kabaka Yekka movement, a traditionally minded group which won the Lukiiko elections in February on a single platform of preserving the Kabakaship from Mr. Kiwanuka, the leader of the rival Democratic Party. Mr. Obote has now to prove wrong his opponents' accusation that this has been simply an unholy alliance of a radical nationalist party with traditionalist group to unseat their common enemy.

He is experienced enough a politician to know how far he should compromise. The amount of power given Buganda as a Federal unit has been little and has still considerable room for negotiation on this matter.

He is ingenious enough to reconcile orthodox nationalism with Uganda's needs and turns a well-worn Pan-Africanist phrase to a new use when in his party manifesto he pledges to

> "...be the guardian of African personality in upholding the dignity, status and prestige of the four African Monarchies and all constitutional heads..."

Wide political experience has made a mature leader at only 36. Like Mr. Nyerere he started schooling late. He entered primary school at the age of 12, after a spear wound had ended his days as a goatherd. And a good deal of chance has shaped his career.

He went to Makerere College to train as a teacher, but Uganda government officials stopped his studying law in America, or economics in Britain, though he had offers in both places.

So, he became a labourer in Kenya, through the worst of Mau Mau emergency. When Kenya political parties were again allowed, he was a foundation member. Then, six years ago; he returned to Lango District, and fierily opposed many Government measures, but was too clever to be ever convicted on a prison offence.

Effective Parliamentarian

When he first came to the Legislative Council the next year, he was still an undisciplined demagogue. Those who have worked with him during these last five years say changes in his approach have been amazing. Slim and elegant, with a black ivory cane, he has made himself into a controlled and effective parliamentarian.

His state of health causes concern. He drives himself too hard. This may be the reason why he is sometimes moody and unapproachable. But at all other times his intelligence and maturity perhaps, to borrow from his own phrase, *"...a gentle revolutionary..."* is best description make him the leader with the best hope of solving Uganda's varied problems.

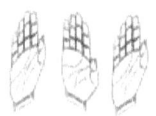

4. On 30.4.62 The LONDON TIMES newspaper column, MAN IN THE NEWS, headed:

MR. OBOTE'S SUCCESS AS MASTER OF THE PARTY MANAGEMENT

Mr. Milton Obote, who has been having talks with the Governor of Uganda about forming a Government is a politician's politician: he has no profession outside politics. When he was a young man his ambition was to study agricultural science, but his family insisted that he should train to be a teacher instead because teaching was a white-collar job. Later he hoped to go to Boston to study Law, or to London for Economics, but the Uganda Government, Mr. Obote says, frustrated both schemes.

In 1950 these setbacks drove him to migrate to Kenya. There he worked as a labourer in a sugar factory, as a clerk in a construction firm and a salesman for an oil company. He also became a founder member of the Kenya African Union.

Returning to Uganda in 1955, Mr. Obote found his home district of Lango in turmoil over the protectorate Government's policy on freehold land titles. He thought that the Uganda National Congress, which he had joined on a brief return to Uganda in 1952, was not taking a strong enough line on this issue. At this point Mr. Obote found his true profession in politics. He re-rebuilt the local branch of the U.N.C., and in December 1957, he was chosen by the District council to represent Lango in the Uganda Legislative Council.

Internal Feuds

The U.N.C. was fragmented by internal feuds, culminating in a split in 1959 which left Mr. J.C. Kiwanuka as leader of the party, and Mr. Obote as commander of a section that included most members of the Party's executive Committee. Mr. Obote merged his former U.N.C. following with Uganda peoples Union a group of non-Baganda Legislative Council Members, to form the Uganda Peoples Congress in March 1960.

During the campaign leading to Uganda's first general election, in March 1961, the U.P.C., emerged as one of the two major parties in the country. It won more seats outside Buganda than its rival the Democratic Party, but because the Kabaka's Government boycotted the elections the Democratic Party carried all the rural seats and was able to form the first African Government of Uganda.

Defeat might have been fatal to the U.P.C., and to Obote's leadership of it. He showed his political resilience by the way in which he held his followers together after election: although party ties were comparatively new in Uganda, the U.P.C. lost only three Legislative Council members to the Opposition. Mr. Obote himself claimed and won recognition as the leader of opposition, and by his speeches in the Legislative Council established himself as the outstanding member there.

Buganda Pact

Last September U.P.C. had the chance to ensure its political future by making terms with Buganda. The deal between the U.P.C. and the Buganda politicians seems to have been particularly the work of Mr. Obote himself. Though it was condemned by his opponents as selling his party to a Buganda clique, the U.P.C.'s move can be defended as a realistic attempt to bring Buganda back into the mainstream of Uganda's politics.

Asked to give his ideas about the next five years in Uganda, Mr. Obote talks of constitution-making in a way which suggests that he is more interested in getting something that works than theoretical excellence. He says that Uganda's greatest problem is to make its people work harder, but he thinks that economic development will have to be Government sponsored, not imposed by the party machine in the way which Tanganyika is trying.

Views On Federation

He thinks that the East African territories should work more closely together (and his experience of Kenya's politics could be a bridge in that direction) but he is not committed to Federation; indeed he places emphasis on the need for Uganda to improve its relations with its northern and western neighbours too.

At the age of 38, Mr. Obote is a man who has got to the top in Uganda's politics by shrewd party management and by parliamentary arts. He seems to have overcome the disadvantages of a volatile temperament. In a year in opposition he has learnt patience, and the necessity of keeping his party's loyalty.

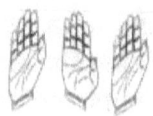

5. *A Writer in AFRICA REPORT'S - a USA based publication of April, 1962. recorded:-*

WHAT IS KABAKA YEKKA?

I have no quarrel with the main analysis of AFRICA REPORT'S report on the February election in Buganda ("Victory for the Kabaka," AFRICA REPORT'S, March 1962, page 13), which I believe to be factually correct. Nor can I, unhappily, dispute the write's main conclusion that

"...the prospects for a stable Central Government by the time of independence in October 1962 remains dubious..."

However, I will try to show in the following lines that the Kabaka Yekka victory in the Lukiiko elections made the prospects for stability much brighter than they would have been had our opponents, the Democratic Party, been successful.

I agree that the Kabaka Yekka victory was a victory for the Kabakaship (not the Kabaka) in Buganda, and that one of the most important elements in that victory was the desire by most people in Buganda to defeat DP. But I think the victory was much more significant, and was brought about by much more far-reaching considerations, than your correspondent allowed for.

DP Advantages Cited

In the first place, although it may be true that "vast majority of the Baganda voted Kabaka Yekka because they were persuaded that the Democratic Party would crush the Monarchy in Buganda," this alone could not have accounted for the unprecedented defeat of the Democratic Party. Remember it was the Party in power in the Central Government and had great advantages of finance, propaganda, and other trimmings of a party machine. The last census of 1959 showed that there were 1,800,000 people in Buganda of whom only 1. million are

Baganda. Buganda is thus far from a tribal Kingdom, at any rate from the point of view of people who voted. It contains, within its borders, representatives of all the Uganda tribes, as well as sizeable contingents from Kenya, Tanganyika, India, Pakistani and Europe.

Had the Kabaka Yekka victory been attributed solely or mainly to the Baganda's tribal loyalty to the Kabaka, the Democratic Party would not have fared so badly in Buganda, especially in the urban and peri-urban constituencies that have large sections of non-Baganda; in some instances, these constituted the national majority of the electorate. Why did Makerere constituency, for example, vote Kabaka Yekka so overwhelmingly, when the Democratic Party candidate--American-Educated Senteza Kajubi--was himself a lecturer at the University and when the combined students and the don voting potential was perhaps something of the order of 1000? How did all the Europeans and Asian residents in this, surely the key constituency, vote? There cannot be two views on this. Most people in Buganda, including the non-Baganda who comprise over 40% of Buganda's population, voted Kabaka Yekka for reasons other than tribal loyalty to the Monarchy.

Pamphlet Quoted

The election pamphlet which I, as campaign manager, wrote on behalf of Kabaka Yekka was our nearest approach to a manifesto. This pamphlet set out to emphasize that the Lukiiko elections would be deciding national Uganda-wide issues for Buganda only. Having referred to the democratic significance of direct elections to the Lukiiko on non-discriminating adult franchise, and increased responsibilities of the Lukiiko under the new Buganda Agreement, I wrote:

> "...Thirdly, and most important the Lukiiko elections will affect not only the future happiness of Buganda, but also the future happiness of Uganda as a whole...
>
> "...They will not be local elections confined to Buganda alone, but national elections affecting the whole country. This is partly

because the Lukiiko will be deciding how the 21 (one quarter of the total) members of the National Assembly shall be elected; and also, partly because whatever happens in Buganda affects the whole country. Buganda is the heart of Uganda. If you have a bad Government in Buganda causing chaos and instability in Buganda, there will be bound to be chaos and instability in Uganda as a whole. If Buganda's economy suffers, the whole economy suffers...."

Unity Stressed

As the person responsible for organising and coordinating the Kabaka Yekka campaign, I travelled extensively throughout Buganda and addressed hundreds of meetings. Many of these were addressed by the Uganda People's Congress members of the legislative council, including Mr. Obote himself. At these meetings................

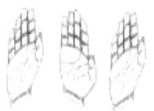

6. The COLONIAL OFFICE information department, on June, 12 1962, issued this text:-

UGANDA INDEPENDENCE CONFERENCE:

(Opening ceremony speech by)

MR. A.M. OBOTE.

The following is the text of the speech by the Prime Minister of Uganda (Mr. A.M. OBOTE) at the opening ceremony of the Uganda Independence Conference at Marlborough House, London, S.W.1 today (Tuesday, June 12, 1962):-

"...Ever since the end of the Second World War, a number of political leaders from what I may call the British Colonial Empire led delegations from their respective countries in conferences of this kind...

"...Only last week you concluded as you stated, one of these conferences...

"...Today marks the beginning of Uganda's turn in the final discussion leading to independence...

"...To the Government of Uganda and me, this conference has three-fold significance...

"...On the one hand it is a tribute to the British men and women who went to Uganda and worked with the people and transformed the country in a manner which has made it possible for us today to talk in terms of the independence of that part of Africa known as Uganda...

"...It is also at the same time and spirit a tribute to the people of Uganda for the part they have played in bringing that country to its present stage of development...

"...Secondly, this conference, in the view of the Government of Uganda, is in fulfillment of the often-repeated British policy of Trusteeship and of social and economic development which aims at preparing the Colonial peoples for independence...

"...In the case of Uganda, this policy was expressed by successive Governors as that of leading Uganda stage by stage to independence...

"...From yet another angle, this Conference is a welcome opportunity for the delegates from Uganda to frame the independence constitution of under which merit, justice and stability would fix the position of the individual in life of the nation...

"...Therefore, the Government of Uganda looks at this Conference as a normal pre-independence Conference and is of the firm opinion that it must be the last before Independence is achieved...

"...On October 9 last year, an important agreement was reached at the conclusion of the conference held in this country on Uganda's constitutional advancement...

"...This important agreement was in three parts...

"...The first part was that Uganda would achieve internal self-government on March 1 this year, and the second part was that a general election to the new National Assembly should take place before mid-April 1962...

"...These parts of the agreement have now been fulfilled...

"...We have now in Uganda a Legislative Assembly to be recognized by all parts of the country as the Central Legislative Body for the whole country...

"...The recognition and consent given so willingly by all parts of Uganda to the new National Assembly, to which the Government of Uganda is now responsible, is an important factor in this Conference, and this is that no useful purpose would be served in re-discussing fields of responsibilities already given to the National Assembly...

"...My delegation is of the clear opinion that discussions should be confined to the reserved powers left last year to the Governor...

"...This, in the view of my delegation, includes even the agreements between Her Majesty's Government and the Kingdoms in Uganda...

"...What my delegation wants from this conference is to achieve the third part of the agreement reached last year regarding the independence of Uganda...

"...This is to complete discussions and to make arrangements still required in time for independence on October 9 this year...

"...The whole country is eagerly awaiting that day and no act from this Conference can be sufficient to put the clock back...

"...I have given a great deal of deliberation to the achievement of independence on the date which is now a household word in Uganda...

"...When this independence comes, there is no doubt that it will be a day of joy both for Britain and Uganda...

"...The ties between the two countries have been close and very strong...

"...The people of Uganda shall inherit to their advantage many things; these include the Legal system, and the English language which has become a common medium of intercourse between the people of Uganda of different home languages...

"...It was because of considerations of this nature that the National Assembly recently passed unanimously a resolution to the effect that Ugandans should seek membership of the Commonwealth on the attainment of Independence...

"...The people of Uganda attach much importance to this resolution...

"...They believe that there is no political partnership in the world accepting so little from members but giving so much in return...

"...It is also believed in Uganda that the Commonwealth is a unique experiment in the direction of securing unity of political action in essentials between free nations without the sacrifice of their several national identities of their control of their national life...

"...Such unity, not based on the domination of a master-state, not even on the rigid structure and sacrifice of individual nationality involved in it, but on common ideals, is something the people of Uganda believe is worth their membership...

"...I therefore hope that in the near future Uganda shall be able to take its place among the independent states in the Commonwealth...

"...To my fellow delegates from Uganda, I would say that the only means of building up a strong Uganda is through the establishment of relations based on esteem and affection between different parts of the country...

"...The Conference shall certainly discuss Constitutional provisions, declarations of rights and Agreements but these can only have permanent value if they are based upon mutual trust and faith in the words we use...

"...The future of Uganda must rest ultimately on the common convictions and ideals of the people of Uganda collectively desire to maintain it...

"...What is needed in this Conference is a union of hearts for the common good of the whole country...

"...It is said that man shapes his own destiny...

"...We are here not to shape our own individual destinies...

"...We are here to establish the destinies of those people who sent us here...

"...Our responsibilities in shaping the destinies of those who sent us here are therefore great...

"...Let us produce for them the Constitution which will ensure a general feeling of orderliness and well-being in Uganda as a whole. Sir, this is the mission which has brought me here..."

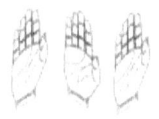

7. Panafricanquotes. Milton-Obote's-9th October 1962-Uganda-Independence-Speech

Milton Obote's 1962 Uganda Independence Speech

'...At the turning-point in the history of Uganda, I hope that all our friends will join with me in bestowing upon the new, independent Uganda our prayers and hopes for peace, prosperity and a growing strength in her now role in international affairs. Uganda has many friends, both within her borders and outside. With the goodwill of all who wish to see her prosper, Uganda will go forward from strength to strength...

'...Let us pause for a moment and look back along the path we have traveled. In the days before this part of the African continent was known to the western world, we became known as a group of peoples who welcomed the traveler, the missionary and the explorer...

"...As the years passed, we reaped the benefit of this friendly nature of ours...

'...The technical progress of the last half-century has transformed our country in countless ways...

"... But, fortunately, we have continued to keep our own customs and culture...

"...It is up to us now, more than ever, in shaping our new country, to achieve a consolidation, in which neither the rapid progress of recent years, nor the age-old customs of our forefathers, are lost or diminished, but rather fused into a new national characteristic in which the best is preserved, while the worst may be thrown away...

National unity

'...What other aims have we, today, on looking forward? One of our first needs must be national unity...

"...The narrow ambitions of a tribe, a sect, or a party must be subordinated to the greater needs of one complete Uganda. In our Government of these past months, we have striven to put the interests of Uganda before all else, and we shall continue to do so...

'...But on attaining independence, this Government has new responsibilities to bear, heavier than those which any previous government in Uganda has borne, and we are conscious of the care and statesmanship with which we must move in taking our first steps in foreign affairs...

"...In the Commonwealth and in the United Nations we shall be among friendly states, both from other parts of Africa and from elsewhere...

"...But the regard in which a nation is held in the eyes of the world depends upon the successful operation of a complex machinery...

'...We have paid attention to the design of that machinery. First, we require political stability...

"...My Government will seek to maintain that stability, by the strict maintenance of law and order, by retaining the confidence of the voters, and by upholding the freedom of the individual...

"...Secondly, we require to safeguard the economy...

"...This we will do by diversifying and improving our agriculture, providing incentives to industry, and creating conditions which encourage foreign investment...

"...Thirdly, we will press forward with social services within realistic bounds and not as dictated by idealism...

"...Fourthly, we need an efficient civil service to operate the Government...

"...Uganda is well provided with well-qualified African officers and we shall continue to ensure that these are attracted into government service by the offer of the right terms, so that a balanced Africanisation programme shall continue...

'...I conclude by emphasising that there is a place in the Uganda of today for all who have her interests at heart, whatever their tribe, race or creed...

"...Let all of us, who wish to see Uganda prosper, join together today in resolving to build a great and united nation...'

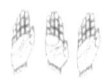

8. The NEW COMMONWEALTH publication, September 1962, E.A. Jones recorded:-

UGANDA'S PRIME MINISTER MOVES TO THE FRONT RANK

Since he took office in April, Uganda's Prime Minister, Mr. Milton Obote, has moved quietly into the front rank of statesmen in Africa. The speech he made to the annual Delegates Conference of his Uganda people's Congress recently was very possibly the most encouraging ever delivered by a Uganda leader, including the Colonial Governors.

His speech dealt largely with the economic problems facing Uganda, and only in passing with party political plans. The political struggle, he indicated, is nearly over, but the economic battle is just beginning.

> "...Our first task should be to avoid considering economic problems on a racial basis....,";

he told the conference.

> "...Let us tackle the subject in four ways. Let us encourage private enterprise, assist the co-operatives, help the parastatal organisations like the Uganda Development Corporation and the Uganda Electricity Board to play their part, and lastly let the Government provide basic services such as trunk roads, hospitals and schools...
>
> "...I charge you all to go out to all corners of Uganda to make this party a partner of farmers, traders, businessmen and educators...
>
> "... Let all men know that Uganda is underdeveloped, that we have formidable tasks to acquire capital and to invest it...
>
> "...Impress upon our people that they must ensure an economy at which investment is attractive...

Tell them:

> '...Strive hard and you will not only be aided, but you will have more to spend, save and enjoy..."

Describing Uganda foreign policy after independence as

> "...the other major subject before the Conference..,"

Premier Obote said that;

> "...Uganda's first duty was to create closer ties with her immediate neighbours and through them, eventually, with the rest of Africa-...
>
> "...an Africa which can never again be the projection of Europe or any other part of the world..."
>
> "...Although Uganda would support the United Nations, she would not rely solely on that organization...
>
> "...She had before her the example of Rwanda, where the United Nations failed to control the situation so now Uganda is paying for the upkeep of refugees who had fled across the border into political asylum...
>
> "...Uganda was not directly concerned with the East-West conflict but we must abhor the arms race and refuse all attempts to use our country as an ideological battlefield..."
>
> "...Uganda's continued membership of the Commonwealth was not for material gain, but for a continued sharing on equal basis of ideals...
>
> "...She would, however, watch very carefully the effect if Britain entered the Common Market...
>
> "... The Conference should examine this subject with care and without emotions..."

The Conference vociferously acclaimed the re-election of the whole party executive. Committees on various subjects reported to the plenary session for approval.

The Foreign Affairs Committee proposed strict neutrality, but willingness to consider sanctions against certain powers. Specifically mentioned were Spain, France Belgium, Portugal and South Africa.

The Committee urged the Government to open Uganda's first embassies in London, New York, Moscow and Peking and to demand the dissolution of the Central African Federation and the cessation of French atom tests in the Sahara. At the plenary session Premier Obote managed to prevent the Conference from endorsing this programme. Its implications had not been fully considered, he warned. He persuaded the delegates to withhold until the Party Executive had considered it further.

It is understood that Mr. Obote favours opening embassies only in London and New York at first and that he intends, during the discussions in the Party Executive to tone down the foreign policy statement into a more statesman approach.

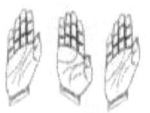

9. *On 27.9.62 a LONDON TIMES correspondent filed this report:-*

EAST AFRICA TALKS ON THE SIX - UGANDA DISTASTE FOR ASSOCIATE ROLE

Mr. Obote, the Prime Minister, returned to Uganda from London this morning. Speaking at Entebbe about Uganda's attitude to the European Common Market, he emphasised that no final decisions had been taken. There would be further discussions with Kenya and Tanganyika before any conclusion was reached.

He said he would not like to see Uganda accept membership of the Common Market, because he could not envisage such relationship with Europe as free from political implications. He hoped the East African Common Market countries could go on trading with the European Common Market countries without entering into associate membership, and he mentioned the examples of Libya and Morocco as enjoying a special trading relationship with the Six without being associate members.

Mr. Obote did not think Uganda's coffee exports would suffer, even if Ivory Coast continued to receive preferential treatment in the European market, as there was already talk of reducing the general tariff on coffee from 16 to nine per cent.

DISAGREEMENT SETTLED

He was happy at the welcome Uganda received from other members of the Commonwealth at the London Conference earlier this month. If Britain did join the Common Market, however, Commonwealth links were bound to weaken because Britain would become "a province of Europe".

Questioned about the difficulties over Uganda's constitution, Mr. Obote said he reported disagreement between the Uganda and Buganda Governments had been amicably resolved.

Everyone now felt that the draft report of the Colonial Office mirrored the decision of the independence conference. The new constitution should be published next Tuesday. Uganda becomes independent on October 9th, 1962

Mr. Obote also said the "lost counties" issue was not discussed in London. He added:

> "...We are internally self-governing now and this is our own affair..."

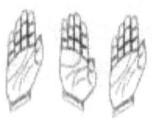

10. The colonial publication EAST AFRICA AND RHODESIA of October 18,1962 reported:-

MR. OBOTE'S SOFT SPOT FOR "IMPERIALIST"

Government's Aim to Foster Tolerance

The DUKE OF KENT, representing the Queen, opened the first Parliament of independent Uganda in Kampala on Wednesday of last week.

He read the speech from the Throne, which stated inter alia:-

"...My Government's first objective in carrying out its responsibilities within Uganda will be to foster a spirit of tolerance and good will between all peoples of Uganda...

"...It will aim to stimulate confidence in the future of Uganda as a united country bound together in common nationhood...

"...It will at the same time pay due heed to traditional beliefs and customs of the diverse peoples of Uganda...

"...It will, under the Constitution, recognize the special status and dignity of the hereditary rulers of the Kingdoms and constitutional heads of districts...

"...In its plans for economic and social development, it will have as its first objective the raising of the living standards of the people. It is determined vigorously to pursue its development programme, in spite of the financial stringency which it faces at present...

"...The orderly development of the expansion of the educational system will be continued...

"...The efficiency and viability of the regional administrations will be improved...

"...My Government pledges itself to respect the independence of the judiciary and the equality of all persons before the law...

"...It will aim at an efficient, impartial and contented civil service, and while Ugandanisation will continue as fast as possible, my Government will continue to employ those expatriate officers whose services the country needs..."

"...The Ministers of my Uganda Government solemnly and sincerely pledge themselves to serve the people of Uganda with faith and fortitude, and to combat unceasingly the evils of hunger, disease, poverty and ignorance..."

Beware of Factions

The Prime Minister, Mr. A. Milton Obote, said in reply that;

"...Uganda intended to be not only a free but a prosperous country, to achieve which condition she would need money and skilled staff...

"...Generous aid was already being gratefully received from Britain and other sources, and he hoped that it would continue, so that related industries could be established as natural resources were developed.

"...To fulfill all our aims we shall the concerted effort of every Ugandan...

"...If we work together we can achieve our highest ambitions and create a nation of which we can all justifiably be proud...

"...But if we think first of groups and factions, then we shall not succeed...

"...I am confident that we have the wisdom and maturity to understand this..."

On the previous day Mr. Obote had told a Press conference that;

"...far from desiring to remove British civil servants in order to effect rapid Africanisation, Uganda might have to go out and recruit more as the country's services expanded...

Outside Investment

"...No group was more needed that foreign businessmen, It would disturb me if even one businessman decided to leave Uganda..."

He was prepared to run to any friendly country to get money, but the Government's main task would be to teach the people that increased output of their cotton, tea and other crops was much better than constant talk of borrowing money. Agricultural officers would be expected to provide the expert encouragement needed, in preference to a campaign mounted by the political parties.

The country's new-found unity as a nation would require consolidation. The British administration had reinforced the individuality of the Kingdoms and districts, but the blame rests largely on Ugandans themselves, who had taken so long to organise a united political movement. When he had first been elected to the old Legislative Council, he did not always know whether he was supposed to represent his party, his tribe, his constituency, or the interests of Uganda.

> "...It is current practice to condemn imperialism..."

he continued.

> "...while I share this condemnation, I have a soft spot for the protection we have had here. The British Administration has done a wonderful in education and health, in developing water resources and industries, in economic affairs, and in bringing cultural benefits..."

As to the East African *"common market,"* he was in favour of continuing the present common services but felt that there could be little enthusiasm until Kenya was "free" for a federal arrangement.

Will Not Recognize Federation

Looking to Africa as a whole, he disagreed with African nationalists in Rhodesia that the Federation should be dismantled, for African Unity would have to be based on regional groupings.

> "...The present Government of Sir Roy Wellensky had to be removed, and Uganda would recognize neither the Federal nor the South African Governments because there was a great deal of deceit in their recognizing the new Uganda Government without according the same respect to the Africans under their control...

"...A decision will soon be announced about Portugal (whose government had been invited to send a representative to the independence celebrations)...

"...All African nationalist movement and Government would be supported but backing would not be given to any Government which was thought to be receiving its instructions from outside Africa.

"...Non-recognition of the Federation and South Africa would be merely diplomatic and would not involve trade boycotts or the denial of aircraft facilities at Entebbe...

"...The stand taken against the present Federal Government was unfortunate because of Uganda's membership of the commonwealth to which Uganda belonged in the belief that such an organisation provided a forum for informal talks wherein certain principles in common were retained, not for any benefits obtainable..."

Mr. Obote feared that Uganda might lose her independent and neutral image by becoming an associate member of the European Common Market. He thought there were about a dozen alternatives to the present scheme of association.

In the light of Uganda's membership of the United Nations, with particular reference to the conflict between the West and East, he wanted to warn outsiders against using Uganda as an ideological battleground.

After opening Parliament, the Duke and Duchess of Kent made a State drive through Kampala's gaily decorated streets, and that afternoon attended a garden party at Government House, Entebbe, for some 4000 guests.

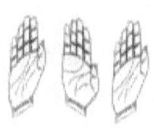

11. On November 22, 1962 in the colonial publication EAST AFRICA AND RHODESIA a comment appeared thus:-

UGANDA AND THE FEDERATION

Mr. Obote's Statement on External Policy

Mr. A. MILTON OBOTE, the Prime Minister, told Parliament last week in his first statement on foreign policy since his country became independent that;

"...Uganda would have no Diplomatic relations with the Federation of Rhodesia and Nyasaland because the Federal Governments policy was to regard and treat Africans in Central Africa differently from the whites...

"...To despise Africans in Central Africa...,

he said,

"...was to despise Africans in Uganda.

Because they felt frustrated the people of the Federation wanted to break it up. He advised them not to do that, but to fight for human rights, so that black and white would be accorded the same rights.

He did not agree that;

"...Southern Rhodesia had internal self-Government or that the British Government and the parliament could not interfere in its affairs...

"...Because South Africa was not prepared to listen to anyone, particularly Africans, Uganda would have no diplomatic relations with that country..."

While recently in New York he had instructed Uganda's Mission to work with other countries in regard to sanctions against South Africa.

"...If she did not change her policies, Uganda might boycott South African goods..."

Mr. Obote added:

> "...We do not consider that South Africa is independent. As Kenya is ruled from London, South Africa is the same, but the people have transferred themselves to the spot; so we cannot agree that South Africa is independent..."

> "...The Portuguese office in Kampala had been closed down because the policies of Mozambique and Angola did not recognize human rights in those territories...

> "...The East African Federation envisaged by the Colonial Government 40 years ago had fortunately not materialised; if it had, Tanganyika and Uganda would not now be independent...

> "...As an independent country must talk with equal partners about Federation...

The Prime Minister was not prepared to talk with London about East African Federation, for it was a purely African matter.

> "...Kenya should be free, and Uganda must support her in her fight for independence...

> "...Uganda wanted friendly relations with all her neighbours and would support all African Nationalists Governments and parties and fight to bridge the difference between the two blocs in Africa..."

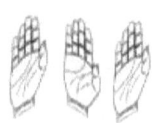

12. November 22, 1962 A colonial publication EAST AFRICA AND RHODESIA reproduced an article it titled:

DANGEROUS MIXTURE

LINKING POLITICS AND RELIGION is a danger in Uganda, the Rev. F.B. Welbourn, Warden of Mitchell Hall at Makerere College, has written in the Anglican paper NEW DAY.

> "...Keep out the Roman Catholics was regarded by most as the policy of the Uganda Peoples Congress and was the real basis for its alliance with the Kabaka Yekka, extremely dangerous politically for both of them. Because Kabaka Yekka was seen as an attempt to maintain Anglican domination at Mengo. It was likely that the Catholics and the Muslims would join hands to oppose it. And because his name has been used for political aims of one party, I fear that the Kabaka, like Charles I and James II of England, will share their fate..."

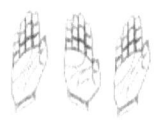

13. In the LONDON GUARDIAN of December 5, 1962 Clyde Sanger reported thus:

PRESSURE IN KENYA

Quicker Pace To Freedom

Pressure has built up swiftly this week among East African leaders to force the pace with Britain over Kenya's independence, which at present looks unlikely to come for another 18 months. A meeting tomorrow in Dar es Salaam of the East African Common Services Authority could add to this pressure.

The Authority consists of the chief elected Ministers of the three territories: Mr. Milton Obote and Mr. Rashid Kawawa, the Prime Ministers of Uganda and Tanganyika; and Mr. Jomo Kenyatta and Ronald Ngala, the two Kenya Ministers for constitutional affairs. Dr. Julius Nyerere will also take part since he becomes executive head as the President of Tanganyika when the Republic is proclaimed on Sunday.

To the surprise of many it has been Mr. Obote who has built up most of the pressure; only two months ago during the independence celebrations he praised the British to the point of generosity. The man who was thought to was so adept at compromise in his own Federal State and ready to understand other people's difficulties has now given instructions that his United Nations delegation should attack British colonial policies "left, right and centre".

After talks with Mr. Kenyatta and other Kenya African Union leaders, he said last night that he would not hesitate to *"rock the bottom of the boat"* to free Kenya from colonial rule. This morning the "Daily Nation" declares Britain is not to blame for the long delays in Kenya, and Mr. Obote would do better by *"knocking heads together among Kenya African politicians."* The newspaper suggests Mr. Obote has recently been so preoccupied with Ugandan affairs that he has had no time to study Kenya's rather different problems.

Before flying to Dar es Salaam today Mr. Obote angrily rejected these arguments. He said that;

> "...when Mr. Maudling was the Colonial Secretary the British Government was following the right policy by making it clear it would impose a solution on any constitutional issues not agreed between the parties within a certain time...
>
> "...But since Mr. Sandy's had taken over the policy had changed...,

he added;

> "...This is the influence of Lord Salisbury and Sir Ferdinand Cavendish-Bentinck. You can see it at work in the House of Lords debate yesterday..."

The Uganda Government is also crossing swords with the United States through its action in declaring Senator Allan Ellender of Louisiana a prohibited immigrant after the Senator had said he had seen no part of Africa where Africans were ready for self-government. Mr. Kakonge said today:

> "...We hope the American Government will issue a refutation of the Senator's remarks...
>
> "... But the American charge d'affaires in Kampala, Mr. Olcott Deming, says his Government has not yet decided to make an official complaint or apology..."

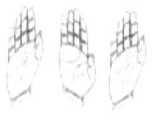

14. In the EAST AFRICAN STANDARD of 20.5.63, below is a staff reporter's excerpt of the official Government News release:

PREMIER STRESSES END TO "SLAVERY"

> "...The African's desire to put an end to political, economic and social servitude was likely to be the central theme of the Addis Ababa summit conference..."

the Uganda Prime Minister, Mr. Obote, said yesterday...

He was speaking at Entebbe before leaving, at the head of a delegation for Ethiopia. Mr. Obote flew to Nairobi where, he said, he hoped to have talks today with President Nyerere of Tanganyika.

He said that;

> "...African nationalism had a double-barreled appeal to preserve Africa from outside control and secondly to construct Africa anew...
>
> "...It wanted to raise the continent to a minimum of equality with the rest of the world..."

No Meaning

> "...It was important that independent African states at the conference should not only review their independence but should also assess their relationships with such countries which still had desires either to rule parts of Africa or to control their economies and their culture...
>
> "..Our attitude (to the conference) is in conformity with our policy that our independence has no meaning unless we have a basis of co-operation with other African countries, and also unless we find a basis jointly with the other African states which would help to advance the social and economic status of our peoples..."
>
> "...There was also the question of those parts of Africa still being ruled from abroad or, as in South Africa, by a minority of

settlers. Uganda did not recognize South Africa as being independent..."

Needed Changes

Mr. Obote described his trip as:

"...A compound mission of love for Africa, belief in her potentialities, and faith in her ability and determination to carry through the required changes...

"...Uganda's contribution cannot be measured,...

he added,

"...but our determination to assist and move ahead with our sister States cannot be doubted..."

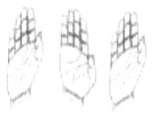

15. *The B.B.C. monitor sheet ME/I856/B/I ON 10.5.65 filled the following excerpts entitled:-*

OBOTE'S ADDRESS "PROGRESS THROUGH CO-OPERATION" CONFERENCE.

The African conference on "Progress through co-operation" was opened at Makerere this afternoon by the Prime Minister, Dr. Milton Obote. Welcoming the delegates on the behalf of the Government and the people of Uganda, the Prime Minister expressed pleasure at the council on the World Tension's decision to hold the meeting in Uganda. He said:

"...You have come to work on problems of great concern to world developing countries...

"...The interest and desire of developed countries to assist African Nations, whether motivated by humanitarianism or selfishness, has been a significant and welcome factor...

"...However, there is evidence that this factor is becoming increasingly a serious source of instability in African Nations, and between one African nation and another...

"...When a country becomes independent, social services and economic resources become urgent and demanding, and offers of help from developed countries are welcomed, a disturbing trend, however, soon develops...

"...The providers of aid begin to compete for the ears either of the Government as a whole or the individuals in and outside Government, and in this task soon begin to act as an instrument of instability...

"...This situation may develop to a point where the providers of aid assume and expect immunity from criticism of some of their policies by the recipient of aid...

"...Because of this mistaken approach by both the East and the West to human relations, most African states are walking on a tight rope...

"...With great respect to the great countries in the East and the West, I would say that the world is not in a condition today, and

I doubt it ever was, when one should refrain from expressing honest criticism simply because of favours received or hoped for...

"...Those nations which are loosely banded together as non-aligned often feel very strongly that some of the actions of the big powers do not take account of the facts of their independence and right of self-determination...

"...In spite of this, certain historians reviewing the present era may well judge that it was the existence of a powerful body of opinion not automatically aligned to a power bloc that saved the world from a nuclear holocaust...

"...It would be a poor reward if the results had been that development assistance to the non-aligned had been reduced or stopped..."

The Prime Minister suggested that the power blocs should seek a new field for co-operation among themselves in helping the poorer nations and not parcel their aid tightly between specified projects. As an example of this move, he said:

"...Supposing we in Uganda wanted to experiment with growing rice on shore of one of our lakes, it might turn out that the best combination for the project would be American equipment and some Chinese advisers...

"...The whole question is whether we would be likely to get assistance for a project put together on this basis...

"...If one could do so it might be of value not only to us but also to other nations...

"...Britain offered us at the U.N. conference in Geneva to extend the Commonwealth preference to all developing countries if the other developed countries would reciprocate...

"...The other developed countries would not reciprocate and therefore no action is likely to be taken on this matter...

"...The result is clear. The inability of the developed countries leaves African nations to look to the various ex-colonial powers...

"...The inability of the ex-colonial powers to accommodate some pressing needs of their ex-colonial territories becomes an obstacle to promoting co-operation among African nations.

"...The fundamental difficulty is Africa's size and language problems...

> "...Huge investments in communications will be necessary to link the continents internally by road, railway and telecommunications...
>
> "...In East Africa we already have a great deal of co-operation between Uganda, Kenya and Tanzania, though this may not be appreciated because of exaggerated reports about differences of opinion between us...
>
> "...Our joint services and common policies include transport, communication, trade and taxation...
>
> "...Inter-council agreements on the allocation of manufacturing industries are most difficult to achieve but we have made some progress in East Africa...
>
> "...Perhaps our basic difficulty has been the inheritance of the colonial methods and types of co-operation which have all somewhat different effects in individual countries...
>
> "...But the will to co-operate has overcome all obstacles, and I have no doubt we shall continue to work together...
>
> "...Perhaps the greatest single factor in getting co-operation within East Africa is the political structure of Uganda with its federal constitution...
>
> "...Shortage of skilled personnel remains a big problem and so does the tendency to cling to the conservative methods and not give way to change..."

To participants outside East Africa, Dr. Obote said:

> "...Your experience elsewhere is valuable to us and your prompt advice would be appreciated..."

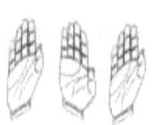

16. Recorded in the colonial publication EAST AFRICA AND RHODESIA, June 24, 1965 was:-

DR. OBOTE ON "AFRICA'S GREATEST DANGER"

Politicians Ready to Betray Their Countries for Cash

"...AFRICA'S GREATEST DANGER, is that there are always ready politicians who are prepared to serve the interests of foreign countries..."

said Dr. Obote, Prime Minister of Uganda, when he addressed the Royal Institute of International Affairs in London a few days ago.

In the course of a long speech Dr. Obote said:

"...We take a firm stand on colonialism, fervently desire to see all subject peoples move to their independence without delay, and are prepared to speak out against all forms of discrimination wherever it is practised...

"...We are opposed to the use of force to settle international disputes, and in our policy of negotiation in settling international disputes.

"We uphold the principles of freely elected democratic Government based on the will of the people, and we have spoken very bitterly against manoeuvres where some nations seek to place in Government nationalists of a particular country not elected by their own people to positions of authority...

"...This applies particularly to our neighbours...

"...Uganda does not allow its territory to be used for the purposes of subversion or the overthrow of another Government in any country...

"...WE have maintained right from the date of our independence the policy of preventing nationalists of other States who come to Uganda from using facilities afforded them in our country as a platform for attacks against their Governments...

"...We are members of the Commonwealth of Nations, and we value the Commonwealth ties and associations...

"...Like most African independent States, we are members of the Organisation of African Unity..."

"...We subscribe fully to the principle of its charter..."

"...We have maintained a very close working understanding with our East African neighbours, and although it has not been possible to effect much-talked of East African Federation, we nevertheless believe that, with the withdrawal of obstacles, our belief in closer association with our neighbours may in future mean political federation..."

Could Become An Ideological Battleground

"...Our greatest ambition is to develop as quickly as possible...

"...As we cannot expect to develop our resources unless we have peace in the world and stability at home, we are obviously the last country to go out of our way to create a situation of instability or to promote circumstances around our country which might lead to lack of peace in the world...

"...The cold war has not yet subsided...

"...There are distinct possibilities of our country being made an ideological battle-ground...

"...We have from time to time warned all countries having relations with us that we would not allow them to reduce our country to be used as a battle-ground for ideology...

"...It is because we want to steer clear of the basic ideology dividing the West and the East that we have adopted the policy of non-alignment and associated with other countries that wish to pursue the same policy...

"...In subscribing to the principle of non-alignment, we have tried to make it clear that we shall remain free to support any nation on any specific matter irrespective of whether that nation is in the Western or Eastern bloc...

"...We must equally remain free to criticize any nation on any specific issue.

"...We reserve the right to take appropriate measures in developing our economy and social services...

"...This right includes any decision taken by us to follow any particular pattern...

"...Where such pattern coincides with a pattern either in the East or the West we shall make it clear that our decision has not been based on copying from abroad but has been dictated by our needs and what we consider to be the quickest means by which to develop our resources...

"We have sought economic aid from West and East because we want to consolidate the principles of being able to do business with all countries in situations beneficial to us...

"...It has been our experience that aid can be given without strings attached...

"...No country, however, has come to us openly and demanded conditions which would have forced to break off relations with other State...

"...We consider it our responsibility to watch against hidden strings in the aid we are receiving either from the West or the East, and we stand ready to draw attention of any country which may give us aid with strings to our inability to accept such aid...

"...We are now writing a development programme which will lead us to negotiate agreements on greater development assistance than hitherto...

"...We shall have three things in mind...

"...First, that it is in the interest of all countries that there must be peace in the world; secondly, that the task of nation building means the maintenance of security, the promotion of understanding and co-operation, and a united effort within our own country; thirdly, that whatever aid we receive must be used only to improve the standard of living of our people...

Interference by Other Countries

"We are likely to run into some problems which will not be good for our people because certain countries in a position to give development assistance are taking more and more interest in how we implement our basic principles in foreign affairs...

"...We must take serious objections when other countries make demands that we should do certain things in a particular way...

"...Certain nations desire that we should follow their particular economic theories and systems...

"...This we are going to reject...

"...WE consider such demands as attempts to reduce us to a colonial status, which would easily cause instability in our country. Other nations desire that our foreign policy should be framed as part of theirs...

"...We cannot speak of being independent if our foreign policy is to be framed in that manner...

"...We also wish to be free to accept proposals from either side, while retaining our freedom to criticize.

"Some big powers regard criticism by us as an act of reject and comment on issues that divide the World Powers, unfriendliness...

"...For nationalists of any country to think that their Governments is always right, and that any disagreement from a small country is not only wrong but unfriendly, is a point we consider to be unrealistic and dangerous...

"...It opens the door through which forces which are destructive and can cause confusion and instability can operate...

"The line normally taken is that of seeking for politicians who would agree with a particular policy as expressed by a foreign country and who would work with that foreign country...

"...To me such a manoeuvre can only mean an insult to the nationals of a developing State...

"...No developing country can call itself free and sovereign when its Government is supposed to play the role of 'his master's voice'...".

Traitorous Politicians

"...The greatest danger in Africa today, as I see it, is that there are always ready politicians who are prepared to serve in a Government and make that Government serve the interest of foreign countries...

"...There are some politicians who consider that assistance by foreign countries to place them in Government is not wrong to seek; and sometimes they believe that, having got to position of authority in the Government through the assistance of foreign agents, they can find ways of resisting pressure from foreign Governments...

"...I do not believe that it is possible for any politicians in Africa cheap enough to be used by any foreign State and to be placed in a position of authority to change and pursue any policy not acceptable to his foreign masters...

"...There are examples where leaders and members of Government have been assassinated either because they refused to subscribe to pressure from outside or because they resisted such pressures after they were placed in position of authority by foreign countries...

"...The Congo is the clearest example of the dangers of the work of foreign agents in Africa...

"...We in Uganda have had a bit of brush with the Congo...

"...We have received the worst Press possible, but, possibly because of vested interests, the writers of articles which have appeared in the Press appear not to have been interested at all in examining the facts and getting generally informed of the real situation...

"...We are about the only country in Africa that has given material assistance to the Congo Government...

"...We have a long border with the Congo, and we consider peace and stability in the Congo as basic to our interest...

"...We desire trade with the Congo, but trade cannot flourish where you do not have law and order and peace...

"...It is not in our interest to have the Congolese conflicts near our border..."

Relation with the Congo

"...We have loyally implemented resolutions on the Congo passed by the organisation of African Unity...

"...Because, however, of vested interests, we have received the worst Press possible in the Western world in our relations with the Congo. Impossible stories have been published in the Press...

"...We know why such stories have been published. It is not that we supported rebellion in the Congo...

"...It is because we must be forced to support one man who is supported by certain Western Powers and has been placed in position of authority by those same powers...

"...What is happening in the Congo today leads us in Uganda to believe that the period of great nationalist movements which led to independence of a large part of Africa is being turned into a period of the scramble for Africa...

"...The difference is that instead of sending from overseas persons to go and rule over Africa, as was done in the last century, it is now found cheaper and convenient to pick upon individual African politicians to be agents to be supported in every respect by foreign States...

"...This development makes us in Uganda to consider the matter of colonialism as a live issue...

"...We therefore take a very firm stand on the question of colonialism...

"...We will consider any puppet Government in Africa on the same footing as we consider Angola, Mozambique, South Africa, Southern Rhodesia and South West Africa...

"...We will continue to oppose any Power that seeks to introduce colonialism not only in our country but also in any other independent areas of Africa...

"...We will continue to speak against any country that assists Portugal or the South African minority Government...

"...We will do this because it is part of the struggle we waged in our own country for independence; because foreign influence in any other part of Africa is a danger to us; because our ambition is to meet the aspiration of our people in providing for them economic opportunities and social services and that cannot be done vigorously and in circumstances of freedom unless influences from outside are eliminated...

"...We must have a free Africa- free from colonialism and enjoying peace and stability...

"...We must have in each of the African States a Government acceptable to the citizens...

"...We must improve the standard of living of our people and achieve their aspirations for progress, social justice, freedom, and prosperity..."

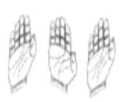

17. In the SOCIALIST INTERNATIONAL INFORMATION, July 10, 1965 extracts from a speech to the Danish Social Democratic Party Congress, was published thus:-

POST-INDEPENDENCE PROBLEMS IN AFRICA

MILTON OBOTE

"...I have no doubt that some of the issues you will be considering here will have meaning beyond the boundaries of Denmark...

"...I say this not only because of the existence in Europe and elsewhere of parties which shares basic principles with you, but also because of the importance of Social Democracy in the world...

"...It is with this in view that I wish to take this opportunity to present to you some of Africa's problems as we see them in Uganda...

"...Great transformations have taken place in Africa since the end of the second world war...

"...Uganda, which I have the honour to represent here today, is one of the African States which achieve independence, like many African state, as result of great nationalist movement which started after the war and gained momentum...

"...I think it is true to say that Africa today is a continent of nationalist movements...

"...Before independence the main problem facing an African country was always how to achieve independence in the shortest possible time...

"...This necessitated and called for great efforts on the part of African leaders to start popular political parties based on social justice and strong enough to present the views of the people...

"...On the achievement of independence these parties and movements have all been faced with problems of maintaining that independence, and how to channel the attention and efforts of the people to tackling the basic issues of economic and social development...

"...To us in Uganda, independence has meant challenge in two ways...

"...First, we believe that we must use our independence to rally the country in a united effort leading to the achievement of economic prosperity and abundant social services...

"...Secondly, we consider it a duty and a responsibility to conduct our foreign relations in such a manner as to ensure that political independence is achieved by those parts of Africa which are not yet independent...

"...In our struggle to raise the standard of living of our people and provide the much-needed social services, we are faced with numerous problems...

"...The greatest of these are two- one is lack of capital, and the other is trained manpower...

"...There is no point of going into reasons why wee in Uganda and the other African States are in this position...

"...It is sufficient to say that Africa's role in world affairs has changed and is changing...

"...In the last century Africa's role was that of a market for the manufactured goods from the metropolitan powers, and a producer of raw materials for the industries established overseas...

"...We therefore inherited at independence an economy which is basically the production of agricultural primary commodities, but the world prices for manufactured goods have been rising...

"...The position today is therefore that although the African people are producing more and more of these agricultural products, they are getting less and less for their increased produce...

"...This state of affairs creates difficult conditions for African Governments, and it is a credit to them that they have nevertheless maintained stability of the states and the popularity of the nationalists' movements...

"...In spite of the falling prices for the agricultural products, great changes are taking place in Africa which- if world peace is maintained- may result, in a comparatively short period, in a far better standard of living for the African peoples than was thought possible in Africa...

"...I consider them to be basic because I believe that what is required for the development of economic resources and social services must come first from within Africa itself, and secondly from the developed countries...

"...From within Africa, strong direction from the centre is requires in order to give opportunity to the people to participate effectively in economic projects, and to associate themselves with the social services which are needed for their welfare...

"...In this connection it must be remembered that the African peoples do not have big industrialist amongst them who can open opportunities as in the case in other countries...

"... In the absence of such industrialists, the Government in Africa have great opportunities to provide a steady economic and social basis, based on cooperation of the people. In the case of Uganda, emphasis is being laid on the development of the cooperative movement in agriculture, animal husbandry and in the processing industries, as well as in the marketing of agricultural produce...

"...These efforts which are observable in almost all African countries, can be greatly speeded up by the effective participation and willingness of the developed countries in several ways...

"...First it is important that the developed countries should look into the problems of stabilising the prices for agricultural products and other raw materials from Africa...

"...Our experience both at Geneva during the United Nations Trade and Development Conference and elsewhere, is that favourable trade terms for developing countries are very difficult to obtain...

"...What most developed countries apparently wish is to give development assistance but the terms under which this assistance is given are not always favourable...

"...It is most given on a project basis and this makes planning very difficult because the African country receiving the aid is never in a position in advance which project in her development programme will attract aid...

"...Then there is the problem of 'import content', which developed countries insist upon whenever they give aid to for large projects...

"...Import content means that the recipient country has to import large amounts of materials at great cost even if these same materials are available locally and are less costly...

"...This makes projects very expensive and at times uneconomic...

"...The other unfavourable item in the terms of aid which African countries receive from developed countries is the insistence by the developed countries that the recipient country should pay what is known as 'local costs'...

"...These can be very high and the total effect it has on an African country is that of postponing desirable projects in order to raise sufficient funds to meet local costs on a limited number of projects for which aid has been obtained...

"...This in turn leads to piecemeal development and a disjointed development programme...

"...Development programmes which African countries want are greater than it was in the case of Europe after the Second World War...

"...It is a historical fact that Europe was able to rebuild real economy and industries through the Marshall plan. In the case of Africa, no single developed country or a collection of them has suggested anything of that kind...

"...This has left African countries so open that they are forced to seek aid can be obtained both from the west and the east, the seeking of that aid from one quarter or the other can easily be misinterpreted, and once that happens a country is likely to walk straight into cold war problems...

"...This is always apparent where a country has received all the aid either from the east or from the west alone...

"...The total effect of this situation slows down a country's ability to plan ahead and to concentrate on essential development matters...

"...Everywhere in Africa where this condition has arisen, serious problems have followed-issues of ideology have arisen; the widely accepted policy of non-alignment in foreign relations has been either undermined or weakened, and the dedication and determination to coordinate policies and actions for the liberation of parts of Africa not yet independent have been compromised...

"...It remains true, however, that African leaders are aware of these problems and have given great thought as to how to work together effectively for the realisation of effectively for the realisation of effective cooperation...

"...The Organisation of African Unity was founded in Addis Ababa in 1963 in order to promote understanding, cooperation and unity in Africa...

"...Specialist commissions within the organisation have been set up...

"...A special committee was also set up to coordinate the activities of member states in the liberation of the whole of Africa...

"...The O.A.U. is likely to grow in strength. It is presently experiencing great stress...

"...There are signs that some powers are frightened of the growing unity in Africa and the possible strength which the O.A.U. could give to Africa...

"...This may lead to some weakening of the Organisation but remain with the hope that the spirit of the great nationalist movements which the Africans created, and which have brought independence to a large part of Africa, will assist the O.A.U. in overcoming present difficulties...

"...I am convinced that what gave Africa political freedom which African states now have is a contract with destiny...

"...The terms of that contract are dedications to the African cause and a determination to serve the African peoples in all activities which would lessen hunger and disease, and wipe out illiteracy..."

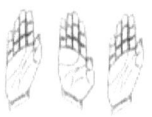

PART II

1966 – Weights on Dr Obote's nape

"...The hopes or rather the wishes of the B.B.C. may have been exemplified by the following reports or otherwise some 'ultra-plots' which matured into the 1971 COUP..."

I am using this quote, to draw attention to the post-1966 era. The documents herein collated belonged to people who had a given end game in mind. Their scheme for the political 'game' was akin to that of a marathon event whose distance is already known, and the winner decided. In this case the 5-year marathon was to run in 1971 and the winner already determined by 1965.

The documents I have collated and posted here for this period suggest that political competitors in the above described event were hopeful but not overly confident that the weights on A.M. Obote's nape were heavy enough to topple him. A three-layered scheme was thus hatched to topple him from power. I hasten to add, that this was much in the like of a three-lap athletic track event.

The first lap was about the manufactured of evidence which were embedded in newspaper publications and radio broadcasts that were emitted to the court of public opinion. Here I am minded to refer to someone I call 'COO', a legal mind, who during the 2006 Apollo Milton Obote Conference debate in London, dealt with this issue of 'creative evidence', but on a matter unrelated to the subject I am discussing here. The AMO Conference was to discuss the way forward for UPC, but the discussants were instead animated by the issue of genocide and human rights violations in Uganda under the rule of Yoweri Museveni. 'COO', a then delegate from Canada cut the chase and dropped a hint that

'...we must learn how to create evidence..." "....to be used in courts of law such as the ICC...."

Manufacturing evidence is a high-level operation in which only the most gifted in the art of deception and creating evidence excel and win. This art plays out in courtroom theatres, where astute judges determine the point at which the law is broken.

The period post-1966 is best captured as a period in which evidences were created, not for use in the judicial process but to cause the fall or demise of A. M. Obote. There is no way of telling that Obote was conscious of this, and what he would or could have done about it. He probably felt teased, but not threatened as he exuded confidence that he was capable of debating and reasoning with anyone, in short that he could hold his own in any adversarial dialogue.

The principals who adduced and disseminated the manufactured evidence also created the audience to feed on and string along with the created evidence. A.M. Obotes' own statement, does not reveal if he had 'a good understanding' of this process or procedure, or indeed consequences. It can be assumed that if he did, then he might have concluded that vilification was part of the game. This attitude was to prove very expensive to both Obote and the country.

The second lap was about participants in the race. Both sides in the race were aware it was to be concluded in 1971. A.M. Obote as his vilifiers was well aware of this. The difference is that while A.M. Obote went *'hell for leather'* for the tape, the vilifiers were working on alternative plans to dope; trip him or physically break his neck, if the political weights on the nape did not topple him over.

The third lap was about putschists who were outside the political race but were being groomed by interested parties abroad to be crowned as winners. These carried the day in 1971 to deny victory to all the political racers or participants and the celebrants at the winning tape. Now this was a surprise because A.M. Obote had assured all and sundry to quote

> "...am probably the only African leader who is not afraid of a military coup..."

The political other participants had no basis for disbelieving him and therefore also lowered their guard against the possibility military coup that had variously swept elected nationalists governments from political power, elsewhere in Africa.

For Milton Obote the political race was the general election slated for 1971 where he had hoped to beat his vilifiers. His calculation must have been blinded by the strong need and urgency he must have felt to consign all his vilifiers to history as complainers; or to constrain them in their vilification after '...*the people have spoken....*' Well A.M. Obote was not to have the last lough, and the vilifiers were to settle for mere crumbs from the table.

The putschists carried the day in 1971 to the surprise of all political racers. A.M. Obote's neck was not broken nor was he toppled over by the political weights on his nape.

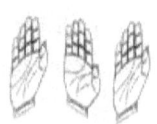

18. Inside the B.B.C. on the 31st March 1966 a PRIVATE and CONFIDENTIAL Memo Ref:05/RNH/CH:-

Dear Mr. **********,
As requested, I enclose a copy of your completed script on Dr. Milton Obote.
Yours sincerely,
+++++++++
        Secretary to ^^^^^^^^

PRIVATE AND CONFIDENTIAL

SUBJECT: DR. MILTON OBOTE---AN APPRECIATION
SPEAKER: ********** NT 29329
ORIGIN: 3D BIOG 401
DATE: 29TH March 1966
LENGTH: 2'40"
Producer: @@@@@@@@@

Dr. Apollo Milton Obote was one of Africa's shrewdest Prime Ministers. His political skill was largely responsible for bringing Uganda peacefully into independence in 1962 after a stormy period during which the powerful Kingdom of Buganda had threatened to secede. Having started life as a goat herd in Lango, when he was born in 1926, Dr. Obote's rise to power was swift, remarkable, adventurous. Once, without weapons, he had an encounter with a leopard; on another occasion he was attacked by two snakes; another time he was threatened by three armed Mau Mau. But this quiet spoken Ugandan, lived to become cool, unruffled, pipe-smoking politician.

At the age of 23 he abandoned his University studies at Makerere College, after completing only one year of his studies and for the next eight years he worked in Kenya as a labourer in a sugar plantation and later for an oil company. During this self-imposed exile he learnt his politics in the Kenya African Union. When he returned to his Native Lango in 1957 he was still virtually unknown. But within one year he was a member of the Legislative Council, and a year later he took over the leadership of the Uganda Peoples Congress. He quickly succeeded in converting it into the dominant nationalist movement, and by arranging an alliance with the Buganda traditionalist party, the Kabaka Yekka, he was able to secure the Premiership in 1961.

This alliance was broken five years later when he failed to hold together his ruling party with the result that he was driven to suspend Uganda's Constitution and to assume all power in his own hands.

In home affairs, his policies favoured the radical nationalists against the traditionalists. In foreign affairs he was a militant Pan-Africanist, a firm believer in non-alignment, and a staunch champion of the Commonwealth. Although he was keenly interested in the idea of an East African Federation he chose to move towards it with deliberate caution.

His health was always a source of concern and he frequently drove himself into states of complete fatigue. Referring to his Christian name, Apollo Milton, Dr. Obote once said:

"...I have always wanted to resemble Milton rather than Apollo..."

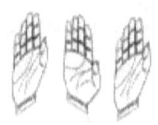

19. In the TIMES NEWSPAPER DATELINE 23.2.66. titled:-

DR. OBOTE TAKES FULL POWERS IN UGANDA - FIVE MINISTERS ARRESTED

Dr. Milton Obote, the Prime Minister of Uganda, who nine days ago denied being implicated in a plot to overthrow the constitution, today assume full powers of Government and imprisoned five Ministers.

He issued a statement in Kampala, the capital, saying that he had taken this step independently

> "...because of my understanding of the wishes of the people of this country for peace, order and prosperity..."

He did not name the five Ministers arrested, but said they had been placed in detention pending investigation into their activities.

Dr. Obote tonight claimed the situation in Uganda was under control. He appealed to the security forces, judges, magistrates, civil servants, both Ugandan and expatriate, and members of the public to carry on with their normal duties.

HELP FROM COUNCIL

In his statement on his one-man coup, Dr. Obote said that in carrying out the duties of Government he would be assisted by a council, whose members would be named soon.

Sources here say Sir Edward Mutesa, is still President, as he never had any executive powers.

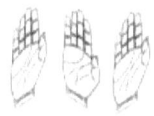

20. In the TIMES NEWSPAPER DATELINE 23.2.66

Our Commonwealth Staff writes:-

Last week Dr Obote answered charges in Kampala that some officials and army officers wanted to overthrow the constitution. He said

> "...I cannot condone anyone who wished to overthrow the constitution for which I have worked so hard..."

For some weeks there has been considerable tension in Kampala, after accusations against the Prime Minister and his closest associate in the Cabinet. Mr. Adoko Nekyon and Mr. Felix Onama of having received looted gold and ivory from the Congo. Both Mr. Nekyon, Minister of Planning and Community Development and Mr. Onama, Minister of Defence, denied the allegations.

On February 4, when Dr. Obote was touring up country, a resolution was passed by parliament calling for the suspension of Colonel Amin, Deputy Commander of the Army, for allegedly supplying the loot. Colonel Amin was allowed to go on leave. The fact that such a resolution could have been passed suggests that Dr. Obote is in serious difficulties with his own party.

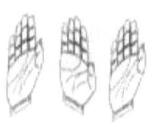

21. *In the TIMES NEWSPAPER DATELINE 23.2.66*

NINTH SCHEDULE   Article 132(3)

Part 1

DECLARATION BY THE GOVERNMENT

WHEREAS in the interests of national stability and public security and tranquillity, the Prime Minister on the 22nd day of February, 1966, took over all powers of the government of Uganda as a temporary measure:

AND WHEREAS we the undersigned are desirous that there should be as quickly a return to normality:

NOW THEREFORE in order to maintain national stability, public security and tranquillity, and to ensure a speedy return to the normality which existed before the events leading to the action taken by the Prime Minister on the 22nd day of February, 1966, we the undersigned do hereby declare that any action taken by the Prime Minister does not and do not affect and shall not affect or be deemed to affect any of the following provisions of the Constitution, that is to say:-

(a) the powers, dignitaries, status and privileges of the Rulers of the Federal States and Constitutional Heads of the Districts;

(b) the constitution of the Federal States and the Administrations of the Districts and the Councils and Boards of the Municipalities and Towns;

(c) the powers, duties and functions of the courts, the judges, and Magistrates;

(d) the National Assembly;

(e) the smooth working of the Civil Service;

(f) the Armed Forces of Uganda, the Police Force and the Prisons Service.

We hereby further declare that as a temporary measure there is hereby established a Security Council of Uganda, of which the Prime Minister shall be the Chairman, and a Cabinet of Ministers holding portfolios who shall be appointed by the Prime Minister.

We further declare that the suspension of the other parts of the Constitution is only a temporary measure for the promotion of unity, peace and the good of government of Uganda.

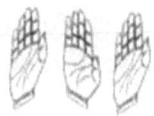

22. In the TIMES NEWSPAPER DATELINE 23.2.66.

1st Cabinet Ministers under the Republican Constitution

A.M. OBOTE - Prime Minister.

A.A. OJERA - Minister of information, Broadcasting and Tourism.

C.J. OBWANGOR - Minister of Justice

L. KALULE-SETTALA - Minister of Finance

J.W. LWAMAFA - Minister of Regional Administration

J.S. LUYIMBAZI-ZAKE - Minister of Education

S.N. ODAKA - Minister of State for Foreign Affairs

B.K. BATARINGAYA - Minister of Internal Affairs

F.K. ONAMA - Minister of Defence

A.A. NEKYON - Minister of Planning and Community Development

L. LUBOWA - Minister of Commerce and Industry

J.K. BABIIHA - Minister of Animal Industry, Game and Fisheries

G.L. BINAISA - Attorney General

W.W. KALEMA - Minister of Works and Communications

23. ON the 25.2.66 in the DAILY TELEGRAPH, Eric Downtown wrote:-

FOREIGN PLOT CHARGE BY OBOTE

Dr. Milton Obote, Uganda's Prime Minister, announced tonight that he has suspended the constitution. He alleged that there was a "...*foreign plot against Uganda...*"

This action follows reports of growing unrest throughout the country after Dr. Obote's sudden move two days ago arresting five Ministers. Yesterday he proclaimed that he had taken all powers of Government "...*in the interest of national stability, public security and tranquility...*"

"Coup" Attempt

Explaining the suspension of the constitution, Dr. Obote said:

> "...*During my tour of the Northern Regions of Uganda earlier this month an attempt was made to overthrow the Government by foreign troops...*
>
> "...*Some persons who held Government positions asked foreign missions for massive military assistance of foreign soldiers and arms...*
>
> "...*Even up to this morning some persons were asking for foreign Governments to invade Uganda...*
>
> "...*If drastic measures are not taken now some foreign powers might be tempted to give this massive assistance for the selfish interests of a few people in high places...*"

Tribesmen Restive

Armed Buganda tribesmen are tonight demonstrating near the Presidential palace after reports that President Sir Edward Mutesa, their Kabaka, had been involved in disturbances.

The Government spokesman, Mr. Kigozi, addressed the restive crowd on the outskirts of Kampala, telling them that the

President Sir Edward Mutesa, their Kabaka was safe and being guarded by soldiers. He appealed for calm.

His followers tonight are in a sensitive mood. They began rallying near the Presidential palace this afternoon when rumours began circulating of differences between Sir Edward and Dr Obote.

Warning Drums

Warning drums were sounded in some Buganda villages, taxi drivers drove at high speed through tribal areas shouting to Buganda followers to be ready to help Sir Edward.

The first public criticism of the Prime Minister's moves came today from Mr. Ochieng, the opposition Chief Whip. He said Dr. Obote was acting unconstitutionally and defying parliament.

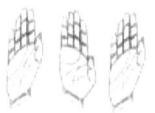

24. On 25.2.66. the LONDON TIMES correspondent reported:-

DR OBOTE SUSPENDS CONSTITUTION

Dr. Milton Obote, Prime Minister of Uganda, who two days ago assumed full powers of Government, tonight announced that he had suspended the constitution to ensure *"stability and Unity in the country"*, because of an earlier attempt to overthrow the Government by foreign troops.

> In a statement he said:
>
> *"...During my tour in the Northern Region early this month, an attempt was made to overthrow the Government by foreign troops...*
>
> *"...Some foreign missions stationed in Uganda were requested by persons who hold positions in the Government under the constitution of Uganda...*
>
> *"...These requests were made outside the provisions of the constitution and were for massive military assistance, consisting of foreign soldiers and arms...*
>
> *"...In effect this was an invitation to foreign governments to come and invade our country, because of the selfish interests of a few individuals in high places..."*

An official of the Ministry of Justice has named five Ministers who have been detained and said they appeared before the Chief Magistrate yesterday. They appeared before the Chief Magistrate yesterday. They are Mr. G.S.K. Ibingira, Minister of State, Dr. E.B.S. Lumu, Minister of Health, Mr. M.M. Ngobi, Minister of Agriculture, Mr. G.B.K. Magezi, Minister of Housing and Labour, and Mr. B.K. Kirya, Minister of Minerals and Water Resources.

KAMPALA, Feb.24.--Mr. Daudi Ochieng the opposition chief whip, today appealed to all Ugandans to uphold the constitution. He said the Prime Minister could dismiss re-appoint new Ministers, as laid down under the constitution, only by submitting names to the President for approval.

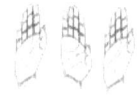

25. Date of publication: 2nd March, 1966.

NINTH SCHEDULE   Article 132(3)

Part II

DECLARATION BY THE GOVERNMENT

PURSUANT to the Declaration made by the Government dated the twenty-fourth day of February, 1966, and in exercise of all other powers thereunto enabling it is hereby declared by the Prime Minister acting with the advice and consent of the Cabinet that,

(a) the executive authority of Uganda shall vest in the Prime Minister and shall be exercised by the Prime Minister acting in accordance with the advice and consent of the Cabinet; and

(b) the duties power and other functions that are performed or are exercisable by the President or the Vice-President immediately before the twenty-second day of February, 1966, shall vest in the Prime Minister and shall be performed or be exercised by the Prime Minister by and with the advice and consent of the Cabinet.

Dated this 2nd day of March, 1966.

A. MILTON OBOTE,

Prime Minister.

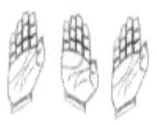

26. On 4.3.66. the LONDON TIMES correspondent reported:-

DR. OBOTE ACCUSES PRESIDENT

Dr. Obote, the Prime Minister of Uganda, alleged tonight that Sir Fredrick Mutesa, the President, had summoned foreign diplomats last month and made a request for troops to be sent to Uganda.

Dr. Obote who last week suspended the constitution and seized full powers, claimed in a Radio and Television broadcast that the Permanent Secretary to the Prime Minister of Buganda was away

"...on the same mission of military assistance..."

The Prime Minister said he and his colleagues intend the present situation in Uganda as a temporary one, and he would be holding discussions aimed at a return to stability. Yesterday he assumed the powers of President and Vice President.

Meanwhile Sir Frederick Mutesa, in the first pronouncement since Dr. Obote seized power, said in a letter to the Prime Minister today that he could not be a party to *"an illegal exercise"*.

It was also learnt here today that Sir William Nadiope, the Vice President, had left Nairobi for unknown destination.

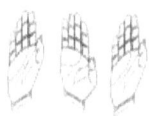

27. The KENYA WEEKLY NEWS April 29, 1966 in it's cover profile, A.C. DUFFIELD wrote:-

UGANDA'S NEW PRESIDENT

HIS EXCELLENCY THE PRESIDENT OF THE REPUBLIC OF UGANDA, is a man of steel. His strong character can be seen in every photograph that has been published, but the camera cannot convey the true picture of his sometimes-conflicting characteristics. It would need a modern Orpen to depict even a little of Dr. Milton Obote's personality. He can change in an instant.

He can converse with peasants or princes without either condescending or being obsequious. A cultured man of the world highly educated and with a brilliant brain he appreciates good music, art (not the pop variety) and real literature, and can talk about them intelligently with experts. But his real interest is in politics and the welfare of the "Common Man".

FIGHTING SPIRIT

Dr. Obote is a convinced socialist, perhaps in his views rather to the left of "African Socialism", but he is certainly not a communist. He believes in international co-operation, in the Pan-African future, in the "African personality", but he is first and foremost a Nationalist, and his primary concern is Uganda and its peoples.

He is strongly opposed to tribalism as a political force, but insists that tribal culture must be maintained and the best of tribal traditions fostered. He himself departed from Langi tradition when he married a charming Muganda lady.

In normal conversation Dr. Obote is not overbearing and listens with interest to other people, even if their opinions are completely opposed to his own, without becoming aggressive.

But in a political gathering. His fighting spirit comes to the fore, and he can be devastating.

As is well known, he has little use for the popular Press, and at a Press conference he has been known to thump a table, shout and display an almost violent temper. Those who know him well, and realized that his temper is normally under perfect control, suspect that he may be *"putting on an act"* on these rare occasions.

In debate in parliament, Dr. Obote is placid, courteous, incisive, aggressive or completely dominating according to circumstances. Amazingly *"quick on the uptake"*, he can seize on a point and tear into pieces his opponents argument.

He is respected, rather than loved, by his colleagues, who know that he is a born leader, convinced of the rightness of his cause; most of them would follow him in any direction he decides is the best for his country and his party (in that order). There are some people who are cautious, and wonder if that direction might lead to totalitarian dictatorship.

Saving grace

But Dr Obote is a democrat at heart (not of the Russian variety). He led a *"loyal opposition"* during the days of internal self-government, when Mr. Ben Kiwanuka was Prime Minister. At the General Election before independence, his Party was returned with majority of seats, but with fewer votes than the D.P. received. The U.P.C. has strengthened its position since then; no one can forecast the result of what may be a general Election this year, but it is highly probable that Dr. Obote will accept the people's verdict, whatever it may be.

He has saving grace that is not too common amongst politicians, African or Western - a keen sense of humour. During his last election campaign, he regularly quoted from **"Paradise Lost"**.

"...Better to rule in hell than serve in heaven..."

The writer once (bravely) asked him why he never quoted the preceding line. Dr. Milton Obote knows his Milton, and once declaimed dramatically:

"...To rule is worth ambition, though in hell;
"..Better to rule in hell than serve in heaven."

He then laughed, and said:

"...It would hardly be politic, would it?..."

Of course, Dr. Obote is ambitious; all statesmen of every nation are. There will be nothing to fear if Dr. Obote's ambition is for the future of his country rather than for himself. Most of us believe that.

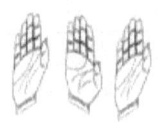

28. June 2, 1966. The colonial publication EAST AFRICA AND RHODESIA in an article recorded;-

KABAKA ESCAPES WHEN PALACE IS ATTACKED BY OBOTE TROOPS.

Baganda Ignore Call From Militants For Mass Rising On Monday.

THE KABAKA OF BUGANDA, Sir Edward Mutesa II, escaped when Uganda Government troops forced an entry into his palace on Mengo Hill, just outside Kampala, after hours of fighting on Tuesday of last week.

That was revealed on Friday by President Obote, who told journalists:

"...I know no more than you about his whereabouts..."

Conflicting rumours then circulating in Kampala suggested that he was in Kenya, in Ethiopia, in Burundi, or on his way to London.

The President emphasized that the security detachment had been sent to the Palace, not to arrest the Kabaka, but to search for illegal arms. Met by machine gun fire from the Palace, they had to defend themselves.

"...Because of the causality risk, they did not force the pace, and that is why it took all day to take over the Palace..."

"...Heavy guns were brought up late in the evening, when last-ditch defence in one building containing machine guns could not be overcome by other means..."

President Obote said that his reports were that only 20 people had been killed in the fighting at the Palace, none being members of the Uganda Army. There had been twenty deaths elsewhere in Buganda and some 600 arrests in the Kingdom for rioting, attacks on the police, breaking curfew, and robbery.

He defended the operation as comparable with that which President Kennedy of the USA had had to undertake against Alabama. The Uganda Government could, he added, not allow any province of the country to rebel, whatever opinions might be held in that province.

Queen and Sister Arrested

By the weekend it was believed in Kampala that the Queen of Buganda and a sister were under arrest; that the Kabaka's escape had been made during the a lull in the fighting caused by torrential rainstorm; and that he had been accompanied by several Ministers including the Katikiro (Prime Minister).

A group of Ministers in Buganda issued a statement late on Saturday calling upon the people of the Kingdom to co-operate with the Central Government in restoring peace and order. They ordered chiefs and civil servants to remain in their posts.

Strong military patrols were then still active throughout Buganda, in which the situation remained tense. Further arrests were made, and many women, children and elderly were reported to be moving away from the Kampala and the neighbourhood.

An attack was reported on a police station at Mayanja; a policeman was stated to have been hanged by a mob not far from Jinja; and sporadic firing from the outskirts of Kampala continued to be heard at night.

The Central Government ordered all holders of firearms to surrender them immediately at the nearest police station.

Legislation was rushed through parliament to deprive Buganda and other Kingdoms of the regional powers granted to them in the Independence Constitution four year ago.

The mass rising of Baganda threatened for Monday if the Central Government had not left Buganda territory appears to have been completely abortive. The Buganda Government had itself appealed for calm and peace on the previous day.

Students who reached Tanzania at the week-end said that at least six of their number had been killed in the fighting at Mengo. Some complained that Baganda had tried to force them to fight against the Government troops, others that villagers had compelled them to help in cutting down trees to make roadblocks and to tear up railway lines and pull down telephones and power connections.

Heavy Casualties Reported

Heavy casualties occurred when units of the Uganda Army attacked the palace of the Kabaka of Buganda on Wednesday of last week. First estimates were of 1000 dead on Mengo Hill. During the action a Red Cross worker said that more than 200 bodies had already been collected in a police mortuary from the fringes of the engagement, among them those of the troops, police, Buganda defenders, women and children.

A reporter who telephoned Army Headquarters for information was told:

> "...If you come here you will not leave alive, especially if you are white..."

A television team of an American and two Germans had their equipment, valued at about £2000, smashed by rifle butts, and they were forthwith put on an aircraft leaving for Nairobi.

In a 90-minute speech in Parliament that day President Obote mentioned that two Europeans had been killed and three injured. He did not refer to the fate or the whereabouts of the Kabaka, who was then generally thought to have been killed.

He accused the Kabaka of a *"three-pronged plan for rebellion"*. The first stage had taken the form of appeals to African States to promise diplomatic recognition and moral support. The second had been the demand by the Buganda Parliament that the Central Government should quit Kampala, which is within Buganda, the Kabaka having packed his parliament with hooligans who shouted down any attempts to express reasonable viewpoint. The third move had been the Kabaka's appeal to the United Nations for intervention in Uganda.

The president added that the troops who had stormed the Kabaka's Palace that day had found within a large quantities of arms which had been illegally imported into the country without the knowledge of the Government.

Arms Issues From Kabaka's Palace

Next day the following statement was broadcast from the Government-controlled station in Kampala:-

"...Yesterday morning a group of Buganda ex-servicemen, who had been selected by Mengo, attacked a unit of the Uganda Army at Makindye, near Kampala...

"...The Army unit successfully repulsed the attackers in an incident in which two persons among the attackers died and six were arrested...

"...Some of the arrested persons stated that the weapons they were using when they attacked the Army unit were distributed to them from the Palace of the Kabaka...

"...Army and police units in other parts of Buganda also arrested other persons in possession of dangerous weapons, whose stores were again stated by the persons arrested to be in the Kabaka's Palace at Mengo...

"...In one of the incidents three elderly European civil servants were attacked, and two have since died...

"...The third is in hospital...

"...In other incidents attempts were made at over-running police stations in the rural areas of Buganda by armed persons...

"...In these incidents eight policemen and another 10 civilians lost their lives...

"...In view of these developments the Government was duty bound to get to the source of the supply of the weapons used in the incidents...

"...Statements by the arrested persons have now been fully confirmed by the amount of arms of various makes and calibre which have been captured by the security forces at the Kabaka's Palace at Mengo...

"...It is important to note that the arms captured at Mengo today were illegally obtained without knowledge of the Government, and could only have been brought in the country not only by illegal means but for the express purpose of overthrowing the Uganda Government by force of arms...

> "...When the security forces went to the Palace at Mengo this morning to investigate the statements of the arrested person referring to these arms, persons in the Palace opened fire...
>
> "...The security forces returned fire and finally took over the Palace...
>
> "...It is now clear once again that the arms which have been used in the various incidents, as well as those found to use against the Government to give effect to his threat to secede from Uganda..."

Mr. Onama, the Defence Minister, told the House that Members who wanted to know the whereabouts of the Kabaka should ask the Minister and the chiefs in Buganda who had misled Sir Fredrick Mutesa and were responsible for the current troubles.

Opposition M.P's. asked for elections as soon as normal conditions were restored, so that the country might show whether it accepted the new Constitution.

Lukiiko Resolution An Act of Rebellion

The following statement on the security situation had been issued by the Uganda Government on May 23:-

> "...The Government has considered the resolution passed by the Buganda Lukiiko on Friday, May 20, and has concluded that this resolution amounted to an act of rebellion...
>
> "...The Government has further considered the contents of a letter dated May 20, said to have been written by Sir Edward Mutesa in the name of the Kabaka of Buganda to the Secretary-General of the United Nations...
>
> "...Here again the Government concluded that the attempt by Sir Edward Mutesa to say that the Government of Uganda must leave the soil of Buganda--which is part of Uganda--by May 30 constitutes an act of treason...
>
> "...The Government reiterates its statement issued on Friday, May 20, and reaffirm that Uganda should remain one country under the executive authority base on its headquarters at Entebbe, and that actions and attitudes such as those expressed by the Lukiiko and in the contents of Sir Edward Mutesa's letter, both last Friday, must be stamped out in the interests of stability, good Government, and the sovereignty of Uganda...

"...The Government has furthermore information to the effect that the Katikiro of Buganda has today issued statement which amounts to inciting to violence the people of Buganda...

"...These three instances - the Lukiiko resolution, Sir Edward Mutesa's letter, the statement of the Katikiro-all amount to a deliberate, systematic attempt, not only to undermine the authority of the Uganda Government, but also to subvert the foundation of law and order...

"...It is in view of these instances and developments that the Government has decided to have under protective custody three saza (county) chiefs whose activities have been known to endanger peace and good Government...

"...The chiefs have today been detained, and the Government is determined not to hesitate in taking similar action against any person or persons conducting themselves in a similar manner...

"...The police have today received reports that after the meeting of the Lukiiko last Friday a few of its members sought to bring chaos by misleading innocent men and women to resort to violence...

"...It was a result of such activities that some 50 men were also arrested near Makindye for attempting to obstruct security forces in the course of their lawful duties...

"...The Government has taken a most serious of this incident, particularly because some of the men arrested were found with dangerous weapons which they attempted to use against the security forces, which made the security forces retaliate...

"...The Government has therefore now taken the decisions to declare the whole of Buganda to be under a state of emergency...

"...This is to come into immediate effect...

"...During the state of emergency the security forces will have powers to arrest without warrants any person or persons...

"...Members of the public are warned to be in their houses except those whose duties require them to work at night...

"...All persons who are employed in essential services must report to their place of work during curfew hours, and the security forces will assist them in every possible way...

"...The curfew should be observed between the hours of 7pm and 6am...

"...The Government has been forced into taking this drastic measure because the situation warrants it...

"...Government Would Have Forgiven The Kabaka's Treason...

"...It will be recalled that Sir Edward Mutesa committed treason by attempting to negotiate without authority for foreign troops. It was the desire of the Government to forgive and forget that treasonable offence...

"...In accordance with its kind of decision, which in other countries would never have been forgiven, the Government introduced a new Constitution last month, which left the provision of the Kabakaship intact...

"...The only major changes which the new constitution introduces in Buganda have been the removal of the highly-paid civil servants such as Saza Chiefs from being a member of the Lukiiko...

"...The only other change has been the bringing to an end of the system whereby the Ministers in the Kabaka's Government and the Chiefs draw revenue from official land paid by the Buganda tax-payer fully for their services...

"...In these changes nothing can possibly be said to have affected the position of the Kabakaship or the Kabaka himself, unless of course Sir Edward had some vital interest in keeping the Saza Chiefs in the Lukiiko and in perpetuating the double payment of Ministers and the chiefs by the tax-payer in Buganda...

"...The Government further wishes it to be known that the UN cannot interfere in our internal affairs...

"...The first letter which was sent by Mengo (the seat of the Kabaka's Government) to the U Thant, the UN Secretary-General, was sent partly in ignorance and partly in hope that Mengo was doing something...

"...It must be clear to most people in Buganda by now that this was the same tactic used in the abortive appeal to the Privy Council on the subject of the "lost counties...

"...The letter of May 20, however, is of a difference...

"...This was an act of rebellion...

"...It is the view of the Government that the people of Buganda as a whole cannot be blamed for the resolution passed by the Lukiiko last Friday and the letter of the same date...

"...The state of emergency in Buganda will aim, therefore, as its primary objective to bring under control the few persons who committed acts of treason or rebellion...

"...It is possible that these few same persons may try to encourage members of the general public to support them by breaking the law...

"...The Government wants everybody to keep the law, to abide by the terms of the emergency declaration, and to realise that those who committed acts of treason and rebellion will themselves be unable to come forward against the security forces..."

The statement was also broadcast in Luganda and other languages.

Leaflets then began to be widely circulated throughout Buganda calling on the people to compel the Central Government to obey the Kabaka's order to move from Buganda soil by the following Monday, 30.

A number of police stations in Buganda had meantime been, substantial quantity of weapons and ammunitions falling into the hands of militant Baganda, who were heartened by rumours that their hereditary leader had not been killed but had escaped to a neighbouring country.

Refugees from Kampala who reached Nairobi during Thursday stated that, after the Kabaka, accompanied by 12 personal bodyguards, had slipped away, using the *"gate of death"* in the Palace wall which is traditionally used only on the occasion of the funeral of a Kabaka. A car then carried them to safety--in, it was believed, Burundi.

Crippled Judge Thrown into Ditch

Mr. Justice Sheridan, a High Court, who is crippled by poliomyelitis, was reported to have been dragged from his car about 80 miles from Kampala by men armed with bush-knives who threatened his life but contended themselves with throwing him into a ditch and stealing his car.

Dr. William Woolf, who has been engaged in TSETSE control work, was severely wounded in a bush knife attack at a roadblock 30 miles north of Kampala.

Gangs armed with bush-knives made other attacks on cars and lorries, one group seizing a consignment of tin valued at about £40000.

The situation was, described as generally quiet in an official announcement that the meetings and processions had been forbidden.

The Kenya Government prohibited entry by Uganda residents, the Ministry for Home Affairs describing the regulation as *"a defence against panic"*. Checks were established at all points of entry by road, rail and air.

Telephone and telegraphic communications with London were interrupted for a brief period.

A Congolese carpenter in Kampala told journalists that he had seen the bodies of two sisters of the Kabaka in the ruins of the Palace.

Commenting on the Lukiiko resolution *"purporting to say where the Government of Uganda should be seated"*, an official announcement stated:-

> "...The Government holds very firmly that the independence and executive authority of Uganda cannot be shared with the Lukiiko, and that its actions and attitude must be stamped out for the good of the country...
>
> "...The Buganda Lukiiko has no power, constitutional, executive, or otherwise, to effect any resolution against the Government of Uganda...
>
> "...As a sole executive authority for the whole of Uganda, the Government re-affirms its determination that the whole of Uganda shall remain firmly under the administration of the Government at Entebbe...

"...Every measure will be taken without fear or favour in carrying out this and other responsibilities of the Government at Entebbe..."

Dr. Obote said that he had now documentary evidence that Sir Edward Mutesa had decided by April 12 to mount a full-scale rebellion against the Government of Uganda. In addition to making appeals, which were abortive, to African States for diplomatic recognition, he had sent emissaries outside Africa for the same purpose. He intended the Province of Buganda to secede from Uganda, despite the fact that it was an integral part of that sovereign state.

Sir Edward had directed county chiefs to propose a resolution committing the Lukiiko to the idea of rebellion, but that endeavour had failed; and there was no shred of evidence that that was the view of the people of Buganda as a whole.

Mr. A.K. Sempa a former Minister of Uganda, and a few county chiefs then decided that the best way to commit Buganda to Sir Edward's personal rebellion was to plot for removal of the Kabaka's council of Ministers. Hooligans were to shout down dared to speak against the motion. That was passed on the previous Friday, when the resolution was passed purporting to order the Government to order the Government and the sovereign Parliament of Uganda out of Buganda. That was an open declaration of rebellion.

Insurrection Planned Last Year

As to the letters written to the Secretary-General of the United Nations by Sir Edward, not one of them had ever been posted to New York. They had been written solely for propaganda purposes in Buganda. In any case, UN was prohibited by its charter from interference in the internal affairs of a member State.

As to foreign reactions to what had happened in the Lukiiko, not one Government had indicated any change in its relations with Uganda since the introduction of the new Constitution.

"...I am now fully satisfied, as my colleagues in Government, that persons in Mengo, including Sir Edward Mutesa as the leader, have for a long time, even before the beginning of this year, been planning for an insurrection and for control of Uganda as a whole...

"...For this reason we as a Government are fully determined to bring this misery to innocent people, to keep Buganda as an integral part of Uganda, and to maintain the Parliament of Uganda Supreme..."

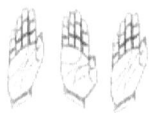

29. A version of the above appeared in a LONDON newspaper dateline Feb 22, 1967 under the title:-

DR. OBOTE RESOURCEFUL REBEL

Dr. Milton Obote, the Prime Minister of Uganda, who is 41 led his country to independence in October, 1962, after only five months in power. He has had varied life ranging from a goatherd and a labourer to teacher and politician. He has now assumed absolute power in Uganda.

He is quiet outspoken and the very image of a cool reflective statesman, but is in fact is a tough, resourceful revolutionary determined that his country and the African continent will not be a mere projection of Europe or any other part of the world.

Sixteen years ago, he was a labourer, a man of drive and apparently physically fearless. Without weapons, he has faced on various occasions a leopard and two snakes, and three Mau Mau fighters intent on shooting him. He also survived a spear in the back and clubbing by a thief.

Forced into Exile

He studied political science and economics at Makerere University College but gave up in 1950 and plunged into the trade union movement to learn first-hand the condition of the lowest paid workers. He helped to establish the Kenya African Union Party, banned with the outbreak of the Mau Mau activities in 1952, and was forced into exile until 1956. He entered the Uganda Legislative Council in 1957 and became Prime Minister in April, 1962.

In his foreign policy he has welcomed Soviet policies in Africa and supported China over the Vietnam war and Chinese entry to the United Nations. But in January, 1964, when the African soldiers of the Uganda Rifles mutinied, Dr. Obote turned to

Britain for aid and 450 British troops from the strategic reserve in Kenya flew in to help.

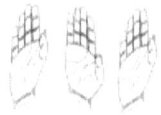

30. EMBARGO: NOT TO BE PUBLISHED BEFORE 6pm Nov. 17.1967.

PRESS RELEASE:

The Kabaka's Message On The Occasion Of His 43rd Birthday cannot be a happy one.

"...Ever since the Battle of Mengo Hill, on 24th May last year, when the Army attacked my Palace, things have been getting worse and worse in Uganda...

"...My brother David is one of the many people who have been in detention for more than twenty months now...

"...A fortnight ago the state of emergency was extended for yet another six months...

"...There is tension throughout the country and the people are anxious and unhappy...

"...Looking back from this point in time, it is difficult to answer the questions as to what Uganda has achieved after all the spilling of blood and the sowing of bitterness and hatred...

"...Much of what has happened is claimed to have been done for the sake of unity, stability and prosperity...

"...What is happening in Uganda and elsewhere in Africa points to the fact very forcibly, that in order to achieve those noble goals, greater efforts and better intentions are necessary...

"...Those efforts and intentions do not exist in Uganda today...

"...I now live in exile in this country, because I tried to resist that which those in power called a "Revolution"...

"...At that time I clearly saw, as well as the next person, that unless good men spoke, evil might triumph...

"...Under the emergency and the strict curb on free expression, people have not been able to speak effectively...

"...That explains the silence that has enshrouded the abolition of the Kingdom...

"...It also accounts for the absence of audible protests against the postponement of the general elections to the National assembly and to the Local Councils for the next five years...

"...Most people in Uganda Know that there is virtue in being patient...

"...They also know that things cannot go on indefinitely as they are now...

"...There must be a radical change of heart...

"...Drastic measures have been tried and are still being imposed, but there is always a limit to what people can endure...

"...In the interests of Uganda realism must be tried...

"...It is only by facing the situation realistically and fearlessly that peace, sanity and stability will be restored in that tortured country...

"...My people expect me to participate in the reconstruction of Uganda in which the rule of law will prevail...

"...Change is certainly drawing nearer and nearer every day; God has surely not forgotten to be gracious..."

London 17.11.68

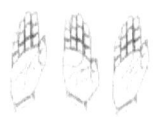

31. *A.C. DUFFIELD in the KENYA WEEKLY NEWS December 27 1968 comments on the strengthening of Uganda's Administration and notes that:-*

THE PRESIDENT APPOINTS

Dr A. Milton Obote

A number of changes in Ministerial, civil service and parastatal posts were announced at end of November and it is now generally agreed that they are all to the good and will have the effect of increasing the efficiency of the administration and accelerating the work of development.

The most interesting is the appointment by the President of Dr. Milton Obote as Minister of National Service. His Excellency carries a great weight of responsibility and has multifarious duties to perform, and it is an indication of the importance he attaches to the newly created Ministry that he willing to assume the burden of building it ab initio. He has appointed a loyal backbencher, Mr. J.O. Anyoti, as Minister of State for the Service and the Ministry will have two Permanent Secretaries- Mr. N. Oluoch (Technical) and Mr. E. Galukande (Economic).

The Details

Details of the National Service organisation have still to be worked out, but undoubtedly the President will be very concerned with the big problem of school-leavers who are unable to proceed to higher education. At the end of this year it is expected that there will be some 68,000 of them from Primary Seven. It is hoped that National Service will provide them with some experience in agriculture, animal husbandry or as leaner artisans which will convince them that they can work for progress and enjoy a full life without wearing a white collar. School-leavers will, of course, be only a minority of those who will be affected by National Service, but they will be an important minority.

The heart of the administration is the President's office, and this has undergone a complete streamlining which will speed up communications and benefit the whole administration. One of the most efficient of Uganda's Civil Servants, Mr. Frank Kalimuzo, heads the office as the Permanent Secretary and Secretary to the Cabinet. Secretary for Administration is another efficient and experienced Civil Servants, Dr. G.R. Katongole, who has previously been Permanent Secretary in the Ministry of Information and Broadcasting and more recently held similar post in the Ministry of Culture and Community Development. Mr. A.M. Sibo has been transferred from Permanent Secretary of the Ministry of Information, Broadcasting and Tourism to the President's Office to head the section that will deal with Economic Affairs and the East African Community, and Mr. Ali Picho, who holds a Master of Law Degree from Moscow University, has been appointed Secretary to the Research Section. Mr. Henry Kyemba continues as His Excellency's Principle Secretary.

For a year and half, Dr. S.J.L. Zake has been riding two horses and it is a tribute to his great ability that both have not only kept up the pace they had single riders, but have changed from fast canter of steady progress to a rapid gallop (but without overreaching!).

Dr. Zake, Minister of Education, took over the additional job of Attorney General when Mr. Godfrey Binaisa, Q.C., resigned. Dr. Zake was well qualified for the post; called to the Bar in London, he later gained a Master's Degree in Constitutional Law in the United States and his fine Legal brain was invaluable in the drafting of the 1967 Constitution. Now he has been relieved from the onerous double burden and will devote his whole time to the ministry of Education where, Heaven knows, there are enough problems to deal with.

Successor

His successor as Attorney-General is Mr. Lamech Lubowa, who vacates the Labour Ministry. Before independence, Mr. Lubowa was partner in the legal firm, Binaisa, Ibingira and Lubowa; when U.P.C. came into power in 1962, all three were appointed to the Cabinet I wonder if this is a record? I believe that in the U.S.A. sometimes two members of a legal firm have been appointed to Cabinet rank in one administration, but I have never heard of before of a whole partnership joining a government, or of two members of a firm becoming Attorney-General during the life of a parliament.

Binaisa resigned in 1967; Ibingira has been in detention since February, 1966, and now Lubowa becomes Bwana Mkubwa of the Law Development. He has been away from legal practice for six and a half years, but he will have experienced lawyers in his office to hold his hand until he gets into full stride and I don't think that will be long. Lamech Lubowa is an extremely capable man and will not leave any loopholes in new bills for the benefit of his colleagues in legal fraternity.

Hell-for-leather

In the Labour Ministry Mr. Lubowa has been succeeded by Mr. F.Y. Lakidi, formerly Minister of State for Public Service and Cabinet Affairs. Mr. Lakidi is a man with very great drive who goes hell-for-leather for his objective. His new responsibilities will bring him into closer contact with rather more difficult people than in his previous post. He was given some very sound advice by the experienced Lamech Lubowa in the process of taking over, particularly on the problems of dealing with clamant trade union leaders and obstinate employers. Perhaps there is no ministry other than Mr. Sam Odaka's where tact is more the first essential than the one Mr. Lakidi now heads. I used an equestrian metaphor in referring to Dr. Zake; here is another for Mr. Lakidi; a bridled tongue makes for steady progress; taking the bit between the teeth can lead to going off the course!

I have no doubt that the new Minister will be able to deal tactfully with difficult customers and the Ministry will retain its excellent reputation for furthering good labour relations.

I might be taken to task for rather outspoken criticism in the U.S.A. and Britain.

I wonder how long an opposition leader in any developing state would remain out of detention if he made such a scathing attack on the Government in power as was lunched recently in Britain by the Tory leader Ted Heath (a possible future Prime Minister). He said of the Labour Government:-

> "...I indict them for misapplying funds...
>
> "...I indict them, above all, for gross negligence...
>
> "...This is not a government of evil and wicked men...
>
> "...It is simply a government-if that is not too strong a term- of men and women bankrupt of ideas and totally lacking in competence...
>
> "...The task is simply too much for them..."

This virulent attack was delivered in a political speech that was not covered by parliamentary privilege. Heath has not been detained or sued for slander.

On the same day, the Chairman of the Tory Party, Arthur Bamber, said;

> "...Rise up and Show the British are sick and tired of second-rate Ministers led by the biggest political trickster of them all..."

Ideas and Ideals

Uganda has no Ministers that could be classified as second-rate. They are comparatively young men who are extremely competent. Far from being bankrupt of ideas, they are full of ideas and ideals. No one could accuse them of negligence, of false pretences or of deliberately misapplying funds (although in some ministries there may have been some overspending of votes).

It is not necessary to be a Tory to agree with some of the criticism made of the Labour Government, but I think Bamber was wrong to speak of Harold Wilson as a political trickster; it would have been more appropriate to have called him a rabbit.

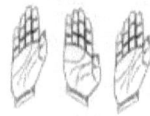

PART III

1971 – The weight on Milton Obote's Right Shoulder.

Dr. A.M. Obote was not a prophet. At least I have not heard or read of his connection with prophesy of the religious kind. Yet he confidently asserted that he would return to political power by means and the power of the ballot. The same ballot he was denied by both local and international political interests in 1971; I hasten to quote "....*for reasons best known to them...*"

The military regime of the 70's and its apologists abroad, together with their local connections, widely publicised the virtues of military rule and bestowed upon the regime all sorts of accolades while hiding its most heinous, hideous and atrocious acts in the management of Uganda. From my reading of published materials and observations both from a distance and from close quarters, this praise of military rule did NOT amuse the people of the country. The relationship between the military regime and the people of Uganda had therefore to be deliberately and carefully managed "....*for reasons best known to them...*"

The political interests superintending over the Ugandan political landscape tried their best during the rule of the military regime to yet again steer an anti-Obote course '...*for reasons best known to them...*".

Anti-Obote political luminaries joined the military junta in the hope that the political space without Obote offered them a chance to steer the country away from the Obote ideas and policies. Since this was never stated publicly they therefore must have joined the military band wagon "....*for reasons best known to them...*"

In due course, some of these anti-Obote political elements fell out with the military regime, or were simply booted out by the military regime. The people of Uganda have never been told the reasons why, nor have the individuals so booted offered any explanations. The nearest explanation I hazard to guess is that they had to be dismounted or were booted "....*for reasons best known to them...*"

Many pro-Obote political elements who belatedly joined the fight to rid Uganda of the military regime did not publicly share their thoughts with the people of the country. Doubtless they must have shared them privately with Milton Obote. I have not been privileged with information that validates the reasons for the sacrifices that such individuals made, including with their lives, to liberate Uganda from military rule. I can only hazard a guess that they did it "....*for reasons best known to them...*"

At least anti-Obote elements who were also anti-Amin publicly shared their thoughts with the people of Uganda. These were "...*men of substance...*" and "...*revolutionaries armed with Mao's Red Book...*," etc. The men of substance were not short of funds to do their errands, sleep in the best hotels, and marry in exotic locations, despite being blanked by mainstream publications. They never publicly shared their disdain for other countrymen who were also fighting the Military Junta with other Ugandans despite the facilities at their disposal. These joined with the Military Juta to ruin efforts to rid Uganda of the military regime wherever and whenever it suited them "....*for reasons best known to them...*"

Ugandans of all walks of life, given their pride and dignity, faced disproportionate challenges to survive under the military Junta. They lived in the hope that all the competing political interests were doing something about ridding the country of the military Junta. By 1979, those of us who were in the front-line to see off the military Junta, faced the verbal wrath of such men of substance as well as their negative actions to keep us out in everything that were associated with the country's so-called development. The men of substance uprooted telephone lines; uprooted electric poles; dug up tarmac roads; trashed hotels; trashed government office-telephones and faxes; trashed

Presidential lodges and official government residences. They trashed anything associated with officialdom or government, both fixed and moving. I can only surmise that they wanted us out of any form of governance, possibly including the one that was being ushered by 'compatriot liberators'. I have been around, but have not heard, even once, from political luminaries why they think the people of Uganda are angry with them. This silence is "....*for reasons best known to them...*"

By 1979 the Uganda Dr Obote left in 1971 was significantly different and its nationalities were significantly a changed people. The language they used had changed and had introduced new ways of describing things. Their approach to issues had changed and been re-modelled in the way they engaged as groups or singularly. A new attitude to everyday life had evolved out of a new form of economic engagement that had now taken hold which a friend of mine 'Opobo', a soldier who had fought in the war, described as *'grabiosis'*.

From 1976, after the murder of Archbishop Janan Luwum, the prelate of the protestant Church of Uganda, the Friday and Sunday prayer places in the country were always full. I have not heard or read of any published research or comments about this phenomenon. Even social researchers from our institutions of higher learning paid no heed to this phenomenon. Maybe they were too busy learning the new languages or ways of doing things. In my observation the unusual thronging to faith places, was "....*for reasons best known to them...*" In 2012, while in a car ride in London England, Dr 'Biz', an Obote critic, informed me that '....*with Ganda nationality when you see them silent and in prayer, know that something is afoot...*' The pin dropped as to what had bothered me about this excessive attention to prayers during this period. Possibly these practices too rubbed on A.M Obote, who was married to a Ganda lady. He was largely silent between 1971 and 1979.

Dr A.M OBOTE PALM PRINTS

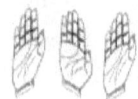

27. William Borders from Dar es Salaam for the LONDON TIMES 11.2.71 reported:

DR. OBOTE SAYS HE WILL RETURN TO POWER WITHOUT AN INVASION.

Dr. Milton Obote, the deposed President of Uganda, vows that he will return, although he cannot say when.
> "...I am not thinking in terms of time, but I am absolutely sure it will happen...",

he said in an interview at the State house of Tanzania, where he has spent most of his time since January 25, when Major-General Idi Amin seized control of Uganda.

Dr. Obote seemed relaxed and confident as he spoke of
> "...the terrible mess..."

into which he said General Amin had led himself.
> "...Don't worry about us...
> " We shall be alright...",

he said, slapping his thigh with a hearty laugh. At other points in the interviews he was sad and quiet, especially when discussing his family.
> "...My mother and father-I think they have been killed...
> "...They were in Akokoro, our village in the North...
> "...My wife and three children are hostages in Kampala...
> "...The eldest child is six and half year sold, but they have five fully armed soldiers in the house...
> "...I am damn certain they will all be killed..."

Dr. Obote said that
> "...since the coup the Ugandan Army had killed thousands of people, civilians as well as soldiers, including his brother Michael Obote..."

The former President said that he had not sent any messages to the

> "...many soldiers who bravely continue fighting in the bush against General Amin...."

He also said that there would be no military invasion of Uganda to reinstate the former Government.

He talked about his overthrow, which he called

> "...a one-man operation, not a real Army coup...",

in the ornate parlour of his apartment in the former British Governor's residence, which now houses the offices of President Nyerere of Tanzania.

Commenting on Britain's decision last Friday to recognize the new Government in Kampala, Dr. Obote said:

> "...The British should know better what the real attitude of the people of Uganda is toward Amin..."

Ghana has also granted diplomatic recognition to General Amin, but most of the other African states have followed a cautious middle course. Kenya and Ethiopia the two countries beside Tanzania that Dr. Obote has visited since his overthrow, have said nothing on the subject of recognition.

> "...When I visited them, I just told them I thought that this was not the time to make a move, although I emphasized that the decision was theirs...",

Dr. Obote said of his talks with the leaders of the two states, which are among Uganda's most important neighbours in East Africa.

The former President spoke of General Amin, who was his Army Chief of Staff, with no particular passion, although he said:

> "...Amin would have me killed within 24 hours if I went back now..."

General Amin has said that he will hold elections in Uganda soon for civilian post of head of government, but Dr. Obote said:

> "...Let's bet on it, as long as Amin is alive there will be no elections in Uganda...

"...He will not be there very long though...

"...A head of state has many headaches, and Amin is not prepared for them...

"...He thinks you can be head of a country in the same way you are head of on Army, and just arrest everyone who disagrees..."

NEW YORK TIME NEWS SERVICE.

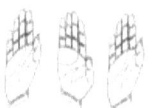

28. *A publication TO THE POINT, 10th February 1973, reported:*

UGANDA - A Nasty Story

Reports that Uganda's President Idi Amin and Libya's Colonel Moammar al-Gaddafi are planning an invasion of Tanzania are doing the rounds in East Africa. The reports have it that the two leaders want to restore the rule of the Sultan of Zanzibar, Seyyid Jamshi Abdullah, who is the brother-in-law of Gaddafi. Reports filtered out of Uganda by men close to Amin say the move is designed to consolidate Arab and Islamic influence on the East Coast region of Africa. In an effort to square his accounts with the Arabs, General Amin is said to be the champion of the whole plan.

TO THE POINT's enquiries among members of Amin's Cabinet have revealed that once the plans are concluded, Amin will eliminate all Ugandans not willing to adopt the faith of Islam by sending them to Arab oilfields as labourers. Apparently, the plan to invade has been subjected to preliminary studies and found to be feasible. What remains to be done now is a more detailed study of military intelligence reports. Libya is preparing to provide the intelligence service and other requirements for the exercise. The reports have it that Saudi Arabia has promised to boost Amin's spending power for military equipment.

Despite agreements between Tanzania and Uganda to stop hostilities, Amin's Airforce continued to bomb Tanzania's civilian population after the Mogadishu Treaty had been signed last year following the alleged invasion of the pro-Obote guerrillas.

In Nairobi a Ugandan soldier who fled to Kenya and who prefers to remain anonymous, has told TO THE POINT that General Amin plans to post unwanted soldiers to the Tanzanian border and then to kill them and the civilians opposed to his

Government. The deaths would be explained away by saying that Tanzania guerrillas had invaded Uganda.

The refugee soldier confirmed a report that the Ugandan Army has copied Army uniforms in the hope of using them for an invasion of Tanzania to restore the Sultanate on Zanzibar. Highly placed sources connected to the Ugandan Cabinet have told TO THE POINT that Arab troops have pledged to fight their way down to Dar es Salaam and later to the Indian Ocean Island.

If the plan succeeds, East Africa will be faced with another violent conflict. Perhaps in an effort to divert international attention, General Amin is continuously accusing Tanzania's President Nyerere of planning an invasion of his own country and has carried this claim to the extent that Somali Government officials have visited the border area with Tanzania to make sure that the Mogadishu Treaty in not violated.

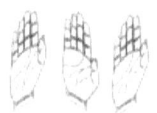

29. *B.B.C. monitoring service bulletin ME/4885/B/2, 23rd April 1975, Kampala home service in English 1400gmt, 21st April 1975.*

UGANDA: AMIN'S DENIAL OF ANY INVASION PLANS

TEXT OF THE REPORT:

A military delegation which was led by the Chief of Staff, Maj-Gen Musitafa, to Turkey today (21st April) briefed Gen Amin on its mission at Nakasero officers mess.

The delegation to Turkey included one which was in Egypt led by Colonel Ibrahim of the Marines. The Major briefed President Amin on how Turkey captured Cyprus in 1974 and how Egypt recaptured the Suez Canal and the Barlev line in October 1973.

After the briefing, Gen Amin told the officers of Tanzania's fear of an alleged invasion by an unnamed country. The fears are in a Reuter report issued today. Commenting on the alleged Tanzania invasion, Gen Amin said he still considers President Nyerere of Tanzania one of his best friends. He reiterated that had he been a woman without grey hair, the General would have married him.

He said Uganda has no plans to invade Tanzania, and Uganda, therefore, is not a neighbouring country in the Reuter report that plans to invade Tanzania.

General Amin observed that Nyerere now wants to win back the confidence of his 400 rebel soldiers who failed to topple his government on 24th December last year, and they have since been operating against him in a forest. He said Nyerere now fears that they will topple him while on his European tour or at the Commonwealth conference in Jamaica. He now aims at boosting the morale of his armed forces and winning the confidence of his rebel soldiers with an invasion pretext. Gen Amin assured Tanzanians that he has nothing against them, nor the reason to invade their country. He said he is instead ready to assist them when approached.

The General also observed that Tanzania is facing troubles, one of which is lack of food. He said Tanzania's Ujamaa policy, which she thought would make her self-reliant, has completely failed and she has no food. He said she is importing it from outside, including USA.

Gen Amin told officers that if Nyerere visited Uganda, he would be accorded a welcome befitting a Head of State and that Uganda, like Tanzania, is a member of the East African Community and the OAU.

The alleged invasion was contained in today's Reuter report, which said that Tanzania Government warned last night that a neighbouring country was planning to invade Tanzania and annex a border district. In a brief statement issues by the Tanzanian Information Ministry, the Government said that she had received reliable report of the planned aggression. The neighbouring country was not named. The Government statement said Tanzania warned any potential aggressor that it was ready to defend its border and freedom. Let the provocateurs know once he invades, he will have set in motion a war which will not be confined to the borders. The Tanzanian Government- owned newspaper 'Daily News' said today that the armed force had pledged they would hit hard at any enemy who dared to violate the country's territorial integrity. The pledge was given by officers and trainees at Tanzania's military academy in Monduli during a ceremony yesterday. The threat of invasion and the counter-charges from Uganda have plagued the relations between the two neighbouring countries in the East African Community for four years.

Gen Amin and the officers also saw a film depicting Turkey's military power and skill employed in capturing Cyprus. Gen Amin said it was a very good film and should be shown on UTV tonight after the news for public information. Gen Amin also directed that arrangements be made for the film to be shown in all

Battalions in Uganda. Gen Amin observed that Uganda has weapons used in Turkey over Cyprus and knows all the tactics employed. He also advised liberation movements in South Africa, Rhodesia and South West Africa and the PLO to employ such tactics in their liberation war.

The General said Uganda plans to invade nobody but if she was invaded, Uganda may set a world military record in winning the war and capturing the enemy in the shortest time, that is six days it took Israel in 1967, Turkey took 11 days, Cambodia which took eleven years. He stressed to the officers that to win any war, officers and their men must have excellent discipline, co-operation and loyalty.

Maj-Gen Mustafa gave the General an album with pictures of their discussions with the Turkish leaders both in Istanbul and Ankara. In the cover of the album is an engraved portrait of President Atartuk, who toppled the Ottoman Empire, started the Turkish revolution, formed the first Turkish Cabinet and Parliament, and his policies are still in force in Turkey up to date. Gen Amin also said he was happy with the military delegation to Egypt which was led by Colonel Ibrahim of the Marines.

The General was met on arrival by Maj-Gen Mustafa, the Commander of the Air Force, Brigadier Guwedeko; the Commander of Infantry and the Commander of Eastern Command, Colonel Gowon.

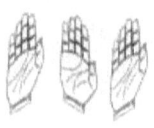

30. *Dar es Salaam home service in English, and for abroad, 1600 GMT 21 Apr 75 BBC ME/4885/B/2, 23 Apr 75.*

TANZANIAN COMMENT ON THREAT OF INVASION

TEXT OF COMMENTARY:

"...Once, there was a child who cried for a razor...

"...But his parents would not let him have it...

"...He cried and thought the razor was good for his play, and continued crying for it until he was given one by his parents...

"...He started playing with it, but when he got cut, he realized the razor was not something to play with...

"...The parents knew that the results of their child playing with the razor were not good, and when they gave it to him, they did so to teach him a lesson to remember...

"...There have been of late of a country on our border invading Tanzania and grabbing a full district to teach us a lesson...

"...The leader of that country had said Tanzania would remain the only target for his forces which, when they strike, they will smash deep into Tanzania...

"...This is not the first time he had said it...

"...Since the so-called leader usurped power, he has constantly threatened to attack Tanzania...

"...But the sophisticated weapons, which he has recently acquired from his pay-masters, would give him the capabilities to follow up the threats with this action...

"...It is for this reason that we did not take his threat lightly this time and, therefore, if he crosses our border, he will find out people vigilant to defend our freedom and the borders of our country...

"...The leader has been crying for the razor for much too long now and, this time, we are going to give it to him...

"...We are going to teach him a lesson, which he will live to remember..."

"...Let him cross the border..."

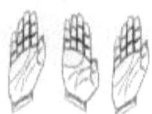

31. Dar es Salaam January 1979: Press Release by Dr Apollo Milton Obote, recorded as:

1979 STATEMENT ON THE UGANDA SITUATION BY A. MILTON OBOTE

1. Uganda enters into the ninth year of the rule of terror and the killings on the 25th. of this month -January, 1979. The country's economy and social services are near collapse. For every Ugandan inside that country, it is a tormenting, cruel and oppressive new year. Ugandans abroad and the exile are equally tormented and gravely anguished by the events at home and the palsy of exile.

2. During the past eight years Amin made it a practice to mock those he killed, taunt Ugandans in their miseries and deceive the world that neither the destruction of lives of Ugandans on a colossal scale nor that of the economy and the social services were issues at all. To him my being in exile in Tanzania was and remains an issue of stupendous proportions, repeatedly he has imputed to me the massacres and murders committed by him and his regime, which fearfully amount to genocide. He has likewise repeatedly accused Tanzania of allowing me to send guerillas into Uganda to commit those crimes. In the past two months Ugandans and the world at large have been repeatedly told by Amin that I was the reason of his invasion of Tanzania. It is possible that there are still people who, and institutions or even Governments which accept either wholly or in part some of these imputations. I have decided to break my silence in order to restate to the Ugandans the issues involved in the tragic situation in which Uganda finds itself today. I am indeed most grateful to the Government of Tanzania for granting the permission to do so.

3. It is now known the world over the Amin the murderer; bur what the world knows of Amin is much less than what Ugandans know of him. His eight years of the rule of terror has been characterised by wanton murders and massacres. It is because of

this fact that Amin and his regime have earned the most chilling but highly appropriate title of *"murderer"*. He heads a regime which has institutionalised murder squads.

4. Two international organisations have documented, though only partially, the extent of the destruction of lives during Amin's rule. They are International Commission of Jurists based in Geneva and Amnesty International with headquarters in London. Their reports show that murderer Amin has no remorse whatsoever for the crime of genocide he has unleashed in Uganda. Amin will most certainly continue to kill Ugandans so long as he remains present position.

5. Besides being a murderer, Amin is a most consummate liar. His lies service his crimes either by duping the intended victims or covering up an accomplished act of murder or massacre. I think the best description of Amin as a liar was given in an open letter written to him in June, 1974 by Mr. Wanume Kibedi who was once Amin's Foreign Minister (1971-73), He wrote:-

> "...As a person who has known you closely for years, before and after your present position in Uganda, I can state with utmost conviction that you speak the truth only through sheer accident, without intending to do so...

> "...Even when telling the truth would do you no harm, or would actually do you a lot of good, you still prefer to tell lies...

> "...The people of Uganda know that out of any ten statement that issue forth from your mouth and are alleged to be statements of fact, at least nine of them are false, and the tenth is at best half-truth..."

6. One of the instances of Amin's lies cited by Kibedi open letter is of pertinent significance in the present situation. It falls squarely within liar Amin's preparations to invade Tanzania. This is what Mr. Kibedi wrote in 1974:-

> "...d. On several occasions in January and February 1973, you issued statements alleging that guerrillas had been sent from Tanzania to assassinate me, Rugumayo (then Minister of Education) and other individuals...

"...On the 4th. of February 1973, you put a number of such alleged guerrillas on Uganda Television and made them 'confess' to their plots to assassinate me and others...

"...The story which those 'guerrillas' told on Television was obvious fake...

"...When I made my own inquiries into the matter, I easily discovered that when the men were at the television studios, you telephoned them to give last-minute instructions on what to say...

"...In fact you were plotting and organising a scapegoat for our eventual 'disappearance...'

7. What flows from Kibedi's apt description is Amin's use of scapegoats in his bundle of lies. In any given situation, be it uneasiness in his Army. Opposition by the people to his rule or his personal decision to have someone killed, he would tell heaps and heaps of lies to pave the way for murders or massacres. After the killings he would again come out with more and more lies to cover up those crimes. In every case of murders or massacres acknowledged by him or his regime there have been lies, often contradictory, accusing guerrillas, Tanzania or some other scapegoat of those killings.

8. Amin's most popular scapegoat over the past eight years have been Tanzania and myself. In the case of Tanzania the purpose has been to divert local and world attention from serious internal problems. There have, for instance, been serious divisions within the army, stretching back to 1971 in which many soldiers lost their lives. On such occasions fighting within army barracks in Uganda were ascribed as to invasions by Tanzania. The near collapse of the economy does not only exacerbate unease in the army but also generates popular discontent against the regime. Consequently, group within the Army and the civil population have over the years made attempts against Amin's life. The more serious of these attempts have been blamed on imaginary agents or guerrillas sent from Tanzania.

9. There is plenty of evidence to show that the recent invasion of Tanzania was a desperate measure to extricate Amin from the

consequences of the failure of his own plots against his own Army. The immediate story begins in early October, 1978 when Amin was told of a plot by some officers and men from the Simba Battalion in Mbarara in Western Uganda. The plot was to have him arrested or killed on or about the 9th. October 1978. Not long before, Amin had sent murder squads composed of men from the infamous State Research and the Marines regiment to massacre soldiers of the Chui Battalion at Gulu, Northern Uganda on the ground that those soldiers supported General Mustapha Adrisi. Someone within Amin's inner circle sent a warning to the Chui Battalion. On their way to Gulu the murder squads were ambushed and wiped out. Amin ordered the incident to be given maximum publicity on the Radio. The radio told Ugandans that a group of armed robbers had been killed by troops of the Chui Battalion. Unfortunately for Uganda, the chief robber himself was not amongst them. Amin even praised men of the Chui Battalion for what he called a splendid action.

10. When the Simba plot became known, Amin chose to plot revenge on Chui for humiliating him. He ordered men of the Chui Battalion to go to Mbarara to put down a *"mutiny"*. That was when Radio Uganda (Uganda Broad-Casting Corporation) first announced that Tanzanian troops of Battalion strength had invaded Uganda but that Ugandan troops were not engaging the Tanzanians! In fact, the Chui Battalion was moving from Gulu to put down an imaginary mutiny at Mbarara and the Mbarara troops were later tipped to expect an attack from a force which was not disclosed. The battle which Amin expected to develop between Chui and Simba Battalions never took place because the two units had discovered the plot to have them kill one another.

11. Amin became desperate. He now had at Mbarara two *"unreliable"* units--Simba and Chui. He ordered his most loyal and best armed regiment, the Marines, reinforced by a Brigade of the newly passed out troops to go to Mbarara and disarm Simba and Chui Battalions. The subsequent battle saw the annihilation of the Brigade and the Marines withdrew having been seriously mauled. Radio Uganda kept on with the lies of an invasion by

Tanzania while in fact killer Amin was busy planning and ordering his own troops to massacre themselves. The defeat of the Marines by the Simba and Chui compounded Amin's desperation. He changed his tactics.

12. The new tactics was the actual invasion of Tanzania to be spearheaded by the Malire regiment. Malire began to move out of their barracks on 20th October, 1978. Troops were told that they would be free to take any booty, and loot, women, movable property, cattle and anything they could carry. The rest of this criminal aggression is known. I need only add that the rehearsal for the subsequent wanton destruction of lives and property in Tanzania by the gangsters were carried out a few days before the invasion of Tanzania when the killer troops ransacked houses, plundered and loaded on to lorries whatever they could take from Ugandan homes North of the border with Tanzania.

13. The world knows how happy Amin became when his troops went on a slaughtering rampage of Tanzania citizens. Amin proceeded to proclaim part of Tanzania as his domain. Hundreds of heads of cattle were driven to Mbarara and distributed to soldiers there as bribes. Amin spoke and continues to speak of a second phase which would take his troops deep into Tanzania. In his utterances, he wanted Ugandans and the world at large to believe that his aggression against Tanzania and his conflict with the people of Uganda, constituted one and the same issue. That certainly is not the case. Ugandans must know that their struggle against killer Amin is different and separate from Tanzania's sovereign right to force out the aggressor from Tanzania soil. The fact that Amin is the cause of both conflicts does not make the struggle one. The Tanzania objective, as I see it, is to drive out the aggressor and to ensure that he does not repeat his aggression or mount his so-called Second Phase. This is Tanzania's sovereign right. As Ugandans, our first objective is to rid ourselves of the regime of death.

14. To confuse the issue and the situation, liar Amin has been ranting that Tanzania means to impose me as President onto the people of Uganda. One could ignore the rantings of killer and

liar Amin and leave him to wallow in his hallucinations. However, when a liar like Amin accuse the victims of his wanton aggression of mounting resistance to that aggression for the purpose of installing an individual as President of Uganda and some people begin to believe and sympathise with the aggressor and liar, the absurdity of the accusation is heightened to the plane of conspiracy against the people of Tanzania and Uganda. Those who believe and sympathise with Amin in his lies know that they have chosen the wrong country as king-maker of Uganda. A Ugandan who believes those lies can only be a supporter of genocide in Uganda and acts of aggression against Uganda's neighbours. Anyone else who believes Amin must be against Tanzania' sovereign right to force out the aggressor and also against the people of Uganda to free themselves from the killer.

15. It seems incredible that some people and nations should feel that they have a duty not to condemn what Amin has done to Ugandans and Tanzanians and at the same time to have no concern at all to the people of Uganda and Tanzania in their respective struggle to control a Killer. The well-being of over eleven million Ugandans, in this context, would appear to be of no importance. Tanzania, the argument the argument would seem to go, must not do anything which would make it impossible for Amin to amount a second aggression, for to do so Tanzania would be a President onto Ugandans. In other words, Amin's supporters would appear to hold the view that in her determination to safeguard her territorial integrity, Tanzania must leave room for a second aggression. As for Ugandans, those who support and sympathise with Amin would seem to barely recognize our existence but not our sufferance. Worse still Amin's sympathisers appear to see no reason and no natural rights for Ugandans to put up resistance against their Killer. All these, in my view, smack of a conspiracy against both the peoples of Tanzania and Uganda.

16. Let me now turn to Amin's second most popular scapegoat, and that is myself. Amin's utterances about me give the

impression that his coup d'état took place only recently when in fact it was eight years ago. After eight years of being in control of all the instruments of government, including murder and terror squads which he created, he still regards me personally as the greatest danger to himself and his regime. The first conclusion I draw from the fact is that Amin has, failed to consolidate his coup and holds the country only by terror. The credit for this failure goes to the people of Uganda for their continuing rejection of a fascist, retrogressive, and murderous man and his regime. The people of Uganda have since 1971, learnt the vast difference between a government with all the deeds, failures or mistakes on the one hand, and institutionalised gangsterism on the other. All evidence points to increasing and unrelenting resistance and struggle against Amin and his regime by the people. And yet he continues to single me out.

17. I am an individual. I do not claim to have special civil rights different from those of my fellow Ugandans. I believe that every human being has a birth right to personal safety for himself and his family equal to every other person. I equally believe that the right to self-government belongs to every people within the community composing that territory must as a whole, control that government.

18. I have no personal office in Uganda to gain or regain. I am anguished by the incessant killings in Uganda by Amin and his regime. It is, I believe, my fundamental civil right as a Ugandan, to join other Ugandans and put up resistance to a regime which takes pride in extensive and wanton killings of its citizens. To opt out of such struggle is to be treacherous to a national duty to which every Ugandan, without exception, is called upon to undertake. It is only cranks (of which Amin is the best example), imperialists of whatever hue and their agents, and perhaps those Ugandans who entertain personal grudge and envy towards other Ugandans who would bring forth spurious reasons for wishing to exclude any Ugandan from the national struggle and resistance against Amin.

19. I am one of those Ugandans who believe that resistance against Amin's regime is a national struggle which must never be personalized. Having been the leader of a national party and from May 1962 to January, 1971 the head of government of Uganda, I could have found ways and means to personalize around me that national struggle and resistance; but I have never succumbed to that temptation. Instead, together with other Ugandans, I have urged the masses in Uganda to lead the struggle. That is why I have, in eight years, spoken publicly against Amin once on the African continent and that was in January, 1971 in Dar es Salaam.

20. In a document which a group of Ugandans and I produced and circulated inside Uganda in July, 1971 we analysed the situation as it existed then and proposed methods of organising resistance. Surprisingly that analysis of seven and half years ago is still fundamentally valid. The most prominent issue in the Uganda situation in so far as Ugandans are concerned, has been, since January, 25th 1971 to date, the destruction of lives. Paragraph 9 of the July, 1971 document attempted to outline to the masses how best they themselves could correct the situation and stop the killings. I quote the paragraph in full:-

"...9. Within our country, the belief and hope are strongly widespread that we are organising a force that will overthrow the regime...

...The unfortunate aspect of such belief and hope is that many of our compatriots are of the opinion that our number runs into thousands...

"...The other unfortunate aspect of the same belief and hope is that our success is so strongly assumed by compatriots inside who oppose the regime that they have not attempted to organise any co-ordinated form of resistance...

"...Further, we who are outside have not had a single battle with the enemy...

"...The situation where the enemy speaks of imaginary battle with us, of wiping out our units on those non-existent battles and of our units inflicting damages which turn out to be the works of the enemy, must in time be reversed...

"...The first steps are for compatriots inside to fully realise and appreciate the fact that ours shall be an internal armed struggle in which the Ugandan population must shoulder responsibility...

"...To that end, we draw attention to the following and call for their articulation by compatriots inside:-

(i) That political education in our country had not developed by the time of the coup, to a degree where the gun in the hand of the oppressor, autocrat or puppet is a toy when such a dictator is faced with a determined will of the people. The task to generate that will of the people and to demonstrate it must be that our compatriots who are politically conscious and active. The situation inside the country is such that will probably take years to get the masses to rise up against their oppressors. The important thing is for compatriots inside to start now on this long road. Instead of falsely leading the masses to wait for "liberation" to come from outside, begin all activities which will generate a determined will of the people to liberate themselves.

(ii). That the objectives of our struggle and resistance are not for the advancement of individual or group causes, are not for what each and every one of us may or should gain in the event of success; are not for the purposes of ensuring for any Ugandan the position he held before the coup; are not for the purposes of revenging the dead or punishing individuals or groups. Ours is not a struggle and must be a struggle against individuals or groups or any part of Uganda. Our struggle is for the stability, freedom and independence.

(iii) That the crimes committed during and after the coup were committed by Amin and his clique and not by their relatives or tribes and that however high the degree of our revulsion to the massive killings, when the regime falls, the police and the courts must be the only proper bodies to deal with this grave matter.

(iv) That our struggle must be basically waged by the people of Uganda as a whole. In this regard, leaders and their followers should be urged to submerge their political differences so as to establish a national front against the regime of death.

(v) That the people constitute the most important single factor in the struggle and that they are the source of inspiration and strength. Every person who joins the struggle must be made to *understand that he will be contributing to the common effort to enable the people to free themselves from oppression, nightmares of killings, and to enable the people through their representatives to establish, control and manage national institutions and likewise to develop and manage the national economy and social service. Above all to enable the people to elect and remove leaders and control national and local governments.*

(vi) That the only course open to us is armed struggle and resistance waged by the people themselves. We have no arms, but the regime has plenty. It should not be impossible to acquire arms from that source. Our present weak position will not be so for all times if this programme is articulated and implemented. The regime's terror will certainly slow down developments favourable to the national cause and it may be years before units are raised in accordance with this programme appear on the scene. In anticipation of that time, it must be imperative that whenever such units or individuals from within them come into contact with the masses anywhere in Uganda, no harm of whatever description should be done to the masses by any such units or individuals. Where such units are not welcomed, a method must be found to win the confidence of the people in that area..."

21. It is quite clear from the above quotation that when the other Ugandans and I wrote the 1971 document, we had no other objective whatsoever except to make our contribution to a common effort by Ugandans to save their lives. For years therefore, I have held the firm view that the conflict between Killer Amin and the people of Uganda is a matter for Ugandans to resolve. That does not mean that Ugandans would not take advantage of any other conflict between Amin and other countries. In 1976, for instance, when Amin promoted a conflict with Kenya by claiming a large part of Kenya, Ugandans took advantage of that conflict. The result, which Amin knows, has been a virtual division of the Uganda Army into one loyal to Amin and the other loyal to General Mustapha Idrisi is still alive, but dead or crippled Amin will never have a united Army. His mistake in the field of foreign relations was to mount a wanton

aggression against Tanzania. By so doing, he has set alight a trend of events which he cannot control. His army is now in disarray. Many of his henchmen are now sending their wives, children and property out of Uganda. He has found it impossible to pay for his war of aggression and has arrested, possibly killed, all Senior Officials of the Bank of Uganda and the State-owned Commercial Bank. In short, he has created a situation which could enable soldiers and the people to rise up in arms against his bloody rule.

22. Ugandans, like all other people, disagree on many issues but the need to get rid of Amin, I find only complete unanimity. Killer and liar Amin knows that Ugandans are determined to rid themselves of him. He knows that in all corners of Uganda he is a marked man. He knows that terror alone has sustained his bloodthirsty regime and he is very scared. His movements are secret and there is no routine in whatever he does. There are over thirty houses in and around Kampala and Entebbe in which he hides. In any one night he would hide in three or more houses. At night he travels in small cars whose registration numbers are changed even between destinations. Sometimes, and like a fugitive, he would spend half a night until sunrise at a petrol filling station. His most trusted bodyguards are foreigners. When hiding in the Airport building at Entebbe, troops of no less than a battalion strength, sometimes more, have to keep guard. On occasions, troops are kept there to make it appear that he was around when in fact he was hiding somewhere else. He has become so scared of and fearful for his life that desperation sometimes makes him fly in a helicopter at night from one hiding place to another.

23. Over the years, we Ugandans, have tended not to realise fully the task of overthrowing a discredited and inhumane regime is ours and ours alone. At times some Ugandans have nursed the idea that foreign troops would do the work but none has appeared. It would be a grave mistake for Ugandans to misread or misinterpret Tanzania's position and objective. To think that

Tanzania's position and objective are interwoven with ours is to make a grave mistake.

24. I take this opportunity to restate and reaffirm the correct path of Uganda's struggle as given in February, 1972 in a document which was produced jointly by compatriots inside Uganda and some of us outside. I quote:

> "...(i) The general and specific characteristics of the Amin regime are well known throughout the country. The magnitude of the Crimes, Massacre, Murders, Robberies, Rape, Looting and Theft are now known to the people. Recruitment of Foreigners on a very large scale into the Army is known. Tortures of the citizens by murder squads are now public knowledge. The telling of open lies is known. All these and many others are fuels in the hands of Ugandans to fire the national struggle and resistance.
>
> (ii) The most expensive way of bringing about a change is the use of a force not composed of Ugandans. Such a force provided it's of a superior striking power can be expected to topple the regime. But a government that will be installed immediately thereafter will have no moral standing. Because of absence or lack of moral standing, such a government will also lack authority and the support of the people sufficient to safeguard life and property of the citizens. The result could be considerable loss of lives. A government established by actions of a force not composed by Ugandans is bound to be more indebted to the country which provided that force than to the people it would purport to govern and serve. Material assistance is wholly acceptable.
>
> (iii) A change brought about by a comparatively few people or narrowly based groups can easily lead to an autocratic rule. The few who would participate actively with their lives as the maximum offer for the "liberation" of the country could after the success of their action, drift and begin to resent any sharing of power with the masses.
>
> (vi) There is no doubt that people are expecting some Ugandans in the army and the so-called guerrillas from outside to "liberate" the country. No one in his right senses would. if that were possible, discourage such groups. There have, however, been considerable killings in the barracks which call for extreme

care by the officers and men who are determined to act for their country. Suggestions by such officers about any successor administration is an easy matter provided the reason for their action is to release the people from oppression and killings. That is the only answer that can be given at present or any future plans originating from officers of the Uganda Army.

(v) The main force for change must be organised from within. There should be no wishful thinking that there are foreign troops who will liberate the people of Uganda. Ugandans outside may be able to help but no one should be led to believe that Ugandans outside, on their own, can change the situation. Let us resolve that even if it would take ten years more, the only method which will change the situation as well as to ensure the unity, dignity and power of the people in the liberation of Uganda by the people of Uganda. Time is on the side of the people and in time, the people will raise the necessary force. The masses must form the basis of that force.

(vi) Start and expand a country-wide cell organisation. Start cautiously but do not relax efforts; go on expanding in as discreet a manner as can be devised cells, in villages in housing estates, in places of work, in colleges and schools, in each trade union and co-operative society, in every organisation. The regime's atrocities will not make this task easy. Difficult as it is, it is the only sure road to end these killings and to bring about national independence and democracy as well as stability. Let the people exercise democracy in these cells thus preparing themselves for the future...."

25. The call to the people of Uganda to liberate themselves is even more relevant today. We must, particularly at this crucial time in the tormented life of our country, be on guard. I would urge my compatriots to close ranks so as to prosecute more vigorously than before resistance against Amin. The propaganda about Tanzania being King-Maker is a ruse to confuse the issue at stake and thereby make Ugandans to slacken their efforts. For eight years, Amin has used such tactics on numerous occasions that possibly only a foreigner but no Ugandan would fail to see through it. The only effective answer to such lies is for Ugandans to combine their efforts, close ranks and to create a formidable

force to knock-out the killer regime and set themselves free to reconstruct their country. The duty for all of us now is to start the liberation of Uganda afresh on a platform of unity.

26. Let no Ugandan forget that Amin has over the years accused other countries of preparing to invade Uganda. All such countries are very different from Tanzania which has never had a colony or a satellite. Most Ugandans know that since independence, Tanzanians have adopted and follow the highest set of principles to be found anywhere in Africa. That is why not only from Africa but also from abroad oppressed people have come and continue to come to Tanzania; they do not come in order for Tanzania to appoint them Kings, Presidents or Ministers and then re-impose them onto their respective peoples. Nothing remotely of that kind has happened in the past and will not happen in Uganda. Let every Ugandan know that there is no government in Africa today which respects the will of the African people in their respective countries more than the government of Tanzania.

27. It is well known fact that the government of Tanzania is always very scrupulous in keeping the terms of the inter-African State agreements. I give one pertinent example. In 1972 I and other Ugandans were involved in action against Amin's regime. The action led to the Mogadishu Agreement signed in October of that year by the foreign Ministers of Tanzania and Uganda. The government of Tanzania has to the best of my knowledge, adhered strictly to the terms of the agreement both by letter and in spirit. Thus, contrary to Amin's lies I have had no training camps in Tanzania for guerrillas. I have neither recruited nor caused any other Ugandan to be recruited for military training in Tanzania. I have sent no force into Uganda.

28. I call to witness all the past Chairmen of the OAU since 1973 and also the documents of the deliberations of the OAU Council of Ministers since 1973. The chairmen are General Yakub Gowon, President Siad Barre, Idi Amin (himself), Prime Minister Seewoogur Ramgoolam, President Umar Bongo and the current Chairman, President Jaffer Nimeiry. None of these would say

that during their respective period of office the Uganda regime ever produced evidence of any conspiracy by me or Tanzania against that regime. Further, there is no record of any complaint by Amin regime regarding any untoward activities on my part having gone before the OAU Council of Ministers. Any serious conspiracy by me with or without Tanzania's assistance would have come to light years ago and the OAU would certainly have had record of it. I give these facts to show that resistance against Amin, has for years, been basically internal and will continue to be so until the end.

29. Before concluding, let me take this opportunity to thank and join all those Ugandans who have condemned Amin's aggression against Tanzania. I most unreservedly condemn the bastardy war of aggression against the United republic of Tanzania launched in October, 1978 by the dictator and murderous Amin. I also most emphatically condemn the violation of the territory of Tanzania and the plunder and destruction by the evil forces of fascist Amin.

30. I want to state categorically and authoritatively that at no time have the people of Uganda ever claimed any part of Tanzania or placed in dispute the borders between the two countries. It was Amin who, being saturated by the desire to export his thuggery and gangsterism as well as his propensities for bloodshed, that laid claim to Tanzania territory and other territories of the neighbouring states, with Kenya, Sudan, Zaire, and Rwanda. In consonance my fellow compatriots, I disassociate myself wholly from all these baseless claims and concomitant lies of Amin.

31. I express the total and whole hearted solidarity of the people of Uganda with the people of Tanzania and I fully support and applaud the determined measures taken by the CCM and the government of Tanzania to ensure once and for all that this evil aggressor- Amin- does not repeat his atavistic act of destruction in Tanzania.

32. On behalf of Ugandans who fled to Tanzania since 1971, I firmly place on record their and my deepest and unforgettable appreciation and gratitude for the fraternal receptions and hospitality which the people, Party and government of Tanzania have accorded to Ugandans who have sought refuge and assistance in Tanzania as the direct result of oppression in Uganda perpetrated by the murderous regime of fascist and dictator Amin.

33. That oppression and these murders and massacres in Uganda cannot go on and on. Centuries ago, a Greek Philosopher, Thucydides, raised the question which has been uppermost in the minds of Ugandans during the past eight years and will be the same in the ninth year of terror. He said,

> " It may be in your interest to be our master, but how can it be ours to be your slaves?"

For eight years it has been Amin's interest to kill us. For eight years it has been Amins' sympathisers' and supporters' interest to make us flee our country and create widows and orphans by the thousands every year. How can it be in our interest? There is only one answer. It is a Uganda-wide rebellion.

DAR ES SALAAM

JANUARY 1979.

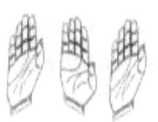

32. IAN RAITT PUBLIC RELATIONS

14 Buckingham Palace Road London SWI
Telephone O1-828 5961
Cables Ianraitt
Telex 21120
Ref 1175.

With Compliments.

Will try to speak to you about this.

Marketing Public Relations Representatives Promotions

THE SITUATION IN UGANDA

A Statement by Professor Yusuf K. Lule.

Next week, on Wednesday 10th December, the people of Uganda go to the polls to elect a new Government. In normal circumstances this would be a matter for rejoicing, with democracy apparently about to be restored after dark years of Amin tyranny. Tragically this is not the case. Instead a situation exists where a new leader- Milton Obote - is about to be imposed on the people of Uganda through the machinations of a foreign power - Tanzania with apparent acquiescence of the Commonwealth Secretariat and, perhaps most sadly of all, the British Government. The ballot box is being abused to legalise this farce.

Those of us who, like myself, were prevented from returning to Uganda to contest the election, have sought the views of Her Majesty's Government on these events. We have been told that Uganda is an *"independent sovereign country"* and should have a *"stable democratically elected Government"*. We agree - but is this really possible with 10000 Tanzanian troops in Uganda supporting Obote and his Uganda Peoples Congress (UPC) and

Julius Nyerere publicly dictating terms and conditions from Tanzania? Where, are we entitled to ask, is our independence now? HMG's reply is to provide a number of ballot boxes and an observer as part of the Commonwealth Observer Team. Our answer is that it is too late. The elections have been won and lost before a single vote has been cast.

I would therefore like to draw public attention to the following facts - facts that on several occasions and in various ways have been brought before HMG.

1. Uganda's Military Commission overthrew and imprisoned President Binaisa in May this year in order to thwart free and fair elections and to pave the way for Obote's return. The chairman of the Commission is Dr. Obote's chief confidant. The majority of its members are his supporters. Before this 'coup d'état' arrangements were being made for a neutral military force from friendly countries in the Commonwealth or the Organisation of African Unity to maintain law and order before and during the elections: for a neutral electoral commission and for the Commonwealth supervisory commission during the elections. All these arrangements were scrapped by the Military Commission.

2. To achieve these objectives - the return of Obote and the UPC under a cloak of legality - the Military Commission took the following steps:

- Appointed a predominantly UPC electoral Commission which proceeded to draw up new electoral rules and electoral boundaries favouring the UPC. This has resulted in gerrymandering of the 126 constituencies.

- Imposed new arrangements for the registration of voters which did not conform to any legal requirements. The registration Officers appointed were mainly UPC supporters.

- Removed or transferred a number of District Commissioners and central administrative staff replacing them with UPC supporters. These UPC men will now act as returning officers and election supervisors. They will be responsible for the safe keeping of all ballot boxes and the counting of the votes.

- Reversed at Obote's request an all-party decision to have one ballot box for all candidates. There will be four ballot boxes, one for each party, a relatively easy task now for the election supervisors to manipulate the votes.

- Allocated to the Northern Regions (parts of which are traditionally UPC) which has a population of 2.5 million out of the country's total population of 13.5 million, 34 parliamentary seats from a total of 126 parliamentary seats. This is a much larger share than the population warrants. The remaining three regions with a population of 11 million where Obote has virtually no support, were allocated 92 seats.

The Military Commission has backed up these measures by using its military muscle and by sanctioning a systematic campaign of harassment, intimidating and even imprisonment against other contesting parties, in particular the Democratic Party.

- In West Nile District of the Northern Region where the UPC has little support, an excuse was made to send in units of the Uganda Army and the District was closed to everyone except UPC candidates and their agents. Such has been the level of intimidation that thousands of refugees have fled across the border to the Sudan and Zaire. Perhaps not surprisingly UPC have announced that all their candidates in the West Nile have been returned unopposed.

- In Lango no non-UPC candidate was allowed to present his papers. Prospective candidates were stopped at roadblocks or attacked by UPC mobs for the purpose.

- In Kasese non-UPC candidates were arrested the day before they were due to present their nomination papers and held in custody during the nomination period.

There are proven examples of the disqualification of legitimate non-UPC candidates who would have stood a strong chance of being elected in any reasonable fair situation - including the former President, Mr. Binaisa, who because of restrictions on his movements was unable to appear at the nomination centre. The net result is that 23 UPC candidates have now been returned unopposed.

In view of the above, the Commonwealth Observer Team has an impossible task. The irregularities which will determine the fairness or otherwise of the election, have already been committed, but Britain, which surely has a certain conscience if not responsibility as our former colonising power, gives tacit approval to these arrangements. Ugandans have suffered before under minority government under Obote which led, in turn, to the monstrous Amin regime. It seems, despite all these lessons, that we are about to enter a new, dark era in the history of our country.

YUSUF K. LULE.

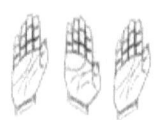

PART IV

1981 – The Weight on Milton Obote's Left shoulder

The weight on Obote's left shoulder was built up during the periods of his rustication when he was in exile and absent from the political stage in Uganda. Then he had chosen to keep silent. That silence nevertheless spoke most subtly to the masses of the people of the country. The 'moss' that gathered during the period of rustication in the 70's however covered the fact that behind the silence A.M Obote moved at dusk through narrow grass-covered paths for purposes he did not disclose as long as he was at the designated place when checked upon by those who were interested in his rustication during his exile years. Dr A.M. Obote then attracted some significant amount of 'mosses' as he quietly traversed the narrow political paths allowed for him to navigate. In this period other Ugandan political players sprouted and struggled to bloom.

Revolutionaries: In the 1970's there arose, in the struggle for liberation from military dictatorship, a Ugandan breed of self-styled revolutionaries who claimed to be more progressive than A.M. Obote. These attempted to act impulsively and independently against the military regime. They sought support from the African region and elsewhere in the world during the then obtaining cold war era.

Sycophants: Correspondingly there arose a group of self-serving political sycophants who worked to weave themselves around A.M. Obote. They thought that Dr. Obote then was a lone figure whose stature they could take undue advantage of. They made false claims then to be re-inventing Obote's party and political image.

The first backlash to this development was from an old party faithful 'A' and an insensitive 'B'. An insensitive 'B' in this category went to see 'A' with a message from Dr A. M. Obote. 'A' politely listened and thanked 'B' for the message. Sometimes later, 'A' called me, (the author that is) in his office quite revolted. To quote, he said to me;

> '....how can 'B' come to tell me about Obote? I know Obote, he knows me and has my contact...
> "...How dare Obote do this – that is if 'B' was sent at all...
> "...Is this the way they are going to do things! This is not acceptable to me and if that is the case I will not be a party to their UPC...'

For this slight, I suspect, 'A' indeed never looked back or embraced The Party again. Say no more.

Overall the political reaction from party members to the divisive rise of the sycophants was negative.

When Dr A.M. Obote returned to the country from exile and mounted conversations with his party members he formed the view that the party had to be re-built all over again. He noted that,

> "...the people at the welcoming party and the follow-up rallies so far attended ....
>
> > "...my view is that they only wanted to see how I looked like...
> > "...I did not see votes...
> > "...We have to do something different if we have to win the election...'

I did not understand this sycophancy business and its consequences until I read Acut Lwani's 1996 write-up on this subject, which on reflection, surrounded and gated Dr A.M. Obote during the various periods as phased in this publication, but with a sharper cutting edge post-1981.

Old political parties: In the Uganda of the 1980's there were new and unfamiliar forms of adversarial politics riding on the back of old political party labels ala new wine in old bottles. Consequently, it became necessary for all political formations:

- to wait or take part in the reconstruction or re-constitution of the political processes after military rule, and fractured transition governance;
- to keep faith with the party-political processes of transmitting ideas that win the hearts and minds of the masses of the people by demonstrating the politics of organized, principled debates as a means of reaching democratic decisions;
- to publish party-political manifestos and platforms that enable the population to make informed political decisions about the country.

Even with the political rustication of the 1971 to 79 period, it was evident that the UPC and Obote still stood neck and shoulder above the rest of the country's political parties.

Men of substance: This was a phenomenon that had emerged around 1976 and matured by 1979. These were propertied Ugandans who felt that it was now their turn to rule the country after the fall of military dictatorship. They had a swollen-eye view of themselves. They now sought to take over the commanding heights of politics in the country without consent from the people. They somewhat had acquired financial clout, made influential friends and won fellow travellers with whom they could curve out commercially beneficial deals once they got to political power in Uganda.

I remotely heard about this phenomenon but did not know its essence. I was faced with a real example when in 1979, then Minister Akena p'Ojok sent me to London to stop the 'men of substance' who were bent on de-grading the London Office of Uganda Airlines, then managed by a Mr. Lubega. One non-descript *'man of substance'* ' Mr. 'B' who was a resident in London and waiting for repatriation to Uganda, was running riot in the Airline Office. Despite my impeccable credential, so I thought, Mr. 'B' eventually confronted me saying *'Do you know who I am?'* I experienced firsthand what *'men of substance'* meant. Say no more about this.

Evidently, *'men of substance'* (an exclusive men-only club) *'...with constituencies abroad...'* had curved out a political platform to determine the political direction of the country shamelessly using UK and USA-based public relations firms to back their political stints.

Non-descript exiles: These were a new hybrid-tribe who had forged solidarity while in exile in various countries. Hybrid because the forged solidarity was not paralleled, synched or aligned with the social and cultural particularities that were evident in the country. Their category was distinct from those who had stayed in the country during the military dictatorship. Each of these groups came to access different possibilities in the country.

In 1986, in one frustrating moment of anger with former exile, Adoko Nekyon, the then General Manager of Uganda Airlines, I had the audacity to ask him a question

> *'...are you saying that you people go to work and the rest of us merely accompany you...?*

This was to underline my anger at the new privileged group and former exiles who were then taking lucrative leading positions throughout the country.

Post-1981, a new political race with unknown end was triggered. All the described above were entrants in the political fray. The consequence was a widened and boundary-less or unbounded pursuit of political objectives, which included even the clergy of all denominations competing for political space or influence. These groups built linkages with and got well connected to global circles of finance and economic interests.

Constituencies abroad: This was a new Ugandan phenomenon intended to impact direct influence on the political direction or political leadership of A.M. Obote. They used expletives such as 'directionless', inept leadership, etc., as an extension of de-campaigning A.M. Obote, all to suggest that the choice of political governance of Uganda should have been left to '...*the men of means and their friends abroad...*' This context fitted the 1982 acerbic remarks made by the then USA Assistant Secretary of State for Africa, Chester Crocker, after a meeting with Cardinal Emannuel Nsubuga of Uganda, that was widely inferred as proof that A.M. Obote was not good for Uganda.

Dr. Obote was subsequently harangued out of political office by those interests, local and foreign, that sought once again to impose military governance over Uganda.

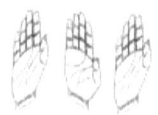

33. Uganda Times dated Tuesday 7 April 1981, Kampala, reported headline by SAM SERWANGA and WILLY MUKASA as:

"DP STRONGHOLDS HARBOUR THUGS"

INTERNAL Affairs Minister, Dr. John Luwuliza-Kirunda yesterday accused DP strongholds "...*of harbouring lawless elements*..." working for the violent overthrow of the Uganda Peoples Congress (UPC) government.

> "...*The thugs are stirring up insecurity in the hope that the popularly elected government will become unpopular before the electorate*...", he said.

Kirunda who was debating a motion of thanks to President A. Milton Obote for his Communication from the Chair, told the House:

> "...*Opposition MP's seem to suggest that insecurity gripping various areas of around is caused by the security forces*...
>
> "...*We have security forces elsewhere in the country. But why is it that there is no insecurity gripping those places? Why does it occur only in the DP strong-holds?*..."

Luwuliza Kirunda MP for Iganga North-East asked.

He said;

> "....*the government was not impressed with the crocodile tears now being shed by opposition MP's*...
>
> "...*Thugs are operating within Mukono, Kampala and Mpigi districts, and the people know their whereabouts*...
>
> "...*Come out and tell the government the hide-outs of these thugs*...",

he said.

He was interrupted on point of order by DP's Abu Mayanja (Mubende North-East) who demanded that the member should substantiate the accusation.

But the speaker, Mr. Francis Butagyira ruled: *"He is still speaking."*

Luwuliza Kirunda then continued:

> "...Supporters of the opposition MP's who happen to come from Kampala, Mpigi and Mukono are harbouring the thugs...
> "...The UPC is tired of inconsistency..."

He said there was not a single member on the opposition who had come out to condemn the killings and acts of insecurity which had characterised life in and around Kampala.

> "...Why don't we hear of bodies by the roadside in Apac or Mbale?...",

he asked:

He challenged the opposition members whether anyone of them had ever addressed the people and condemned insecurity.

Kampala South Opposition MP, Mr. John Sebana-Kizito, rose on point of order and demanded to know whether the Minister was in order to suggest that none of the DP MP's had condemned insecurity when only six days ago he (Sebana-Kizito) held a meeting with people in his constituency to find solution to the problem.

Butagyira ruled: *"He is out of order".*

But the Minister whose speech was repeatedly interrupted by the opposition said there were good examples to illustrate that the opposition supporters backed insecurity.

During the October incursion in Arua, some Ugandans who supported the DP celebrated in Iganga North East and Central on hearing of the attacks.

> "...These were DP supporters dressed in party colours..."

DP chief whip and MP for Iganga North West, Mr. John Magezi, asked whether the Minister was in order to continue debating before he substantiated that *"...DP is trying to use force to remove the legally elected government..."*

Butagyira ruled: *"He is still speaking"*.

Luwuliza Kirunda continuing said the source of insecurity could be traced from the statement which the DP around December 11 and 12 last year claiming the UPC cheated them.

They had called on their supporters not to cooperate with the UPC government, he said. He said the UPC was tired of inconsistency. In 1971, there were people who talked of Democracy, while struggling to get posts in the Amin regime. But by then Amin was killing people in thousands, and the same people talked of magnanimity of Amin.

> "...They are now crying crocodile tears...", he said:
>
> "...Freedom of press has responsibility...
>
> "...We must have a responsible Press...
>
> "...It is the irresponsible press which shall not be allowed to thrive...
>
> "...If somebody thinks he will print what appeals to our enemies and expect to thrive, I declare war...";

Luwuliza Kirunda determinably told the House.

The Minister said he had before banning the Newspapers called the Editors and asked them to be responsible journalists.

> "...In Uganda, where word is taken as gospel truth, the government has the right to ban 'filthy' writing...".

He said very few people had been detained by the government, and some few others were only assisting in investigations.

The Minister noted that some local people were not cooperative in giving information to the Police whenever inquests leading to the killings of the people were carried out.

But at the same time, he was dismayed to hear that some people who were Amin's Ministers at one time were suggesting that "inquests" be instituted.

He added the same people wanted to set free Idi Amin's men - people who decimated Uganda to what it was today.

> "...Some of them will be released, but after they have been screened...".

"...The government will keep persons causing breach of peace out of circulation until reformed...

"...This will be our policy, instead of eliminating them as Idi Amin's government did...",

Luwuliza Kirunda said.

He added the government would only retire somebody if his services were not wanted any more, other than killing him and replacing him with another as Idi Amin did.

Uganda's plight during Idi Amin was enough example to show that foreigners could take control of the running of the country.

He also lashed at the politics of intrigue which characterised the opposition party. If it were not for UPC to stand against the UNLF arrangements this country would have been sunk.

"...Who among the DP members stood firmly to oppose the UNLF arrangements?..."

But P. Kaboha (Kabarole Central) stood on a point of order:

"Is he in order to say that no DP member opposed the UNLF arrangement, when it was Sebalu who moved an amendment motion calling for multi-party politics?..."

Butagyira ruled:

"He was in order when he referred to the opposition MPs?..."

Luwuliza Kirunda then added that Sebalu was denied a chance to stand on a DP ticket.

But DP's Sam Kutesa (Mbarara North) rose on another point of order:

"...Is he in order to say Sebalu was refused to stand and yet he lost in the preliminaries?..."

Butagyira ruled: *"The member was entitled to his views".*

The Minister added that it was the opposition leader and DP President General, Mr. Kawanga Ssemwogerere, who thought Sebalu was not fit and ordered for the holding of another election.

The Minister of Housing and Urban Development, Mr. A. Waligo, on the opposition members to mount anti-insecurity campaigns in their constituencies. In this exercise, he was prepared to share a common political platform if it were announced that it was a combined effort. Waligo said he was sure the Minister of Internal Affairs was prepared to give any assistance including security to any member of the opposition who wanted to participate in the exercise but who was afraid of going back to his constituency. He pointed out that the problem of insecurity would have faced the people of Uganda no matter what government might have been in power.

> *"...The gospel we should spread now is that the responsibility of ensuring security in our country is ours..."*

If anybody reported a matter connected with insecurity to the Police and on one or two cases he received what he deemed was insufficient attention, that should not deter him from the fact that the exercise of fighting insecurity was essential.

As members of Parliament Waligo said; they could help the people of Uganda in several ways. One would be by giving them positive leadership

> *"...which we are trying to do as a government side..."*

and he hoped they would be supported in their endeavour by the opposition.

He called on the members to try and stifle rumours that fan insecurity. That is why he commended the President's forthrightness when in the Communications from the Chair, he condemned acts of insecurity in all its manifestations.

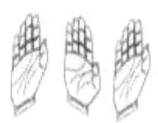

34. The London GUARDIAN of 9.3.81 recorded from VICTORIA BRITTAIN in Nairobi the following under the headline:

OBOTE SEEKS POPULAR SUPPORT

President Obote in a national broadcast, repeated twice over the weekend and clearly reflecting his concern about the armed opposition groups in the country trying to overthrow him, has appealed to Ugandans to back his government and denounce the *"gunmen"* in their amidst.

His appeal came a day after the ambush of two military convoys in the Western Uganda, near Hoima, where the former Defence Minister, Yoweri Museveni, claims to have 5000 soldiers loyal to him. In the ambushes, 19 Tanzanian soldiers and 30 Ugandan Soldiers were killed, according to a spokesman for Mr. Museveni's MOSPOR (Movement for the Struggle of Political Rights).

MOSPOR is the biggest and best organised of the four groups which have announced that they were waging a guerrilla war against the Uganda Peoples Congress (UPC) Government. Earlier this week, two minor splinter groups threatened United Nations aid workers with death if they did not leave the country.

President Obote urged the Ugandan Army and Police to redouble their efforts to break dissident groups and said that he intended to increase Uganda's security forces.

> *"...We must not allow ourselves to be led twice in 10 years to an era of chaos, death and destruction...",*

he said.

However, any fast expansion of the Police force is impossible, according to diplomatic sources. Uganda's Police force is still being re-trained by Britain and Canada since the overthrow of Idi Amin. Diplomatic sources said that Dr. Obote was probably preparing the ground to ask for an extension beyond the present agreement, running to the end of June, for Tanzania's stationing of 10000 soldiers in Uganda.

Meanwhile, emissaries from Mr. Museveni's MOSPOR were reported to have gone to Southern Africa (presumably Mozambique, where Museveni lived in exile and received military training) in search of arms and diplomatic support. It seems highly unlikely that they would be successful in raising the latter from any left-leaning African government as long as President Obote retains the support of President Julius Nyerere.

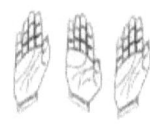

35. *The INTERNATIONAL HERALD TRIBUNE on 7.4.81 quoted the agency ASSOCIATED PRESS, Kampala recording:*

REBELS REPORT KILLING

Guerrillas trying to oust President Obote asserted Monday that they had killed 47 Ugandan and Tanzanian soldiers in an ambush last week, and a government source said 35 people died Sunday in a guerrilla attack on a military camp.

In Nairobi, a spokesman for the guerrilla group headed by the former Ugandan Defence Minister Yoweri Museveni claimed responsibility for the ambush. The spokesman, telephoning from unidentified site in Uganda, said all 47 Ugandan and Tanzanian troops in three military vehicles were killed.

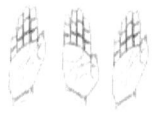

36. *INTERNATIONAL HERALD TRIBUNE* dateline 7.4.81. recorded the following report by GREGORY JAYNES of New York Times Service:

....in the last two weeks;

"...at least 50 bodies have been found in and around Kampala, most of them in forests that were used as a dumping ground for Marshal Amin's victims...

"...wives and children of U.S. Embassy personnel in Kampala were transferred last Wednesday to Nairobi, purely as a precautionary step in response to recent attacks in Kampala by anti-government groups,..."

according to an embassy statement.

What it did not say according to American sources, is that distaste for the government's recent conduct had as much to do with the evaluation as anything. Mr. Obote regained the Presidency in elections last Dec 12. His party, the Uganda Peoples Congress, won the majority of seats and the right to name the head of state for the five-year term.

Rigged Election Charged

The other political parties charged that the election was rigged. One of them the Uganda Patriotic Movement, has begun a guerrilla war against Obote government. The movement is led by Yoweri Museveni, part of a six-member military commission that governed Uganda until the elections.

On March 9 the Museveni rebels asserted that they had killed 73 Ugandan government soldiers in an ambush seven miles outside Kampala. The ambush was later confirmed by the Chief of Staff of the Uganda Army, Brig. David Oyite Ojok, although he did not say how many soldiers were killed.

On March 24 another rebel group knocked out power stations in Kampala, put the official radio off the air and sprayed the city headquarters of the Obote party with gunfire, killing at least one man. The attackers, about whom little is known, call themselves the Uganda Freedom Movement.

Girl of 16 a Victim

The weekend before last, groups of bodies were found in nearby forests. The chief of one of Kampala's mortuaries, where 14 bodies were brought on March 28, including that of a 16-year-old schoolgirl, said all the victims had died of gun-shot wounds.

The chief spokesman for the Museveni guerrilla group - uses the fictitious name Harry Freeman - said in an interview:

"...The people don't mind suffering to see Obote go out. They are suffering now...

"...They forgot long ago about salt, sugar, and soap..."

Evaristo Nyanzi, one of four Kampala representatives in Parliament said:

"...They go around picking our supporters and we don't know where they are..."

37. Lecture Notes for Chartham House, 22 September, 1981.

THE FUTURE OF UGANDA

by
COLIN LEGUM

"...There is a long history of suspicion between important elements in Buganda and Obote, who is still blamed for what happened in the crisis over the Kabaka's deposition and exile in 1966...

"...A number of myths have grown up in Buganda, as well as in this country, over what happened at that time...

"...While the essential facts are easy to recapitulate, the prejudices surrounding them make it more difficult to reach a clear judgement...

"...As an old friend of both Obote and the Kabaka (in whose cause I wrote a book at the time of his unfortunate exile by another old friend of mine, Sir Andrew Cohen), I had a ringside seat in the conflict between the two men...

"...They represented two irreconcilable strands in Uganda's politics...

"...Obote was a nationalist whose overriding interest was to create a unitary state in which in which the disadvantaged Nilotics in the North would have a reasonable opportunity to move from the periphery to the centre of the political system created at the time of independence...

"...The Kabaka was, at best a Federalist, who not only wished to see Buganda's traditional institution of Kingship preserved, but who sought to create a special and privileged place for the Baganda, harking back to pre-colonial times when they were the dominant political force in the country...

"...At independence, a political marriage of convenience was arranged between Obote and the Kabaka for the sole purpose of defeating the then Prime Minister, Benedicto Kiwanuka, whose Democratic Party was seen as a threat by both men, but especially by the Kabaka since Kiwanuka had succeeded in building considerable support among the more modern-minded, especially the Christian, Baganda...

"...However, once the alliance had achieved its immediate purpose of defeating Kiwanuka, the way was open for a power-struggle between Obote as Prime Minister and the Kabaka as President of Uganda...

"...The details of that struggle --for example the Kabaka's struggle to reclaim the so-called Lost Counties from the Kingdom of Bunyoro, and his refusal to allow direct elections from Buganda to the Central Parliament -- are irrelevant to this analysis...

"...What is central is the Kabaka's unyielding insistence on a special status for Buganda...

"...To this end he not only built up his own private army, bur intrigued with members of Obote's Cabinet to bring about his downfall...

"...Finally, he made the crucial mistake of sending emissaries to two foreign embassies to seek support for a military coup against Obote...

"...It was when he learnt of this that Obote sent his Army (under the unfortunate leadership of Amin) to Mengo...

"...The Kabaka's forces were routed and he himself fled into exile and to an early death...

It was the Kabaka who forced a show-down on Obote, not the other way round...

"...Obote has publicly admitted that mistakes were made by himself when, on his return from exile, he held out a hand of reconciliation to the Baganda...

"...While the restoration of the Kabakaship is no longer an important issue - it wasn't even raised by the Democratic Party or the Conservative Party (the old Kabaka Yekka) in their election platform - feelings against Obote still rankle among some Baganda...

"...However, the situation in Buganda is considerably different today from what it was in the days of the Kabaka.

"...The Baganda themselves are no longer held in thrall by the strong centralised Mengo; nor are the modern-minded Baganda dominated, as they once were, by the traditional chiefs...

"...Moreover, the Baganda have become commercially minded and enthusiastic farmers...

"... As much as much as anybody else, they now see stability and economic recovery as being in their own interests as well as in that of the country...

"...In brief, the present-day Buganda is now fully identified with the interests of the rest of the country...

"...The old wish to dominate, or for some special status, has finally disappeared.

"...Obote has succeeded in attracting a number of the younger well-educated Baganda to the UPC, and has appointed several of their number to his Cabinet...

"...If he can succeed in his aim of including many more prominent Baganda in his Government, the way will be open or a genuine reconciliation...

"...Two obstacles stand in the way to this achievement of this goal: the uncertainty among the Baganda about the likely success of Obote's economic policies and the pressure from the armed wing of the Democratic Party...

"...However, it is significant that the dissidents have succeeded in operating only in two of the Buganda Districts...

"...Provided that the economic recovery, now begun, continues, and Obote can convince enough Baganda of the sincerity of his wish to forget the past, than even the problem of Buganda will become tractable..."

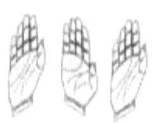

38. OFFICE OF THE PRESIDENT
21st January 1982
REF; PO/16.3
Mr. Thomas Hammarberge,
Secretary General,
Amnesty International,
LONDON.

Dear Mr. Hammarberge,

I wish to thank you for sending Mr. D. Oosting and Mr. M.H. Posner to Uganda. The two delegates arrived on the 11th and left on the 19th January 1982. I met them on the two occasions, and they held several meetings with Ministers, officials, Members of the opposition and Religious leaders and others. Their visit took them to part of the Eastern Region where they attended a political rally and met a number of people.

On the first occasion when I met the delegates, they presented to me a document dated 1st December 1981, which they said was confidential and was not for publication. That statement was a great relief to me as I will indicate herein.

On the second occasion when we met, I re-stated to them the concern I had expressed at the first meeting which was about the unfounded assertions and inaccuracies in the document. The assertions in my interpretation, tended to show that Amnesty International had already made judgement that my government was engaged in massive violation of Human Rights and had arrested and detained thousands of political prisoners in jails, lock-ups, military establishment, *'safe houses'* etc., scattered across the country. Any such accusation, Mr. Secretary General, has no foundation whatsoever.

The document presented by you states inter alia that -

"...The total number of prisoners arrested on political grounds is much higher than those listed here: in mid-1981, an estimated 2000 people were held,.."

An assertion of that kind is a judgement completely unrelated to the facts of the situation and is untrue. We have no political prisoners in Uganda.

In the discussion the two delegates pointed out to me names of persons who are politicians and who had been arrested. I was able to tell them that they were not arrested for political reasons. I was able to tell them that it looked curious to me that a number of politicians who belong to my party, who had been arrested during 1981 for criminal offences, did not have their names with Amnesty International.

I gave the delegates the example of virtually the entire Executive Committee Members of the Kampala West Constituency who had been arrested but whose names do not appear in the document. Furthermore, the document contained even the name of Mr. ELIJAH KITAKA GAWERA with the description;

"released on 6th October on bail."

It was the first time in my long life in politics to find *"a political prisoner"* being released on bail. They did not appear to me to be innocent errors or minor inaccuracies.

I discussed with the two delegates, the meaning of the word *"arrest"* which appears to be the basis of the lists of persons in the document, and I regret to say that I did not get a satisfactory explanation. I am still left with the impression that anyone arrested in Uganda for any offence whatsoever would attract the interest and concern of Amnesty International.

The document begins by making the reader feel that the persons listed were arrested and imprisoned in *"circumstances"* which left no doubts at all in the minds of the officials of Amnesty International to believe that the arrests and imprisonment or detentions of all persons listed were political. I was not able to get from the two delegates the nature of those *"circumstances"*, and I suggested to them that the use of words such as *"arrests" "detained"* or *"imprisoned"* in the document, did not only show a judgement made by your organisation, but also an accusation of the government as a violator of Human Rights. I trust that this was not your intention or belief.

My government welcomed the visit of the two delegates and hope that they benefited from the visit. I still, however, remain with the problem that the arrest in Uganda will still continue to be presented to you, by opponents of the government who have declared, advocated and are in fact engaged in violent activities in some parts of Uganda, as *"political prisoners"*. If you were to continue, to entertain such presentations by such persons, the administration of the Criminal Law in Uganda would be a mockery.

The above point came out clearly when the two delegates met with Ministers. A large number of people whose names appear on the document had in fact been charged with criminal offences. Others, though arrested on criminal offences, had their cases dropped on the recommendation of the director of Public Prosecutions and had been released. I enclose a paper the Ministry of Internal Affairs had prepared hurriedly in response to the assertions and accusations contained in the document referred to above.

In discussions with the two delegates, my Ministers and I were disturbed by the impression the delegate gave to us on the credibility of the sources of your information. It would appear that the government is to be believed less by your organisation than the advocates of violence (your source of information) who, to us, seem to be using your organisation as part of their weaponry.

The list of the persons my government is supposed to have arrested, detained or imprisoned, contained the name of a person who died in a motor accident in April 1980, long before my government was formed in December 1980. He was such a prominent man that I have since wondered how his name was presented to Amnesty International and why your organisation accepted the presentation and adopted him as a prisoner of conscience.

The list also includes people who were arrested long before my government was formed and people who were never arrested at all. Your two delegates explained to us that the document contained some errors, which I accepted; but that doesn't explain the central point, namely, that an organisation with noble objectives like yours may be an unwitting victim of the advocates of violence in Uganda.

This letter comes to you in good faith. My government inherited a situation where there was no law and order for some ten years. We are doing everything possible to normalise the situation and we had to make every Ugandan to be aware that change had taken place from the era of lawlessness and terror to the time of the Government of Law.

We are being opposed by men, some of whom were leading personalities in the days of Amin when Human Rights in Uganda meant nothing. They have combined forces and Mr. Oostings told me that he attended a Press Conference in London before coming to Uganda, when these men spoke openly of their belief in the use of violence as means of acquiring power.

Any help I can get from Amnesty International will be highly valued and will enable the Government to consolidate the gains during the past year, and to eliminate violence and lawlessness of the abnormal nature which we inherited. A blanket condemnation of my Government, without concrete evidence, is a direct assistance to the men of violence and would not help to bring respect of Human Rights in Uganda.

Yours Sincerely,

A. MILTON OBOTE.
PRESIDENT

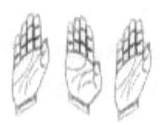

39. PRESS RELEASE ISSUED IN KAMPALA 23rd FEBRUARY 1982.

The Ministry of Defence announced

That the events of last night in Kampala were designed as a desperate action to capture not only Malire Barracks but also to overthrow the Government. This fact has emerged from the statements made by captured terrorists and bandits. There is no truth whatsoever in any claim that this was a hit-and-run attack by the guerrillas. They fled in disarray, but many of them were captured. They abandoned large quantities of arms, including mortars, RPGs, machine-guns and rifles.

Two soldiers lost their lives during the attack. Bodies of the attackers counted so far numbered sixty-seven. There are ten terrorists in critical condition and several others wounded who reported to private hospitals. They have now been transferred to government hospitals from the private hospitals to which they reported.

The attackers did not enter, nor did they cause any damage to any installations, or barracks, and they did not capture any arms. Soon after the attack the army instead of retaliating immediately, was deployed strategically to contain the terrorists within the suburbs of Kampala. The terrorists in the meantime continued to fire indiscriminately. At sunrise the army, which had already surrounded the attackers, responded, killing, wounding and capturing many of the bandits.

The Vice President, who is also the Minister of Defence, had a meeting this afternoon with religious leaders of the Protestant and Catholic Churches. The Vice-President briefed them on the events of last night and regretted the fact that mortars used by the attackers were placed virtually on the doorstep of the Roman Catholic Cathedral of Rubaga. This fact was equally regretted by the Vicar-General who represented the Cardinal at the meeting.

The religious leaders were told by the Vice-President that throughout the night, officers of the government tried to contact them by telephone to warn the religious leaders that the attacks were coming from the direction of the Roman Catholic Cathedral of Rubaga and Protestant Cathedral of Namirembe. This afternoon, is when officials established that for unknown reasons the telephones in the houses of the religious leaders in both areas had been taken off the hook.

This afternoon there was a report on the overseas radio to the effect that the Vice-President was ambushed this morning and that four soldiers in his convoy were killed. This report is absolutely untrue and deserves to be condemned.

Furthermore, the same overseas radio station made gross and untrue allegation that Uganda still has a battalion of Tanzanian Army stationed at Entebbe. There are no Tanzanian Army personnel stationed in Uganda.

Whoever planned the attack of last night should know that it was a complete disaster and a total failure, and Ugandans should have no doubt about the truth of this statement. The events of last night demonstrate what the government has been saying throughout past year, namely that the terrorists are concerned only with destruction. The whole country knows that the first time in more than ten years Uganda has been making successful advances in the establishment of peace, creation of conditions that are conducive to development and the raising of standards of living of every family.

The President as Commander-in-Chief of the Armed Forces has sent a message to the Ugandan forces for their quick response in neutralising the situation, and the exemplary conduct shown during the operations. The President wishes it to be known to the citizens that the policy of reconciliation and no revenge will continue.

The Minister of State in the Vice-President's Office who is holding the portfolio of Minister of state for Foreign Affairs, Hon.

Peter Otai, today met all the Heads of Mission in Kampala and briefed them on the security situation in the country.

The Minister recalled that when UPC Government came to office in the December 1980, security was the number one priority concern of the Government. Terrorists and bandits interrupted peace, which was developing in February last year, when they made attacks on the Military installations and police stations, coupled with indiscriminate acts of killing of innocent citizens through various means including the placing of landmines on roads.

Throughout last year the Government made every effort to contain the situation. The terrorists were flushed out of rural areas and some had to seek refuge in the suburbs of Kampala.

The Minister told the Diplomats that terrorists attacked, in the early hours of today, one military barracks, but were easily overpowered. The army behaved extremely well, and the situation was now completely normal.

The Minister added that Government has decided not to impose a curfew in Kampala and surrounding areas because the situation did not warrant such an extreme measure.

Meanwhile the Minister of Information and Broadcasting, Dr. David Anyoti and the Minister of State for Defence in the office of the Vice-President, Hon. Peter Otai, combed various parts of the city and visited Rubaga Cathedral grounds where over thirty-five mortar bomb shells were found.

The containers indicated that mortars were sixty millimetres type. There were also sachets of chemicals to deflect gravitational force.

According to army experts on the scene, the mortar was placed on the raised ground next to the statue of Our Lady which overlooks Lubiri barracks. One expert remarked that the Cathedral and the statue would now be flattened had the Armed forces returned fire.

The parish priest at the Cathedral said he did not see who operated the mortar, but the noise did not allow them to sleep. He said

> "...we saw the fire in the sky but we did not now where it was coming from..."

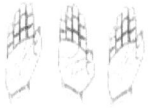

40. The SUNDAY TIMES of 29th August 1982, carried a report by BARRIE PENROSE and NEIL SMITH under the headline:

MERCENARY COUP PLAN FROZEN BY CASH SHORTAGE.

The Fredrick Forsyth-Style exchange (see below) was part of a remarkable conversation by two men planning an invasion of Uganda this weekend. The conversation took place last May between a former Ugandan President, Godfrey Binaisa, and a British mercenary recruiter at Binaisa's expensive London flat.

Binaisa, who fell from power in May, 1980 after a coup by supporters of Uganda's present leader, Dr. Milton Obote, had expected to be back at Government House in Entebbe this week, having ousted Obote in turn after a successful armed invasion.

But he is still living at his apartment in Kensington Gardens Square, West London. For the moment, his plan has had to be postponed because his backers - who he says are from *"the southern states of America"* - failed to raise the £2 million needed to fund the invasion.

It was from London last January that Binaisa launched the new Uganda Popular Front party with another Ex-Ugandan President, Yusuf Lule. Rather than trying to win back power through the ballot box, however, he came to believe that only force could remove Obote.

The man he commissioned to organise the invasion originally scheduled for this weekend was Raymond Ingram, a burly British ex-army sergeant and full-time mercenary recruiter. Ingram, 50, a veteran of Korea and Malaya, runs his International Security Agency from Blacknell, Berkshire, and advertises for recruits in the American mercenary magazine, Soldier of Fortune.

Ingram came to the notice of the Scotland Yard special branch in 1977 when he started a recruitment drive for mercenaries needed *"somewhere in Africa"*.

In 1979, he began talks in Kampala, the Ugandan capital, with a member of Binaisa's then Government who wanted him to act as a security adviser. When Binaisa was ousted from power, Ingram was undaunted and began negotiating with the new Obote Government, which was offering a contract to train Uganda Special Forces.

Because of his earlier connections with Binaisa, Ingram failed to win the contract, which went to another security company called Falcon Star.

Back in London, Ingram agreed to meet Binaisa to discuss a *"top secret"* project which the ex-President had already sketched out with fellow exiles and with supporters in Uganda.

After their initial talk about the invasion plans in the early spring of this year, a series of meetings took place to work out the details. The Sunday Times has a tape recording of the conversation that took place on May 11. On the tape, Binaisa can be heard discussing the finer logistical points, and finance, surrounding the plans.

BINAISA: *"...100 soldiers would not be able to do the job...*
"*...100 are no good..."*

INGRAM: *"...Oh yes they could but it would have to done very quickly..."*

BINAISA: *"...I want 500 soldiers...*
"*...We'll compromise...*
"*...All the men, plus their transportation to Africa, plus the weaponry but not including hiring of the twoC-130 aircraft..."*

INGRAM: *"...Now, will Zaire let us use their gun-ships?...*
"*...If they don't, we are in trouble..."*

BINAISA: *"...I think so, Supposing they don't you can hire them?..."*

INGRAM: *"...Yes, but they are very, very expensive..."*

BINAISA: *"...How are you going to capture Entebbe Airport?...*
"*...Do you want to capture it by helicopters?..."*

INGRAM: *"...Yes, I want to make two attacks...*

> "...One in the centre of Entebbe Airport and the other in the centre of Kampala..."

BINAISA: "...Your people will already be there?..."

INGRAM: "...Oh yes...

> "...We will already have some on the ground in...
>
> "...But then the main party will arrive when we travel from Zaire... "...They will only succeed by surprise...

A group of crack mercenaries would launch a two-pronged attack on Uganda from neighbouring Zaire, using helicopter gun-ships and C-130 troop-carrying aircraft. They expected to be supported by troops on the ground in Zaire and by Ugandan soldiers.

Binaisa claimed that some Uganda troops, who used to serve under Idi Amin, were still loyal to him. He had contacts with them and on the tape names several high-ranking officers who he says, would support the invasion. Two senior officers would be called to London from Kampala.

Ingram dislikes publicity, he says and prefers to conduct business under nom de guerre with Collins and Porter his favourites. But he confirmed last week that he had been planning the invasion for Binaisa.

> "...Provided we don't interfere with the British Government, we would do a service if someone needs carrying out,..."

he said.

> "...But we would not do anything illegal...
>
> "...I am a law-abiding citizen."

Binaisa a Barrister who practiced at the Lincoln's Inn before becoming Uganda's President, said yesterday that he was disappointed his secret had got out:

> "...The Ingram plan, has fallen through, and we don't like to say anything until we reorganise ourselves...
>
> "... But the invasion plan,...

he added,

> "...was not dead...

"...Obote's days are finished..."

"...What we need from the West is better understanding and sympathy for our cause...

"...We have the boys inside Uganda but we need to supply them with weapons...

"...We shall try again sometime next year..."

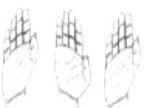

41. *The London TIMES article of Friday, January 14 1984 recorded the following by COLIN LEGUM under the title:*

GUERRILLAS FLEE FROM WRATH OF BUSH WOMEN.

"Madam Christina", a striking young woman still in her twenties was until recently the Director of Intelligence of the Uganda Freedom Army (UFA), one of the three armed groups which for the past two years have been trying unsuccessfully to overthrow President Milton Obote's regime.

She is one of a dozen top guerrilla leaders who have come out of the bush in Buganda in recent months, either as captives or, as in her case, having given themselves up to the Uganda Army.

It is not hard to see why this sharply intelligent daughter of a former MP should have commanded so much respect that led her being referred to as *"Madam Christina"* by the boys in the bush.

Now living in a *"safe house"* in Kampala, 'Christina Mudende' admits she went into the bush to be with her boyfriend, with whom she has now lost contact. If he is still alive, she wants him to surrender. Judging by her own experience, she says he will not be ill-treated provided he can get to a police post without falling into the hands of the Buganda villagers.

"...Ho, those villagers!..."

she says with a shudder.

"...For four days they were after me and a companion when we were escaping from an army ambush...
"...No food, no water, - all that time...
"...They chased us with stones...
"...Those village women they chase you and chase you...
"...They don't give up...
"...They are worse than the soldiers..."

This marked change in the attitude of the villagers towards the guerrillas is seen by the government as its most important breakthrough since the opponents of Dr. Obote took up arms early 1981, alleging that they were cheated in the first elections held since the overthrow of Idi Amin.

The UFA is loosely linked to two other fighting groups -the Uganda Patriotic Movement (UPM) led by Mr. Yoweri Museveni, and a group of former Amin soldiers headed by one of his most notorious former aides, Colonel Moses Ali. Their top exile leaders are two former interim Presidents of Uganda after Amin's overthrow, Dr. Yusuf Lule and Mr. Godfrey Binaisa. A third leader, Mr. Balaki Kirya, has been taken prisoner.

According to Miss *'Mudende'* there is bitter internecine rivalry between the top UFA leaders in the bush. Mr. Andrew Kayira and Mr. George Nkwanga occupy different camps, and, she claims, many were killed in fighting between them on September 6. She also confirms reports of hostility between Mr. Museveni's force of about 1000 men and the UFA.

Miss *'Mudende'* claims that Mr. Museveni is determined to establish supremacy over what he regards as the *"capitalist forces"* of the UFA. She also accuses him of tribalism. He is not from Buganda. Among his 58 officers, she said, there were no Baganda.

She confirmed government allegations that Colonel Gaddafi, the Libyan leader and Amin's staunch ally, has been actively helping Dr. Obote's armed opponents, despite his repeated assurances to the contrary.

She said that recruits from both the UFA and UPM went for training to Libya in 1981 and 1982.

> *"...Some are still there...*
> *"...The first group consisted of 26 men, but only five returned to the bush after training...*
> *"...The rest decamped in Kenya on their way back home..."*

Among the Libyan arms smuggled back into Uganda were Sam-7 missiles which were to be used to shoot down President Obote's executive jet and army aircraft.

> "...The trouble...

she said,

> "...was that we did not have anybody who knew how to work them...
>
> "...They were supposed to have been fired by Captain Luyima (now prisoner); but he did not know how to handle them either... "...When he tried, he found that their batteries were flat..."

Both the Sam missiles have been captured and are now on display by the Uganda Army.

As recently as last month, another arms shipment was discovered in Kenya on its way to the Uganda border. It was landed at Mombasa and is believed to have originated from Tripoli.

In recent months the supply of money and weapons reaching the bush has begun to dry up and they are no longer able to pay the villagers for the food.

The tide began to turn in favour of the security forces last August when villagers in the three districts of Buganda where the guerrillas were based, turned against them. By September, when Miss 'Mudende' fled, the Army was striking heavy blows at the UFA and UPM forces.

It would be premature to suppose that violence is now nearing its end, even though it has sharply declined. Mr. Museveni's forces have not yet been eliminated.

In an interview, Dr. Obote said that in much of Buganda only a small pocket of rebels remained active.

> "...They may shoot at a vehicle on the road or they may still have a few landmines, which they will plant and run away...

he said.

> "...I am satisfied that the worst security situation that could have befallen Uganda has now passed..."

Asked about the allegedly undisciplined state of his army, Dr. Obote replied:

"We have had incidents of harassment of the people by the soldiers...

"...When such incidents come to the notice of senior officers, immediate action is taken and, as a result, a large number of soldiers have either been dismissed or are in jail..."

There still remain the problems connected with training the rapidly assembled Army of about 18000 men. Hundreds of officers are training abroad. At home the Commonwealth training unit has just completed its first year.

The North Koreans also have a small training unit and there is a special force of about 1500 armed police with a private British firm employing mainly former SAS officers.

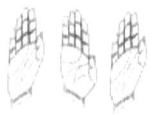

42. The *INTERNATIONAL HERALD TRIBUNE* dateline 14.1.83. recorded an article by COLIN LEGUM titled:

AND A LIBYAN HAND OVER UGANDA.

LONDON--Notwithstanding his repeated assurances to the contrary, Colonel Moammar Qadhafi apparently has continued to provide arms and military training for opposition groups attempting to overthrow Milton Obote of Uganda.

Even while continuing his bid to become the chairman of the Organisation of African Unity, the Libyan leader has supported the political terrorism that has impeded Uganda's economic and social recovery, especially during the first two years of Mr. Obote's rule.

Colonel Qadhafi firmly supported Idi Amin for most of the nine years he ruled Uganda and tried to prevent the dictator's defeat in 1979 by sending in troops to oppose the military forces of the Uganda Liberation Movement and Tanzania.

Although Idi Amin himself is no longer welcomed in Libya (having been forced to find sanctuary in Saudi Arabia), Colonel Qadhafi has nevertheless maintained his animosity to Mr. Obote, who from his exile in Tanzania, led the struggle against Mr. Amin.

Evidence of Libya's role in fueling Uganda's opposition movement is provided both by the source of captured weapons (often with Arabic script) and by testimony from captured leaders of the opposition Uganda Freedom Army and the Uganda Patriotic Movement.

Lieutenant Henry Kalema, another Freedom Army who has surrendered, has disclosed that the weapons used in the guerrillas' November 1981 attack on the Army barracks in Lubiri came from Libya. He said these weapons included 45 rocket-propelled grenades, 15 mortars and 45 rifles.

Mr. Obote has been anxious not to push his troubled relations with Libya to the point of severing them altogether. He has, instead, sought assurances from Colonel Qadhafi that Libya would stop supporting Uganda's armed opposition. But, despite Colonel Qadhafi's denial of involvement, there is no sign that he has finally stopped helping the two guerrilla groups.

President Obote was among the African Heads of State who did not attend either of the abortive OAU summit meetings held in Tripoli last Autumn.

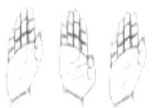

43. The DAILY TELEGRAPH of 31.1.84 in a report by A.J. McILROY recorded the following under the headline:

TERRORISTS BLOCK AID FOR UGANDA REFUGEES.

More than 1000 new refugees, including children who are dying from exposure and shortage of vaccine, have moved into one camp in the Northern Uganda as the Government forces continue their anti-guerrilla campaign.

News of their plight reached Kampala as senior government officials mounted a big security operation yesterday, 25 miles south-west of the capital, in the hunt for the gang which massacred over 30 women and children five days ago.

At Kakoge camp, refugee victims of the latest fighting near Avumbe in the north, mostly women, children, and the old, desperately need help.

In their panic to escape the fierce fighting whenever Government troops and guerrillas clash, they managed to carry only their children and whatever clothing they wore at the time.

International relief agencies are being hampered be fears of ambush and renewed kidnapping. The road north has been subject to attack by bandits and anti-Government guerrillas.

A small group of correspondents in Uganda with the Archbishop of Canterbury, Dr. Runchie, made a spot check of seven camps. They ranged from a few miles outside Kampala, to Kakoge.

They and their guides did not see a single relief worker, and while there was evidence that some food had been distributed in a number of camps on the previous day, they were told it was too dangerous for help to arrive frequently.

A number of relief workers were kidnapped late last year. Two lost their lives in an ambush.

The new arrivals at Kakoge have increased the number at the camp from 1800 to nearly 3000.

There are an estimated 130000 displaced people because of the operation started last year to push anti-Government forces out of the country.

"Terrible shortage"

Catholic missionaries told me:

> "...There is still a terrible shortage of medicines even in these camps...
>
> "...Further north malaria, measles, and malnutrition, are killing children...
>
> "...In its first reaction to the attack by unknown gang which decimated the village of Muduuma on Friday, the subversives using the visit of the Archbishop of Canterbury and its attendant publicity to try to discredit Uganda's Government in the eye of the world..."

A spokesman said terrorist activity had been stepped up significantly to coincide with Dr. Runchie's visit for the enthronement of a new Archbishop on Uganda, and with the country's appearance at the international conference-table in Paris to try to win urgently needed foreign aid from the World Bank.

"Determined Men"

> "...We were just beginning to get some favourable comments from abroad about progress in our economy and an improved, though still difficult, security situation,..."

a senior Government Minister said.

> "...It takes only a few determined men with guns, choosing the right time and place, to undo what we have achieved...
>
> "...We are convinced that is the background to the killing 10 days ago of the four white expatriates, including one Briton, in Kampala..."

The Uganda Government is acutely aware that Mr. Timothy Raison, British Minister for Overseas Development, is currently touring the country on a three-day visit which includes a likely agreement on a £4150000 British capital aid programme.

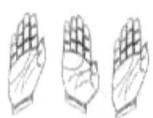

44. The DAILY TELEGRAGH in a dispatch from A.J. MacILROY on 30.1.84 recorded the following under the headline:

DR. RUNCHIE'S PLEA AS UGANDANS ARE BUTCHERED.

Children with deep gashes in their necks and shoulders were being cared for in a Kampala hospital last night after the massacre of about 30 people near the Ugandan capital.

I drove to Kampala's Roman Catholic Nsambya Hospital to see the wounded survivors from the village of Muduuma about 25 miles south-west of the city.

The atrocity was carried out on the eve of the installation of the country's new Archbishop attended by the Archbishop of Canterbury, Dr Robert Runcie.

The tragedy had an added poignancy since Dr Runcie had made the keynote of his Uganda's stay a plea for Church and national unity *"for the sake of the children".*

Some of the unknown killers wore raincoats and others army uniforms, which are frequently stolen and worn by anti-Government guerrillas.

Government Ministers are convinced the recent upsurge of guerrilla activity by forces hostile to the ruling Uganda People's Congress has been orchestrated to try to discredit the Government.

It is currently seeking urgently needed international aid and the presence of the Archbishop of Canterbury has attracted international attention.

Five youngsters

When I reached the hospital yesterday, nurses were clearly shaken by the state of the surviving children.

They took me through the sprawl of low buildings to the ward and pointed to a corner where five youngsters aged between three and 13 stay in small metal-railed beds.

Most were on saline drips. Only one was fully conscious.

They had deep gashes to the necks and shoulders consistent with them fleeing attackers wielding pangas.

They had heads heavily bandaged, and wounds to their arms and legs.

A mother, also wounded, sat on the floor between the beds. She had been weeping. Other women from the village stood close by.

They told me what happened. A similar account was repeated to me soon afterwards in the men's ward by a young man serious and savagely wounded.

I had to crouch close to his lips to hear his words.

The accounts said that the gang, armed with some automatic weapons, came at night out of the bush and held two women and six children in one of the village huts while they demanded money and food.

A man told to get money for them fled, and the gang wreaked terrible revenge.

They run from hut to hut, burning them to the ground and cutting down fleeing men, women and children.

"...They killed many: Over 30...

"The women at the hospital told me...

"...When we came back we found the bodies...

"...Our chief died as well..."

One woman, bandages covering her knife wounds, was staring silently at her child.

In one of the beds I read a chart for *"Patient No.741:"* Resty Kegabane, seven; Religion : Catholic.

She was one of the worst wounded. Another was Bosco Sebulindee,13. His leg was in plaster and he lay naked, sleeping.

Other Attacks

The attack happened only a week after four white expatriates were killed in Kampala: Three Swiss and a Chelmsford man, Mr. Eric Wells, who had been working for the Uganda Development Bank.

Mr. Peter Otai, Uganda's Minister of State for Defence, said yesterday there had been two ambushes during guerrilla activity on the Bombo road north of Kampala. A soldier had been wounded and a guerrilla killed.

Concern over the security situation has led to the estimated 5000 Western workers in Uganda, including about 500 Britons, seeking Government reassurances.

News of the massacre at the Buganda village on the Mudwana road, was spreading through the city as thousands streamed up the red dust path to the Church of Uganda Cathedral at Namirembe, in the hills overlooking the city.

The congregation included President Obote, his Government Ministers, Bishops from America and Britain, Mr. Colin MacLean, British High Commissioner, and many other dignitaries.

Dr Runcie received confirmation of the massacre before the enthronement of the Most Reverend Yona Okoth.

He added to his prepared text the words:

"...We must reverse the springs of violence which have beset this country..."

"Dark Years"

Dr Runcie said:

"...In these dark years you have suffered the violation of every human right..."

He said the years of violence and persecution under the former dictator Idi Amin had bred violence which was also breeding violence. The country had to be turned and the human right restored to all.

Archbishop Okoth said the Church of Uganda supports the measures President Obote's Government was taking to restore security and economy and order.

Mr. Timothy Raison, Overseas Development Minister was also in Kampala yesterday.

He is expected to sign an agreement for a £4150000 total aid programme.

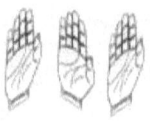

45. The DAILY TELEGRAPH OF 14.2.84 in a report filed by A.J. MacILROY recorded the following under the headline:

OBOTE WINS SUPPORT OF OPPONENTS

A FULL SCALE political follow-up operation is being carried out by the riling Uganda People's Congress in the wake of the Army's advance against anti-Government guerrillas who are pilling back to the Zaire border.

President Obote's party organisation is making considerable ground in the Opposition Democratic Party strongholds in the so-called Luwero triangle that includes Mubende and Mpigi districts.

Most of the opposition's 34 seats in the 126-member parliament are in this 90000 square-mile area from where the guerrillas of Yoweri Museveni's National Resistance Army and other factions have retreated.

The People's Congress Party Youth Movement is spearheading the campaign to win over the population. Every village and refugee centre has a building or even a grass hut bearing posters or painted slogans promoting the party.

Food Messages

Messages tell the people that food, medicine and tools reaching them to the value of many millions of pounds through relief agencies are evidence of the support outside the country for the President and the People's Congress Government.

The initiative has not been without its price. Three party chairmen have been murdered during the recent violence.

The Opposition Democratic Party are trying desperately to counter the current political advantage the UPC holds. They remind their people of the traditional hostility in the Luwero area base on the religious background towards the UPC.

This is a Roman catholic-dominated region and basically Roman Catholics support the Opposition party while the UPC is mainly Protestant Church of Uganda.

Politicians Cheered

But in the past few days I have seen thousands of refugees cheering UPC politicians and officials as relief agencies bring them help.

An estimated 140000 people have been displaced by the protracted guerrilla war. The improvement in the past month in their lot has been remarkable.

In the areas which were the centre of bitter refugee camps, Maazi, is down to just over 3000 people, from its peak before Christmas of more than 10000.

President Obote and his party leaders insist that by clearing the area of the guerrillas they have proved beyond doubt that the UPC is the only party that has the organisation and the confidence of the armed forces and the people to pull Uganda out of its dark age.

Some observers wonder whether in real terms Uganda is not in fact moving towards a one-party state even though President Obote has repeatedly said this has never been his intention and never will be.

PANGAS HANDED OUT

Protests rejected

Meanwhile the Government went ahead yesterday with the distribution of nearly 58000 pangas to returning refugees despite strong objection from the International Red Cross.

Handing out the first batch of 30 pangas and 60 hoes to families at Luwero, Mr. Nathan Karema, District Commissioner, said:

> "...These people need pangas to clear their overgrown gardens to be able to plant seeds before the March rains..."

Two weeks ago 30 people, most of them children, were massacred by a gang wielding pangas and axes.

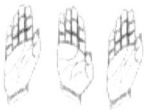

46. *The TIMES of London on 22.2.84 recorded the following from their correspondent under the title:*

BARRACKS and PRISON HIT in UGANDA REBEL RAID

The National Resistance Army (NRA), which is led by a former Ugandan Defence Minister, Yoweri Museveni, has claimed responsibility for the guerrilla attacks on the town of Masindi, 140 miles north of Kampala.

The Ugandan Defence Ministry announced late on Monday that dissident elements had attacked the army and police barracks and the prison in Masindi but had been repulsed. The Ministry gave no details of the causalities.

An anonymous NRA spokesman yesterday said 178 soldiers, 27 police and 18 prison warders were killed, as well as five NRA guerrillas. The attackers stole large quantities of arms and ammunitions, he said.

Roadblocks were operating round Kampala yesterday and no buses from Masindi arrived there. There were rumours in the capital that some soldiers had joined the guerrilla attack.

NRA guerrillas have been operating for nearly three years between Masindi and Kampala. But in the past year they have been driven back by the Ugandan Army, and Ugandan leaders had said the guerrillas were no longer a problem.

Significantly, however, the Defence Ministry announcement said the Masindi attacks were designed to show that the dissidents had the capability to mount an offensive. Masindi has a large army barracks and this is the first the NRA is known to have carried out an operation in that area.

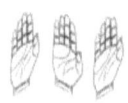

47. In AFRICA REPORT a March-April 1984 issue recorded the following under the title:

UGANDA: Out of Control

In early January, rebels kidnapped eleven Red Cross workers in Mpigi district, 40 miles southwest of Kampala. Nine of the hostages were released two days later, but a French doctor and a Ugandan were held for an additional two weeks before being freed.

Informed sources indicated that, since "...*the government has very little or no control over its armed forces,...*" negotiators from the relief agencies were forced to deal directly with the rebels. The two-week delay evidently occurred because "...*there doesn't seem to be much of an organised authority in the opposition forces...*" Red Cross workers have apparently returned to the area after the release of the last hostages in January, and the Red Cross delegation has actually "...*been reinforced...*" since late last year. The presence of international Red Cross workers "...*has added a certain amount of security for the local Red Cross relief people...*"

The Red Cross had earlier suspended its activities in the rebel-held areas of the north as a reaction to the killing of a driver and a nurse last November, but then resumed its operations after receiving safety assurances from the government.

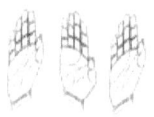

48. The DAILY TELEGRAPH in a report from A.J. MacILROY recorded the following under the title:

"100 KILLED" AT MARTYRS' SHRINE IN UGANDA

Local Roman Catholic and Anglican missions talked to me yesterday of their despair at the massacre by the Ugandan Government soldiers at the shrine for Christian martyrs which is to visited by the Pope next year.

They said the attack earlier this summer at Namugongo, 10 miles from Kampala, had claimed just over 100 lives, with others mutilated.

I was the first Western correspondent to visit the scene of the massacre which figures in a report in the United States - hotly disputed in Kampala - that the Ugandan army is carrying out a reign of terror "...*that goes beyond the excesses of Amin regime*..."

The Uganda Government through its Minister of Information, Dr David Anyoti, spoke last night of its outrage and anger at the criticisms, which it said had been motivated by the political enemies who wanted to bring down the regime of President Obote.

Nothing to Hide

The claims followed a visit to Uganda last month by Senator Charles Grassley. The Uganda Government said it was so incensed at the accusations that it wanted to show there was "...*nothing we wanted to hide*..."

They allowed me to speak unaccompanied to the Catholic and Anglican Missions in a visit that was not pre-arranged.

> "...*The soldiers involved in the massacre were shot at after being told by the local people there were no strangers in the area,*..."

said Dr Anyoti.

"...Bandits (anti-government guerrillas) had broken three months of calm by attacking the important satellite station at Mpoma, about 16 miles away, and the soldiers were searching for them...

"...Seven stayed with their vehicles while two sections moved out in the search...

"...The soldiers had reached this point in their search when the seven were fired at...

"...The bandits know only too well the publicity to be gained for their cause if they can provoke an attack by soldiers on an area of religious shrines for Christians and Moslems such as this was..."

Trial Promised

Dr Anyoti said that the action at Namugongo by the soldiers could not be condoned, Mr. Paulo Muwanga, the Vice-President, told parliament two weeks ago in reply to questions that the army officer responsible for the loss of life was awaiting trial.

"...It will be a public trial and that is better, because people have been killed and the guilty must be held responsible,..."

Dr Anyoti said.

"...Officers and ranks in the Army who offend and are found guilty have been sentenced to prison or otherwise disciplined either by trial or court martial...

"...We are building up an army that was decimated at the downfall of Idi Amin...

"...We have told the United States fully the situation and we have stressed that mass murder on the scale claimed are an exaggeration beyond belief...

'Skepticism in Britain'

"...We have a new no-nonsense army chief, Col Smith Opon-Achak, who has taken over seven months after the death in a helicopter accident of the former Chief of Staff, Brig Ojok...

"...The British military aides and experts are still helping to train our soldiers in Uganda and we are greatly encouraged to see reports from Britain that the Foreign Office is skeptical about the allegations emanating from America..."

Dr Anyoti said the security situation continued to improve and suggestions that the Government had resorted to wholesale slaughter to clear anti-government forces out of the so-called Luwero triangle, a 90000 square -mile central area, was simply not true.

Out of The Blue

The mission in Namugongo agreed that the security situation has improved. But Mgr. Joseph Ssebayiga, parish priest for 10000 Catholics in the area, told me at his mission:

> "...The fear of soldiers remains from the days of Amin...
>
> "...And I am afraid there are arrests still happening of the people suspected of having associations with bandits...
>
> "...The attack on the satellite station was out of the blue; things have been so quiet...
>
> "...But the army came three days later attacking the area and particularly the Anglican mission, burning and stealing from houses..."

The Rev. Sserwada a tutor at the martyrs Seminary, pointed to the initials UNLA (Uganda Army) in red paint on the walls of the buildings where the theological students were dining yesterday.

> "...They shot the Principal, the Rev. Godfrey Bazira, and dumped his body and they killed the seminary manager...
>
> "...Then they took the boys out to question them..."

Namugongo is the site of an execution ground where more than 30 Ugandans were ceremoniously burned to death 99 years ago for refusing to renounce Christianity. Thousands of Christians make their anniversary pilgrimage to the shrine.

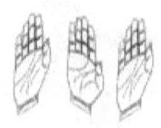

49. *The DAILY TELEGRAPH dateline 19.8.84 recorded the following as reported by A.J. MacILROY under the headline:*

UGANDA KILLERS "ARE DISGUISED AS SOLDIERS"

Men, Women and children are still being murdered in Uganda's Luwero triangle where the Red Cross temporarily suspended relief operations two weeks ago.

The international organisation took this action after a Doctor and two others were wounded when a medical team came under fire at Wabusana, 35 miles east of Luwero township.

They are the victims of the bush war which, with Yoweri Museveni's National Resistance Army being ousted from the region that was once its stronghold, has become a bloody hit-and-run campaign.

The guerrillas' targets are the ruling Uganda People' Congress politicians, officials and their families. Snatch squads are also attempting to *"recruit"* village youths for Museveni's army.

With Museveni's main strength driven back towards the Zaire border, his men travel many miles through the bush dodging army patrols and, according to the government, are so dressed so much like soldiers that their actions are often blamed on the Army.

Although the Army has established control of the region with ample evidence of life returning to normal for the Buganda people, the rebels' continued activity, no matter how spasmodic, is too near to the capital, Kampala, for the Government's liking.

I had firsthand contact with the situation yesterday. I was about to turn off the Kampala-Luwero road towards Kapeka, 25 miles from Kampala, when Capt. Terence Okullo, from Bombo barracks, had me stopped.

"...We do not want you to get caught in crossfire,.." he said as the bandits had already attacked. The road was heavily patrolled by the well-equipped and disciplined troops, the rearguard of a big *"hot pursuit"* operation.

The surrounding lush green countryside was unnaturally quiet, but life was bustling on farm holdings and the people thronged the roadside walking to the market only two miles away.

In an extensive tour of the region, including visits to areas said by some foreign reports to have been the scene of wholesale killings by Ugandan soldiers purging the area of anti-government elements, I found nothing to support American claims of massacres.

On the contrary, the evidence of returning normal life was overwhelming with colourful markets busy, hundreds of schools and churches reopened and thousands of people back on their holdings urgently planting before the rain arrives.

The Red Cross had just agreed, after receiving renewed government safety pledges, to resume food supplies to the two remaining refugee transit camps in Luwero District. At Nakazzi and Kibisi I heard Mr. Nathan Karema, the Luwero District Commissioner, say food was coming.

In the village of Namugegera, about seventeen miles south of Luwero, I visited the disused factory which the resistance movement opposed to President Obote claims was the scene of the mass burials after a March massacre.

I was alone for one hour with villagers, ranging from chiefs to ordinary families and the surprise these simple people showed when asked about the massacre in the area could not have been an act.

Harrowing Story

The villagers did, however, have a harrowing story to tell about an attack which they said was carried out by the *"bandits"* and not the Army.

And Mr. Nusur Jogojogo, the area chief, later told me;

> "...Three months ago seven villagers were killed, three men and four children shot or hacked by men with pangas and guns...
>
> "...They were bandits; there is no doubt about that. Some of them were from our village...
>
> "...They were dressed halfway, I mean they were in army and civilian clothes, all mixed up..."

By the time soldiers arrived the people had fled into the bush. What possessions they left behind, he added were looted by the soldiers.

Mr. Karema told me:

> "...Naturally all Uganda Government and the army is distressed when film is shown on B.B.C television purporting to show a massacre involving the army...
>
> "...The President could not understand that anyone would believe that such large-scale killings could happen or that the reports could happen or that the reports could have been given credence in Britain and America..."

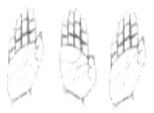

50. The London TIMES recorded this report from Charles Harrison on 28.8.84 entitled:

REBELS CLAIM SUCCESSES AGAINST UGANDA ARMY

The National Resistance Army, the biggest anti-government guerrilla movement in Uganda, claimed yesterday that its forces had killed 213 government troops and wounded and captured others since the Ugandan Army launched an offensive against the guerrillas earlier this month.

The NRA's leader, Mr. Yoweri Museveni, a former Ugandan Defence Minister, said in a communique from inside Uganda that 16 guerrillas had mounted a number of successful ambushes.

Kampala has given no details of the offensive, but reports from Kampala say that more than 5000 troops are involved. Speaking at the installation of the Bishop in Western Uganda this weekend, President Obote repeated that he would not take part in talks with guerrillas and opposition leaders at a neutral venue outside Uganda.

To do so would be to betray those Ugandans who believed in democracy and elections, he said. He attacked the two former Presidents, Mr. Yusuf Lule and Godfrey Binaisa, who are in exile in London, for supporting underground guerrilla movements in Uganda, and appealed to them to return and stand for election.

Referring to recent criticism of his Government and allegations that the army has caused many deaths, President Obote said:

"...A lot is being said about Uganda abroad these days..."

"...But I am not worried because our policies of reconciliation and no revenge are correct..."

The offensive has so far had little success in tracking down the guerrillas.

Troops have been carrying out sweeps through Luwero, Mubende and Mpigi areas where the NRA has been operating for more than three years.

Mr. Peter Otai, the Minister of State for Defence said in Kampala at the weekend that the recent allegations of atrocities by Ugandan troops were *"exaggerated"*. He admitted that civilians had been harassed, ill-treated or killed by the troops, but blamed the guerrillas for creating insecurity.

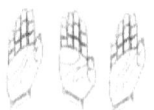

51. The DAILY TELEGRAPH quoting the Associated Press recorded the following report under the headline:

213 SOLDIERS 'KILLED'

A Ugandan guerrilla group claimed yesterday that it had killed 213 soldiers over the past two weeks. The claim was made in a news release given to journalists in Nairobi.

The Politics of Luwero District - The Cover Up

The district of Luwero which lies North of the capital of Uganda, Kampala in the central region of the country, the inhabitants of which are multi-ethnic but predominantly under Buganda cultural influence and outlook, was the cradle of the National Resistance Movement (NRM).

For nearly four years the NRA launched guerilla warfare against the Obote regime that came to power in the 1980 following a general election, the NRA was mainly confined to this district.

No wonder, therefore, since the movement assumed power after a 6-month military confrontation with the Gen. Tito Okello regime, Luwero has become the focus of NRM politics.

The thrust of this politics is a cover-up strategy.

This cover-up strategy is aimed at exonerating the NRA from the atrocities it perpetrated on the people of the area in its bid to coerce them into supporting it and bearing the burden of sustaining it materially.

One of the key elements in this strategy has been done in two ways; firstly, by the government imposing the condition on the newsmen that they clear all stories about Luwero with the Ministry of information and Broadcasting. Secondly, access to the district by the newsmen has been curtailed. News coverage of Luwero is organised by the state. This ensures for the state's purpose that the newsmen are conducted only to places and audience that the government has stage-managed.

The second important element in this cover-up has been a deliberate state policy if denying foreign relief agencies to deliver food aid to the district. This serves the purpose that these agencies do not, during their activities in the area, do not access information, and scenarios that do not tally with the general propaganda campaign of the NRA that the atrocities and destruction in the area was solely the work of UPC and the UNLA.

Thus, these agencies have been kept out ostensibly on the account of the NRM's policy of self-reliance. The real reason however is that they should not witness the cover-up.

Yet another element bizarre in the nature is the shifting of human skulls of the victims of the war between the NRA and UNLA. The NRA's aim is to give the impression to newsmen that there are heaps and heaps of skulls all over the *"Luwero Triangle"*. In most cases this is done so secretly that even the local Village Resistance Council (VRC) chairmen are not informed. The result of this has been that there are reports of skulls beings stolen. This theft has been attributed to former UPC chairmen and youth wingers, who actually do not exist, most of them having been *"eliminated"* through NRM orchestrated *"mob justice"*.

Museveni himself boasts of his army having blown tens of civilians and UNLA buses and lorries. He has also claimed that since his movement started armed struggle it has killed over 6000 troops during the Obote regime and 4000 in its encounter with the brief Tito Okello/Bazillio regime.

The cover-up strategy has become imperative because the supposed support the NRA got from Luwero was not *"natural"*. Yoweri having been a guerrilla in the Mozambique fighting in the FRELIMO outfit had learnt that the most appropriate territory for guerrilla struggle is one covered with large stretches of jungle and forest.

For a specifically this reason Yoweri Museveni chose Luwero district. Through his violent methods psychological warfare, he was able to cow the local population into supporting him. Those who did were hit. This in turn served his propaganda campaign that the Obote regime and the UNLA was out to kill all people in Luwero irrespective of whether they were guerrillas or not.

To a good extent this campaign worked, thanks to the relative backwardness of the pastoral nomadic populace of the area who interpreted the idea of Uganda to mean their small surroundings.

The people of Luwero therefore are beginning to realise that after all if Obote's mission was to decimate all Baganda (people from Buganda region) there is no reason why he should have chosen only the district of Luwero. Luwero is just one of the seven districts of Buganda and its inhabitants are not people of pure Buganda origin. The majority of the inhabitants are Hima (ruling caste of Ankole, Southern Uganda) and Nyarwanda (Rwandese refugees who settled there). Museveni is ethnically close to these two.

At many public rallies Yoweri Museveni has stated that he would apply *"NRA Style"* treatment to all those seen to be dissenting to his movement. He speaks of how deserters and those suspected to be sympathetic to the Obote regime were summarily executed. For him he says *"...it is simple, if you betray the cause of the people we kill or if you kill we kill..."*. Reminiscing on the guerrillas' days, he has admitted that because his guerrilla force was mobile army with no jail places, the only way it could *"discipline"* those it felt had committed offences or broken the NRA code of conduct was by capital punishment and execution.

Wittingly or unwittingly in some of his public pronouncements he has appeared to be apologising for the role he played in the carnage in Luwero. All this goes to show that the supposed NRA received from Luwero did not come naturally.

At the moment a rift between the Baganda on the one side and the Nyarwanda/Nyankole alliance on the other is beginning to take shape.

The Prime Minister, Dr. Samson Kiseka (a Muganda) is working hard to exclude Museveni and the government from reaping political capital out of the rehabilitation of the war ravaged Luwero district. Kiseka personally has opened a bank account to which all financial assistance to Luwero should be deposited. He is thus projecting himself as the architect of the Luwero rehabilitation plan.

The President's behaviour of late indicates that he is aware of the motives of the Buganda group led by Kiseka.

He has physically moved to stay in Luwero where he personally supervises relief food distribution.

Recently during one of his tours in the area he was presented with a memorandum by the elders of Luwero pastoral community (supposedly unwavering supporters of his) demanding that he makes good their loss of cattle.

Museveni himself at a public rally on the same tour acknowledged that his NRA *"borrowed 21000 heads of cattle"* from this community for consumption. On the occasion he pledged a compensation of at least 30% of that number.

It is thus becoming clear to the people of Luwero, that the NRA brought to them uncalled for destruction which it is unable to make good.

The most outstanding evidence of the conflict that has been simmering is the recent attack on the NRA ideological school at Wakiso, 13 miles West of Kampala.

Museveni recently shocked to the marrow, when, during one of his many tours of Luwero, he found relief maize flour poured on the road along which he was to travel to Kapeka (one of the trading centres in the district).

Following this incident, the President gave a stern warning to the people of the area that such behaviour would in future be punished severely. He chastised the natives for not being grateful to his efforts to avail them relief assistance.

This apparent rejection of food aid from the government is linked to the natives' demands for compensation for their herds of cattle that were consumed by Museveni's guerrillas.

The staple food of this pastoral community is milk and they find relief maize unpalatable.

There is also strong demand for building materials on account of destruction done to the buildings during the war.

It is interesting to note that the people of Luwero are not yet quite certain as to where to place the blame for this destruction. So, they have not come out to blame the UNLA.

Last year, during the Tito regime when Lutakome Kayiira (leader of the Uganda Freedom Movement, UFM Buganda based fighting group) and Kawanga Ssemwogerere (leader of the Democratic Party, DP) visited the district, the natives are reported to have acknowledged that they never experienced such magnitude of violence before under the UNLA. The two told them that their problems arose from harbouring guerillas (NRA).

It is astonishing to note that the house in which Museveni lived, at Semuto (about 30 miles from Luwero town) has remained intact like an island in the rubble.

As the conflict simmers on, the Buganda based Federal Democratic Movement (FEDEMU) has vowed that Buganda will never be used as ground for war to attain state power. Their stand is that no non-Muganda should bear arms on the Buganda soil.

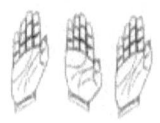

52. Dr Apollo Milton Obote - Memorandum for Clare Short MP, 15th March 1997 through his UK Rep: Joseph Ocwet; wrote:

BRITISH POLICY IN UGANDA -

1. I am shocked and frightened by the position of her Majesty Government in the letter of 24 December 1996 from the Minsters office to you. My letter of 24 October 1996 to the Minster has not even been acknowledged perhaps for the reasons that any Ugandan does not, or even a group of Ugandans in an organised association such as a political Party, do not deserve to be recognised by HMG as having any opinion on the governance of Uganda should they be opposed to the Museveni system of rule which her HMG supports.

2. In her annual visits to Uganda during the past eleven years since 1986, the Minister never formally met even once a committee from any of the political Parties. The message, for that glaring antipathy to Uganda's political Parties, now reiterated to you in a letter from her office is clearly that it is President Museveni alone who knows what is good or not good for Uganda; and that for that reason HMG *"have been right"* since 1986 to give diplomatic support and to finance and to facilitate the infallibility of President Museveni.

3. With the knowledge gained in eleven years of close working relations of hoe President Museveni detests the political Parties, multiparty politics and multiparty elections; it is most frightening that the letter from the Minister's Office should convey the message that it has been, and it is *"right"* for HMG and the British Parliament to finance and facilitate Museveni's programme which has been from the beginning, a brutal programme for the entrenchment of personal dictatorship.

4. The two grounds given at the beginning of the letter for the support by the British government of President Museveni's programme namely, that *"since President Museveni came to*

power in 1986, he has overseen progress towards rebuilding his shattered country and restoring it to constitutional government," are not only specious and disingenuous. That the two grounds are specious and disingenuous is unwittingly supported and confirmed where the letter itself states that: *"The new Constitution enacted in September (actually 8 October) 1995 postponed the issues of adopting a full multiparty system to 1999, when the referendum issue is due to take place."* Why should Uganda be the only country in the commonwealth or Africa where multiparty system is an *"issue"* to be resolved by a referendum when the political Parties, the basic factor in the system, already exist but are suppressed?

5. Contrary to what the letter states, what was *"postponed"* by the Museveni dictatorship in 1995 was not the adoption of *"a full multiparty system to 1999"* but the removal, altogether, of the political Parties from Uganda body politics when a spurious referendum in the year 1999 or 2000 will effect the removal. For that eventuality, the Constitution provides an Article 269 for the continued suppressions of the political Parties so that by the year 1999 or 2000 President Museveni's Party, known as the National Resistance Movement (NRM), but which he claims is not a Party will be the sole voice and, participant in Uganda's politics foe 14 or 15 years. This unfair head start by the NRM which, like President Museveni, is vehemently opposed to the existence of the other political Parties, multiparty politics and multiparty elections makes the referendum whether on the *"issue of full multiparty system"* (as claimed in the letter) or on the removal of the political parties from Uganda's body politic patently a ploy and chicanery designed to entrench the Museveni dictatorship.

6. The matter of *"multiparty system"* has become *"an issue"* in Uganda because President Museveni who, to quite the letter, *"came to power in 1986"* did so not through the ballot but through the gun and much bloodshed and devastations because in the multiparty elections held in December 1980 - observed by a Team drawn from nine Commonwealth Countries including Britain - his Party was thoroughly thrashed. Museveni's Party won only

one seat out of 126 seats in the National Assembly; Museveni being one of losing candidates. Even before the 1980 multiparty elections, Museveni was vehemently opposed to any such mode of elections and the reason was and still is that he is innately a militarist to whom multiparty rule including multiparty elections is anathema.

7. In a letter to Mr. Brian Sedgemere MP in December 1993 (which I cited in my letter of 24 October 1996 to the Minister), the Minister presented the *"issues"* and President Museveni differently. She asserted in that letter of December 1993 that *"President Museveni (was) opposed to premature return to the multiparty system - because of Uganda's multiparty record under Idi Amin and Milton Obote."* The fact and Museveni's own record give a totally different picture and the reverse of the Minister's presentation.

8. In the first place, it is a crude dissemblance to put Idi Amin and Milton Obote on the same pedestal. By his Decree 14 of 1971 dated 17 March 1971, Amin banned all the political Parties then in existence numbering 8. Under Obote 1962-61 and 1980-1985) not a single Party was banned or restricted - not even the Party which was led by Museveni who in February 1981 launched and waged a most vicious war against the constitution and the People. The military administration of which Museveni was the Vice-Chairman which organised the 1980 elections left Amin's Decree 14 intact and permitted only four Parties to contest the elections. It was Obote's government elected in December 1980 which repealed the Decree and in 1984, another Party was formed.

9. The difference between Amin's and Museveni's policies towards the political Parties is that whereas Amin banned the Parties outright at the beginning of his rule, Museveni adopted the policy of attrition involving the enfeebling and the incapacitating of the Parties and cutting off all contacts (public meetings, recruitment and management of Branch offices) between the Parties and the people and debarring them from

contesting any public election. In effect, there has been no difference.

10. That policy has been in existence for the past eleven years since it was imposed in March 1986 and the letter from the Minister credits such oppression as substantive restoration *"to Constitutional government."* The policy was imposed by a mere statement and until 8 October 1995 was never backed by any legislation but was vigorously enforced by the military. How an oppressive policy on governance not even backed by any legislation can be a substantial restoration *"to Constitutional government,"* as the Minister's letter claims is now part of the myth which has since 1986 bled and is continuing to bleed Uganda to death. That an elected government such as HMG should base its policy on myth is most frightening.

11. The 1995 Constitution which, in a letter of 25 January 1996 to Sir Jim Lester MP, the Minister praised and endorsed contains the codification of the oppressive measures against political Parties which were imposed in 1986 and have since, to date, been vigorously enforced. On top of the previous measures of oppression, the Constitution added what amounts to the Sword of Damocles – the referendum – which now hangs over the heads of the Parties. Article 269 of the Constitution which enfeebles, and incapacitates the Parties and which prohibits the Parties from participation or having any voice in public affairs including terms and deployment of external aid and Article 270 which debars and excludes the political Parties from contesting elections, make Uganda, by any form of definition, a dictatorship precisely because there is and there are no outlet or outlets for citizens who do not support Museveni and his NRM to participate and t be active in public affairs.

12. In the circumstances, it is a gross misrepresentation and deception to project Article 271 of the Constitution which provides for a referendum as a means to open the country, after 14 to 15 years of monolithic politics and control, to multiparty politics and multiparty elections. Every major political or constitutional measures since 1986 have been to suppress the

voice – if not the very existence – of the political Parties in the politics and governance of Uganda. For instance, when the Constitutional Commission was appointed to gather public opinion and to draft a new Constitution, the ban which prohibited the Parties to convene and address public meetings or meetings of their respective members only or to hold discussions with the Executive Committees of their respective Branches made it impossible for and ensured that the opinions of their Parties were not presented to the Commission throughout its four years of inquiry.

13. The result was that the Constitutional Commission drafted a Constitution based, except for the submission of some individuals, overwhelmingly on submission by Museveni's NRM – the only free and active political voice in the country. The chicanery in the appointment of the Constitutional Commission when the Museveni dictatorship knew that the only organised and staged NRM supporters would make submissions to the Commission may or may not have been detected by the donor governments which financed and facilitated a trickery to "legally, Constitutionally and publicly" suppress the rights and freedoms of Ugandans who belong to and who support multiparty politics, has since become a serious matter of attacks on donor governments by the multi-partyist politicians inn Uganda.

14. Someone once said that an event of a similar kind happening once is an accident, twice is coincidence, and three times is a trend. The donor governments have, in addition to annual subventions to the Museveni dictatorship, consistently financed and facilitated not three but every scheme designed to entrench the dictatorship. It is believed in Uganda that Britain, the former colonial power, is at the forefront in giving diplomatic support to the dictatorship and in persuading the other donor governments to support, finance and facilitate the entrenchment of the dictatorship.

15. In December 1996 a senior, US official from the State Department told one of the major political Parties while on a visit to Uganda that his department was not happy with the

referendum provision in the Constitution. In the letter from the office of the Minister written in the same month the definitive position of HMG is given as: *"The Ugandan people must be allowed the opportunity in 1999 to choose freely on whether to adopt a full multiparty system as the next stage of democratic reform, or to stick with the present Constitutional arrangement."* The position of HMG is a Catch-22 situation for the political Parties.

16. Having informed Mr. Brian Sedgemore MP in the letter of December 1993 that it was *"President Museveni, who because of Uganda's multiparty record under Idi Amin and Milton Obote, is opposed to a premature return to the multiparty system....,"* the Minister's letter of 24 December 1996 now appears to shift the opposition to a return to multiparty system to *"the Ugandan people"* (who) *"must be allowed the opportunity (in the face of Article 269 of the Constitution) to choose freely...."* on a return to multiparty system or *"stick with the present Constitutional arrangement."*

17. The shift appears very ingenious and appears to have been contrived, despite or in spite of the word *"freely"* in the formula, to ensure that the account of Article 269 which provides for the political parties to have been dormant for 14 or 15 years at the time of the referendum, *"the present Constitutional arrangement"* would win in the referendum. A secondary reason for the shift would appear that the Minister now realises that Idi Amin never rules Uganda even for a single day under multiparty system and therefore to assert as the Minister did in 1993 that Amin's multiparty record was the reason against a return to multiparty system is false. The shift may also be possible because the Minister now appreciates that to present Museveni as holier than Obote on the matter of multiparty rule is a hollow and ingenious propaganda.

18. What is most disturbing in the Minister's formulae for Uganda to return to multiparty system is the conditionality that there "must" be a referendum. When Museveni imposed his system of rule with the gun, his Proclamation of 26 January 1986 stated,

inter alia, that *"The National Resistance Army (NRA) on that day, took over the powers of the government of the Republic of Uganda ...."* The Army, now known as the Uganda People's Defence Force (UPDF), has never returned those powers to the people to be exercised by their representatives elected in a free and fair multiparty elections.

19. At article 271(1), the 1995 Constitution which was enacted by persons at which elections the political Parties were debarred, specifically debars the political Parties from contesting elections, rejects multiparty elections and provides for elections to be *"held under the Movement political system."* The Movement referred to is the National Resistance Movement (NRM), the political wing of the NRA (now UPDF) and its mode of elections permits the NRM to field, Finance and campaign for the elections of its candidates while all other candidates must stand as independents and must not indicate whatever Party they may belong to. It was the NRM and NRA which in 1986 imposed the oppressive dictatorship not after a referendum and it is the same NRM and NRA (now called UPDF) and their supporters and collaborators at home and abroad who insist on the conditionality (which the Minister endorses) that for the dictatorship to end, there "must" be a referendum.

20. The conditionality is, in fact, a subtle means to promote dictatorship imposed by the gun and bloodshed to the level of a democratic system and to the level of the rule of law and then demand that to change it a referendum be held after those who imposed the system (dictatorship) have suppressed the adherents of the multiparty system for 14 or 15 years. That is not, by any stretch of the imagination, a record which can be described as *"substantial progress towards restoring Constitutional government."*

21. During the 1996 Presidential elections campaign – under the NRM system, President Museveni on 6 May made a broadcast carried concurrently on TV and Radio. He was dressed in military gear. The most important point he made was that should the votes go against him, he was not going to hand-over his army (the

UPDF) to any person. He was, in fact, restating the substance of what he had said time and again over the past ten years. However, on 6 May Museveni introduced a new element which was that the military and not the Constitution was supreme in Uganda. The Minister's letter was the referendum to be held because the provision is in the Constitution but President Museveni, his army and his NRM do not regard any provision in the Constitution as capable of ending their rule. That is what Museveni was saying on 6 May, namely that although the elections were being held under Article 271(1) of the Constitution, the system of rule imposed by the military in 1986 would continue even if the votes went against Museveni.

22. The Minister's position that a referendum *"must"* be held, not least, because the provision is in the Constitution also defines the issue to be put to the electorates as choice between *"a full multiparty system"* and *"the present Constitutional arrangement."* Besides the fact that the protagonists of the "present Constitutional arrangement" would have had a head start of 14 or 15 years to deepen their hold on society by various means including corruption now extremely rampant, threats and intimidation, the Minister's position and definition would subject to a referendum much of the fundamental rights and freedoms of the individual so that should the result of the referendum be in favour of the present system the resultant situation will be one which conforms the Uganda Constitution as a Charter of Slavery and exempts Uganda from the provision of the UN Charter on human rights of which Uganda is a signatory.

23. To hold a referendum for a majority to determine whether or not each citizen of Uganda including minors and those yet to be born should enjoy the fundamental human rights and freedoms of the individual such as the freedom of conscience; the freedom of expression; the freedom to hold opinion and to receive and impart ideas and information without undue interference or restriction; the freedom of assembly and association; the freedom to assemble freely and to associate with other persons and the freedom to form or belong to a political

party will, for the first time since the adoption of the UN Charter on human rights irrespective of the outcome of the referendum (because it is a Catch-22 situation), deprive the individual from being the sole custodian of his or her fundamental (inalienable) human rights and freedoms. It will also be an outrage of incalculable proportions.

24. The only reason for the now eleven years war of attrition which the Uganda dictatorship has waged against the political Parties is to deprive the citizen of his or her freedom to participate in public affairs and therefore the freedom to disagree with the policies of the NRM and NRA (now UPDF) from outside the aegis of the NRM and the institutions which have been created since 1986 to perpetuate the dictatorship. It is an indisputable fact of the situation that since 1986 on account of policy, deed, legislation and the Constitution, the citizen who does not support the NRM, has been, under the guise of disabling, enfeebling, incapacitating and debarring the political Parties from participation in the politics of Uganda, deprived of his or her rights and freedoms to conscientiously participate in public affairs. The referendum is designed to be the final act in the elimination of the conscientious voice of the citizen, outside the NRM, from public affairs.

25. For HMG to support, finance and facilitate the empowerment of the majority – even without coercion or intimidation – usurp the conscientious power of the individual in the exercise and enjoyment of his or her fundamental human rights and freedoms just because the military dictatorship is opposed to political Parties, multiparty politics and multiparty elections would amount not only to a perfidious appeasement of the Museveni dictatorship but also raise the question as to whether as to whether or not HMG and the British Parliament believe in the fundamental (inalienable) human rights and freedoms of the individual. How can it be accepted that a majority in Britain should determine whether or not the Minister should belong to a Party active in politics or is it that individual in Uganda is sub-human and not at par with the Minister. If the Ugandan

individual is sub-human, the majority of then cannot be anything else.

26. Although the Minister's position appears to be emphatic that it is only a referendum which may or can return Uganda to a multiparty system, the Minister is also aware that over the past ten years, a number of African Countries once ruled either by single Parties or by the military or a combination of both have returned to multiparty system without anyone of them holding a referendum. This is clearly because the right of the citizen and his or her freedom to form or belong to a political Party for it to be his or her vehicle for his or her conscientious participation in the public affairs of the country is intrinsically interwoven with and inseparable from the freedom of conscience; the freedom of expression including the freedom to hold opinions and impart ideas and information without undue interference or restrictions; an freedom of the citizen to assemble freely and associate with other persons. Subjecting the people of Uganda into a clearly designed Catch-22 situation namely, present oppression or continued oppression if a referendum is held or not held when other dictatorship in Africa, at the insistence of MHG and other donor governments, released their victims without any of them holding a referendum, if it remains the position of HMG, will make HMG a very active collaborator of the Uganda dictatorship.

27. In the case of the former African dictatorships, all that was done was that each repealed the provisions of their Constitutions which provided for either one-Party rule or military rule or one-Party cum military rule. They did not repeal such provisions as a matter of charity or because they suddenly became democrats. They repealed the oppressive provisions because MHG and the other donor governments stopped or threatened to stop financing, facilitating, and entrenching dictatorship. The Minister is obviously very strongly opposed to applying the same policy to the Uganda dictatorship and appears to protect the dictatorship by projecting the referendum as if it will be on matters such as Uganda federating with another Country or Countries, or the re-introduction of the former East African

currency and not non the fundamental human rights and freedoms of the individual citizen of Uganda. The Uganda situation is fundamentally different from the Maastricht situation where violations and threats to the human rights and freedoms of the individual are absent or much less.

28. In addition to the Minister's perturbing conditionality that there "must" be a referendum, there is the Minister's presentation of Uganda's recent and current history which is equally perturbing. Whether on the economy, politics or Constitutional government, the Minister appears to believe that it is Museveni alone or his dictatorship who or which can manage the economy well and ensure economic growth; and therefore that Museveni's system of governance being good for the economy is also an acceptable system unless and until it is rejected in a referendum. Thus, in the letter from the Minister's office to you, it is asserted that President Museveni *"has overseen substantial progress towards rebuilding his shattered Country and restoring it to Constitutional government."* The Minister's presentation of the situation clearly puts Museveni both before and after he became President outside the factors which Museveni is, in fact, the greatest factor who after the fall of Amin in April 1979 has consistently worked against the restoration of *"Constitutional government"* in Uganda and in doing so caused much bloodshed and devastation than all his predecessors put together.

29. This Memorandum has already shown that Museveni's record, since becoming President by the gun and bloodshed in 1986, has consistently been against a return to *"Constitutional government"* and instead for the entrenchment of his dictatorship. That policy has cost Uganda most dearly in lives and property; a fact which the Minister would not want to acknowledge and clearly prefers to put a strong lid on it. The fact is that since Museveni became President in 1986, his army has been waging unceasing wars of conquest and subjugation in various districts from that year to date. There are presently some 200 people form 10 grouping in Uganda jails charged with

treason; the highest number both in total, or at any one time any previous ruler of Uganda ever endured. Some aspects of Museveni's war may be given.

30. Considering that until October 1990 the Command of Museveni's army consisted predominantly of Rwanda Tutsi officers, evidence of genocide committed by the army of conquest and subjugation exists; Museveni himself and his military commanders have, from time to time; given that evidence not as crimes committed but as prowess of the army. In January 1987, for instance, Major General Fred Rwigyema, the man who was to command the army which invaded Rwanda from Uganda in October 1990 committed genocide in Kitgum District, Northern Uganda. The crime was (partially) witnessed by a large number of journalists flown to the scene of crime in two military helicopters to record the prowess of Museveni's army in battle. On alighting at the scene, the journalists were ordered, while the helicopter flew away, to run for safety because (allegedly) *"the rebels were attacking the place."* From where they ran, nit far, the journalist heard considerable gun fire and when called back to the scene, Rwigyema addressed them; part of what he said was as follows:

> *"We killed about 350 and these are the bodies we have counted...*
>
> *"...There are many more bodies lying in the field. These are the ones we have counted so far...*
>
> *"...The number dead could be more than six hundred (600)...*
>
> *"...We were surprised to see the rebels coming to us without taking cover...*
>
> *"...We kept massacring them, but they kept coming and we killed so may..."*

(The Standard, Nairobi 21 January 1987)

31. Far away from the scene of genocide in Eastern Uganda, the man whom the Minister credits with *"substantial progress towards restoring (Uganda) to Constitutional government,"* President Museveni, also addressed journalists flown to his

station from the scene of crime. Part of what he said was as follows:

> "The rebels attacked us (his army) at a place called Corner Kilak, 20 miles south of Kitgum (Town)...
>
> "...They came in while singing and shouting; our people (the army) massacred those chaps...
>
> "...They approached us frontally...
>
> "...This gave us a very good chance because they exposed themselves, so on Sunday we surrounded them and massacred the...
>
> "...We massacred them very badly..."
>
> (The Standard, Nairobi, 21 January 1987)

32. The Minister's paragon in Constitutional rule. President Museveni, comes out from his own statement and that of his field Commanders as a bloodthirsty militarists to who the sanctity of human life is of no importance to the extent that the *"rebels"* who had been *"surrounded"* by a superior force were not forced to surrender but had to be *"massacred"* and *"massacred very badly."* Museveni, in his short statement, used the same word in describing what their army did at Corner Kilak. Museveni is a university graduate in Political Science and could not in 1987 or now be taken not to know the meaning of the word massacre. That Museveni and his Rwanda Tutsi field Commander used the same word more or less at the same time, when each was distant away from the other, was not an going on and had been going on in Northern Uganda since September 1986 namely, widespread massacres – genocide.

33. Museveni's army arrived in Northern Uganda in early March 1986 to find neither opposition and resentment nor celebrations, a state of affairs which puzzled Museveni and his army who expected stiff opposition. There were two reasons for the absence of opposition and both were political. The first was that the military Junta which overthrew on 27 July 1985 the government elected in 1980 and on the eve of another general elections was detested throughout Uganda and more so in the North where the overthrown government had in 1980 won all the

Parliamentary seats. Therefore members of the Uganda Peoples Congress (UPC) in the North, like elsewhere in Uganda, saw the overthrow of the Junta by Museveni as poetic justice but also had no cause to welcome Museveni because he had in February 1981 launched and waged a vicious war against the Constitution, the people and the elected (UPC) government.

34. The second reason was that although Museveni had in February 1986 appointed a large number of leaders and members of the Democratic party (DP), the second largest political Party in Uganda, into his Cabinet; he also left out the Vice-President of the Party who was a Northerner and had been a very close to the leaders of the Junta. The DP leaders in the North therefore adopted the policy of wait and see – no celebrations and no resentment – particularly as Museveni had publicly stated that he would rule for four years after which a general election would be held.

35. From their different positions on Museveni, the leaders of UPC and DP in the North moved quickly in February 1986 to isolate the leaders of the Junta who had fled to the North and together with the Bishops and clergy made the leaders of the Junta and their armed men to decide either to surrender to Museveni or to leave the Country. The leader of the Junta with their men chose to go to Sudan. Thus when Museveni's army arrived in the North in early March, they met neither armed opposition nor exuberant jubilations which, as it turned out, Museveni and his army erroneously or deliberately and maliciously took as a stratagem designed to unleash widespread Northern rebellion. To frustrate the imaginary rebellion, Museveni's army launched a severe programme and operations of persecution and inhumane treatment of the people. Homes and granaries were ransacked or bunt by the army. Young able-bodies men were rounded up and taken by the army; they have never been seen again. Crops and livestock were taken by the army without payment. Persecutions became so much that many men whose homes were along or near roads had to leave their homes and live in the bush.

36. Two Bishops, Benon Ogwal (Protestant) and Cyprian Kihangire (Catholic – now deceased) took it upon themselves, after the activities of the Political Parties had been banned in mid-March 1986, to plead with Museveni to stop the persecution but without avail. Bishop Ogwal was threatened by the army and was nearly killed. He fled and now lives in America. Because of the deepening persecution, some men from the birder with Sudan fled into that Country where they joined the army of the Junta which in August 1986 invaded Uganda.

37. The invasion was easily repelled within 24 hours by Museveni's army which also accused the villagers in the invasion area of having harboured the invaders. For the concocted crime, the army became the accuser, prosecutor, and judge. The villagers of the area were herded in their houses which were then burnt, food granaries were also burnt, and livestock seized by the army. Commenting on the ghastly deeds of the army, Museveni said: *"Those chaps were massacred very badly."* It was the language which he and his military commanders were to use in describing the success of military operations against *"rebels"* - real or imaginary.

38. The Junta's army which invaded Uganda in August 1986 was in fact, two armies. One was composed of professional soldiers who had fled to Sudan with the leaders of the Junta. The second was composed of a small number of peasants – estimated at the time by the political Parties to be less than a thousand – who, because of persecutions by Museveni's army went to Sudan in order to acquire arms and then return to villages and Districts near the border with Sudan.

39. Those men, through armed, lived in the bush, and frequently mounted successful ambushes against marauding and rapacious army. The result was that in November 1986, the Deputy Minister of Defence disclosed in a public statement that the army had been given orders, as measures to deny succour to *"rebels,"* to destroy and/ or poison all boreholes and water well and destroy all food granaries and food stuff not harvested in four Districts in the North namely, Gulu, Kitgum, Lira and Apac.

Thus, to Museveni, the entire inhabitants of those Districts – men, women and children – had become "rebels" to be poisoned or starved to death.

40. In January 1987, a new programme – direct massacres by the army – was introduced. This was because the army could not, in order to accomplish the November programme, scour the hundreds and hundreds of scattered villages and homesteads in a vast area so as to quickly destroy the food and water well therein. The January programme, without cancelling the November programme, required male peasants living in a village or villages and homesteads when summoned, to gather at an appointed place, date and time in order to be addressed by military officers on agricultural production. All who went to such gatherings were massacred. After two weeks of the pogrom in various places, Museveni and his military commanders decided to present one of these heinous operations as a battle between his army and rebels and to have journalist at the scene at Corner Kilak.

41. This memorandum has already shown that Museveni and his field commanders both described what happened at Corner Kilak as a massacre, and that journalist were at the scene. The journalists were flown to the scene in military helicopters which landed at the scene precisely as the "rebels" were allegedly attacking the position. No journalist, however, later write of having seen the attack or of having heard gun fire before the field commander sent them away. No *"rebel"* was taken alive or wounded although, according to Museveni they have been previously *"surrounded."* No journalist saw or reported on arms, not even spears, which the massacred *"rebels"* carried and the field commanders did not display such arms or spears. Museveni said that the *"rebels"* were *"surrounded on Sunday"* but the field commander gave a different account; he said, *"We were surprised to see the rebels coming at us without taking cover. We kept massacring them....."* Both Museveni and his field commander while they admitted massacre also hid the fact that the victims were not rebels but peasants.

42. The peasants had gathered, after being summoned, at Corner Kilak. They were kept at a nearby bushy area, under armed guard, overnight for their massacre to begin the next day after the landing of the helicopter carrying journalists. That is why the journalists arrived at the scene precisely as the *"rebels"* were allegedly attacking the place, which none of the journalists became aware on arrival of any attack or battle, why they were sent away so that none could observe the phony battle or the *"rebels"* coming *"without taking cover"* and why no *"rebel"* was taken alive or wounded.

43. The Corner Kilak massacre was the only military operation which was covered by journalists or to which journalists were especially flown in order to be at the scene when it began and to report it as *"battle"* between the *"rebels"* and Museveni's army. It was not an isolated massacre or operation involving massacre. It was not the first of what may be called *"operation massacres"* and which did not end at Corner Kilak. President Museveni announced the existence of *"operation massacres"* and prepared the Country for what has to happen at Corner Kilak and thereafter at a Press Conference which the New Vision – the mouth daily of Museveni dictatorship – reported as follows:

> *"You see when you give them (civil population) a good beating then those who are using them will no longer use them. Since the month of January (1987), we have given them much beating especially in Lira and Kitgum Districts. And in fact, the week I left (for Yugoslavia) we had given them a good blow in Gulu District."*

(The New Vision, 19 January 1987)

44. *"Good beating,"* *"much beating"* and *"good blow"* were euphemisms for massacres and the expressions *"those who are using them"* was Museveni's way to cover the senseless massacres by his army with false and malicious indirect accusation against political Parties – at least one of them, the Uganda Peoples' congress (UPC) – of resisting his rule. There was no resistance anywhere and the accusation or its falsity was not new.

45. During the six months rule of the Junta from July 1985 to January 1986, the Junta ceded the entire Western Region of Uganda to the remnants and stragglers of Museveni's army and that army arrested, tortured, and killed many UPC leaders in the region. After Museveni became President in late January 1986, his army did the same to the UPC leaders in the Southern and Eastern Region. The UPC leaders were arrested, tortured, and killed not because they were organising resistance or rebellion but precisely because Museveni was and still is extremely obsessed with the idea that unless he destroys the UPC, his rule will not last as long as he wants it to last.

46. In The New Vision report quoted above, Museveni was happy that his army was giving the villagers *"good beating," "much beating"* and *"good blow"* so that *"those who are using them will no longer use them."* He did not name "those who" were using the villagers because there was none. Throughout 1986 and in January 1987 no Ugandan, group of Ugandans or any political Parties had come out to militarily confront Museveni's rule; and the political Parties (till now) and much as they detest that rule has steered away from supporting armed resistance so much so that for eleven years, much as he tried, Museveni has never found any scintilla of evidence connecting any of the Parties with any armed group. Instead of supporting and assisting the emergence at the top of his singular commitment to Constitutional governance, maintained for eleven years under very trying conditions, the Minister still believes that the Uganda political Parties have no role in restoring Uganda to Constitutional governance and must continue to be enfeebled, incapacitated and kept out of participation in public affairs by a dictatorship until a referendum organised by the dictatorship removes them totally from Uganda's body politics in the year 1999 or 2000.

47. From The New Vison report which was published a few days before the massacres at Corner Kilak, President Museveni made public that *"since the month of January"* (1987) there were military operations – operation massacres – which involved the

military giving the civil population in Lira, Kitgum and Gulu Districts *"good beating," "much beating"* and *"good blow."* These (January) operations were the thirds in a systematic scheme of carnage which Museveni's army meted since it arrived in the North in early March 1986. The first was the widespread persecutions in which many were killed, abducted never to be seen again, and homes and food granaries were ransacked or burnt. The second was the operation to destroy all foodstuffs and to poison or destroy all boreholes and water well in the North. Persecutions forced some men in Gulu and Kitgum Districts but not Lira Districts to go to Sudan and acquire arms for the (futile) defence of their homes.

48. It was a futile decision and reaction on several accounts. The Gulu and Kitgum men had no organisation and no leaders or leaders; they were not trained soldiers or guerrillas and had only small arms and limited ammunition. Above all, the decision and reaction afforded Museveni the pretext he desperately wanted and had harboured since March 1986 to stamp his rule in the North with cataclysmic carnage. Museveni's army arrived in the North expecting still opposition but found indifference and proceeded to punish the indifference with scotched earth persecution. The inclusion of Lira Districts in January 1987 operation massacres – as the New Vision reported – when no one from the Districts was either in the August 1986 invasion or ever went to Sudan to acquire arms, expose the January 1987 operation massacres as a deliberate bloodbath policy.

49. After its coup of 27 July 1985, the Junta pursued a policy of extreme violent brigandry in Lira District and in neighbouring and ethnically connected District of Apac. To the people of Lira and Apac Districts, the fall of the Junta in January 1986 was not only poetic justice but also solace and for that reason the people of Lira or Apac could not and did not participate in the Junta's invasion of August 1986. Secondly, Lira and Apac do not border Sudan and the people from the two Districts did not go to Sudan, where the Junta was, for arms. Yet, as disclosed by Museveni and published by New Vision, Lira District was included in the

operation massacre of January 1987 involving *"good beating," "much beating"* and *"good blow."*

50. Operation massacres, which began as Museveni said, in January 1987 in Lira, Kitgum and Gulu Districts in the North, soon engulfed Apac District (North) and several Districts in the Eastern Region. The modus operandi remained substantially the same for several months namely, summoning peasants to a meeting and then massacring the attendants. As the modus operandi became more and more widely known in the Districts, less and less peasants turned up at the meetings. In some cases, very many people, even those not summoned, turned up at meetings with concealed weapons – spear with shortened handles, knives of various types, axes, adzes, etc., – fought hand to hand with and overpowered soldiers and acquired modern weapons.

51. As the operation massacres intensified in several other Districts and in the three which Museveni had mentioned, and the people increasingly either disobeyed the summons to attend meetings or went prepared to fight or die, a fourth additional form of carnage coupled with pillage was brought into play by Museveni's army. The new additional form was the violently savage campaign in which the army openly raised villages and homesteads, massacred the inhabitants, burnt homes and granaries and seized millions of livestock. The North and North-East became, in three years, desolate. The Minister and the Uganda dictatorship concealed the fact and are now desperately distracting attention away from the holocaust with the claim of, to quote the Minister's letter, *"10 years of economic growth"* as if by accepting massacres and devastations the same somehow became factors in economic investment and growth and were therefore much needed.

52. The holocaust made the people desperate for arms. The army appreciated the desperation correctly and worked out an appropriate plan to deal with it. It so happened that in March 1987 at the height of operation massacres (which began in January) and the start of the holocaust, some Ugandan politicians who were out of the Country began to pronounce that they had

formed and were the leaders of organisation of the people (peasants) fighting to remove Museveni in their respective Districts.

53. There were, in fact no District organisations with District leaders either in Uganda or abroad. The peasants managed to acquire some arms and desperately wanted more not to remove Museveni but to defend their homes and properties. Although the pronouncements from abroad followed by some actions in Uganda managed to establish in a few Districts or parts of such Districts semblances of organisations, the objectives of the peasants and those of the politicians remained divergent and were never harmonised and the organisations remained weak or existed only in name. Thus, years later, when some of the politicians who were said to be leaders of organisations with *"armies"* returned to Uganda after signing agreements with Museveni, their *"armies"* did not and have not come out of the *"bush."*

54. The plan which Museveni's army prepared to encounter the desperate desire of the people to acquire arms was massacre. In late July and early August Museveni's intelligence service spread in Soroti and Kumi Districts (Teso in the East), and Lira and Apac Districts (Lango in the North) the false information that the politicians abroad, who were claiming to have armies in those Districts, would fly arms to Soroti airport. A date was given. The people, travelling by night and through the bush in their thousands, assembled on the outskirts of the airport on the appointed date. It was a trap and at first light, Museveni's army opened fire on the assembled crowds. Some estimate put the number of those massacred at around 30,000 while others put the figure as high as about 50,000. No one was taken alive or wounded. On 15 August 1987, Museveni escorted military Attachés of various High Commissions and Embassies in viewing what the New Vision reported as "piles and piles of dead rebels."

55. Massacres, destruction of food to starve people to death, pillage, and devastation have been Museveni's means to the seat of government and also to stamp his rule. In his quest to reach

that seat after the fall of Amin in April 1979 when Uganda was ruled by a weak and fractious coalition from that date to December 1980, he raised a private army for that purpose. The private army was nominally part of the then nascent national army when Museveni was the Minister of Defence in the coalition. It was the private army which he used in 1981 to launch and wage his war of conquest and subjugation and for the establishment of his dictatorship. He achieved his goal in 1986 but only after suborning some officers in the official army to overthrow the elected government and Parliament and the turn against the Junta.

56. Over the years since 1981, Museveni's supporters and apologists abroad have done everything to conceal the most notorious machinery of massacres and terror since the fall of Amin namely, Museveni's army. Museveni's friends abroad have cloaked his army with the accolade of a very disciplined army wittingly knowing that Hitler's SS and Gestapo were also so much very disciplined to have seen nothing wrong, for instance, in Auschwitz.

57. The livestock pillage campaign, for instance, by Museveni's army has never been acknowledge by his supporters and apologists who have all heaped the terror and death on the cattle rustling Karamojong of North-East Uganda. However, while heaping the crime onto Karamojong, Museveni's supporters and apologists completely destroyed their case by writing and claiming that the Karamojong cattle raids in 1987/88 extended as far as West as to Nebbi Districts in West Nile where much havoc was also wrought. The only route to Nebbi Districts from East or from Karamoja was (is) through Pakwach bridge on the Nile and Museveni's army had (still has) a garrison at the bridge. Apart from the guarded bridge, for the Karamojong to raid in Nebbi, they had to traverse Kitgum and Gulu Districts or Lira and Gulu Districts – a distance of more than one hundred miles either way – and do so through territories where Museveni's army was very active. Furthermore, Karamoja has never at any time teemed with extra livestock allegedly or supposedly from other Districts.

58. The Minister's attitude to how the people of Uganda have bled and continue to bleed under Museveni's apologists abroad; only good has happened. On one of her annual visits to Uganda, the Minister went to Kumi District where Museveni was commanding his army in an operation. Uganda Television later showed the Minister and Museveni observing artillery bombardment of a village. Before leaving Uganda, the Minister announced increased British aid. The policy of HMG appears therefore to be that the more bombardment of villages, massacres, pillages, devastations and suppressions of the political Parties, the more British aid which now stands at forty million pounds annually. A referendum which will ensure the continuance of tyranny s therefore strongly supported by HMG.

59. In June 1989, Museveni made two statements which the British High Commission in Uganda could not conceivably have failed to report to the Minister. Both statements showed that Museveni and his army had committed genocide. Instead of the two statements at least shocking the Minister and enabling her to see Museveni in his true colours and to see his goal, the Minister's letter of 24 December 1996 now shows that to the Minister, genocide admitted and confessed by Museveni prove that HMG *"have been right"* to support and continue to support the Museveni dictatorship and that genocide is an acceptable part of the "substantial progress" which Museveni *"has overseen....towards rebuilding his shattered Country and restoring it to Constitutional government."* Thus, to the Minister, genocide does not shatter Uganda, and a dictatorship which commits it *"must"* only be removed by a referendum organised by the dictatorship itself and after the dictatorship has been the sole voice in the politics and governance of Uganda for 14 or 15 years.

60. The Minister's position is reminiscent of the position of the (Sir) Edward Heath government in 1971 to the Idi Amin dictatorship. Amin paid an official visit to London where he was entertained at Number 10 and Buckingham Palace where his reign of murders and terror was less than six months old. The

visit was the greatest certificate of approval which made Amin, on return to Uganda, to literally set Uganda ablaze. London knew, before sending an invitation to him, that Amin had established a dictatorship and that massacres and terror was rampant. In London, Amin asked for and was allowed to buy British arms, the very tools he wanted for bloodbath and terror in Uganda and for threatening neighbouring Countries. That policy of 1971 to fraternise with a mass killer, give him diplomatic support and whatever he wanted, is the same policy which HMG has pursued since 1986 and which the Minister in the letter of 24 December defends as "right."

61. A most chilling and very important aspect of the consequences of what the Minister sees as *"right"* was given in a statement by Museveni to diplomats in Uganda on Saturday 11 June 1989. According to the New Vision of 13 June, Museveni told diplomats that *"as the direct results of ways, there were (at that time) two points seven (2.7) million displaced people who had lost everything including homes and were living in make-shift camps."* Museveni appealed to diplomats for tonnes of maize and beans (food), 12 million meters of cloth, saucepans, blankets, and hoes for the destitute.

62. The British High Commission must have reported the appeal and the staggering number of the destitute to the Minister. To hold as the Minister obviously holds that a system of rule which generates wars and some three million destitute is not only the *"right"* policy but also that the system must be supported and even entrenched by the collaboration of HMG through diplomatic support, annual subventions and financing and facilitation of a chicanery referendum to entrench the system is most shocking and frightening and most heartless and inhumane.

63. The figure of 2.7 million displaced people who had lost everything including homes as *"the direct results of the wars"* was given by Museveni himself and not by his political opponents or detractors. Never before had such a staggering number of the people of Uganda known and experienced so much wars, death, devastation and deprivation as under Museveni; and yet it is

precisely that very tyranny, oppression and holocaust which the Minister praises, has been praising for eleven years, and wants it to continue. Although Museveni has so far massacred and oppressed the people of Uganda to the Minister's satisfaction, the Minister is also wittingly or unwittingly inviting the people of Uganda to abandon all belief in political campaign to change the system and take up arms. This is bound to come the more political Parties are suppressed or when they are removed, altogether, from Uganda's body politic.

64. When Museveni met diplomats on 11 June 1989, he appealed for donations of 97,400 tonnes of maize and 64,800 tonnes of beans to feed 2.7 million destitute in the make-shift camps. It was a most cynical appeal which made and still makes the Minister's policy to be a clear subsidy of and fuel for tyranny, massacres, and devastation in Uganda. The 2.7 million destitute were starving and dying in the make-shift camps not because if famine or some others natural causes but because Museveni deliberately decided to destroy not only the entire stock of their food but also their homes and everything, they possessed including clothes. The Minister praises Museveni for having done so and HMG now subsidises and fuels the tyranny to the tune of forty million pounds annually.

65. The Minister's letter praises Museveni for having *"overseen substantial progress towards rebuilding his shattered Country..."* The Praises contradicts and sits incongruously with the real Museveni who disclosed his real self and policy in a policy statement he made and was published by his mouthpiece, the New Vision on 27 June 1989. The Paper reported Museveni as having revealed himself and his basic predilection and policy as follows:

> *"There was a policy to destroy food stocks that were assisting the rebels to continue disturbing the peace of the ordinary people. This was done after due notice was given to the population through dropping leaflets in the disturbed areas in advance, by helicopters. These leaflets, in vernacular, were*

telling the people to evacuate, the fire areas, where the security forces would clash with rebels, to safe zones.

Now, whether that policy is still continuing or not is no longer major issue because we have cleared out the rebels. The operation is over. It is in only a few areas where we are still operational.

And in those few areas, there isn't any food anymore. So there is nothing to destroy."

66. To regard and describe Museveni, the President who by military operations in which many were massacred, operations which uprooted millions of people from their farms and homes; destroyed their homes and food sticks until there was *"nothing more to destroy"*; herded the millions in make-shift camps to starve and die, seized all their livestock and in the process destroyed all education and health infrastructures to render desolate the erstwhile habitat of the millions, as the President who has *"overseen substation progress towards rebuilding his shattered Country ...."* is for the Minister not only to give Museveni a transparency false identity but also to present evidence that HMG abetted, concealed and are still abetting and concealing crimes against humanity in Uganda.

67. Since September 1986, the official statement and propaganda had been that the army was fighting *"rebels"* but in the statement published on 27 June 1989, Museveni specifically stated that advance *"notice was given to the population .... to evacuate the fire areas where the security forces would clash with the rebels"*. It is also inconceivable that a conscious rebel would have, after reading the warning leaflets, remained in the designated areas of the clash. It is also inconceivable that a Minister of the British Crown actually believed Museveni's trash that he first warned everybody including rebels in a designated area before his army went into the area to clash with the rebels and to destroy the food stocks and homes therein. If the Minister or HMG did not believe the trash, their previous and continued support for Museveni amounts to turning a blind eye to and

abetting and concealing the crime of genocide committed by Museveni's army.

68. The claim by Museveni that leaflets were dropped in the designated areas proved to be fiction. No texts of any leaflets have ever been published officially or by any newspapers either in Uganda or abroad. No one in the affected areas saw or read any pf the acclaimed leaflets. The political Parties are unanimous that their respective members, who either escaped from the areas or went to the make-shift camps, neither saw nor read any of the leaflets. Because it was inconceivable that Museveni would have warned the rebels – if they existed – of impending military operations against them and because all available evidence show that no warning leaflet was written or dropped in any designated areas, it follows that what Museveni said about warning leaflets stands clearly exposed as a cover to conceal genocidal military operations which rendered desolate a vast area of Uganda once populated by some five million people.

69. The Minister's praises for Museveni's economic performance therefore appear also to suggest that to her, the millions of people who either massacred or uprooted from their homes and farms, and their areas rendered desolate were or are not part of the human race and that they did or do not matter at least to Museveni and to HMG. The Minister also seems to hold that what Museveni stated as having been his policy which was carried out until *"there wasn't any food anymore (and until) there (was) nothing more to destroy"*, and which resulted in the herding of 2.7 million people in make-shift camps to starve and die or was not in fact; or else it must remain a great puzzle why the Minister was and is still eager to cover and protect while at the same time sending to Uganda an increasing amounts of British taxpayers' money to repair or to subsidise the repair of the physical structures and productive capacities which Museveni was destroying or had destroyed in parts of Uganda. On the other hand, if the Minister accepted what Museveni had done and had said as fact, if is curious that HMG never publicity censured him

or withheld British aid to him until he abandoned military rule and adopted a more acceptable system of governance.

70. On the economy of Uganda, the Minister's apparent belief that only Museveni and his dictatorship can manage the economy well is grossly contrived and erroneous and is disproved by existing records so much so as to make the belief a sinister scheme to protect and entrench the dictatorship with the British taxpayer's money.

71. Records show that under multiparty politics, government, and Parliament elected in two multiparty elections, the Uganda economy in the 1960s and early 1980s performed and was managed extremely well. The Country Report of the UN National Human Development published in July 1996, for instance, confirms that performance and management published in July 1996, for instance, confirms that performance and management. In summary, the Report states that in the 1960s *"GDP grew at 4.3 percent, subsistence production at 4 percent per annum. Social services, economic infrastructures, and other support services expanded at an estimated rate of 6.2 percent per annum."*

72. The UN Report describes the 1971-1980 (Amin dictatorship) as a period of economic and political stagnation when *"the economy was mismanaged, environmental degradation increased and the overall conditions of human existence deteriorated."* The Report states specifically that that *"was altered and reversed in the period 1981-84 (multiparty politics, government and Parliament) (when) the economy regained its growth path ....the GDP grew at 6 percent per annum."* Museveni thereafter did not inherit, in 1986, a "shattered" Country as the Minister claims; that lot fell on the shoulders of Milton Obote in December 1980 after multiparty elections that month.

73. When Museveni became President in January 1986, he also inherited a body of economic policies, programmes and (costed) project profiles (put in place by a government and Parliament elected in multiparty elections) which were generating 6 percent GDP growth per annum. The Secretary of State Hon Malcom Rifkind, who at the time of that recovery held the office the

Minister now holds was very supportive of the policies, programmes and project profiles; Museveni, on the other hand during the same period, was waging a vicious was not only against the political system but also against and virulently condemning the economic policy which was recording 6 percent GDP growth per annum.

74. In the one District (and its environs) where Museveni's guerrilla army held sway and keep the national army at bay for upwards pf two years, for instance, Museveni's army destroyed coffee farms and factories, burnt and ransacked homes and seized all livestock to feed the army. Museveni's reasoning, which was published in Bulletins, was that to destroy the economy was to weaken the government and lead to its overthrow. Had the elected government not contained Museveni's predilection to bloodshed, despoliations and devastations in the one District in the Southern Region, other Districts in the Region would today be as desolate as Districts in the North and North-East.

75. In the elections of December 1980 Museveni's Party, then known as the Uganda patriotic Movement (UPM) did not publish a manifesto. In fact, only one of the four Parties, the Uganda Peoples Congress (UPC), did publish a manifesto. The situation in Uganda after the fall of Amin followed by twenty months of the rule of a weak and fractious coalition was so daunting and challenging that only the UPC dared to publicly point the way ahead. One of the daunting and challenging issues which had a very strong bearing on human rights and on economic recovery was what to do with the Asians – some of whom were citizens of Uganda – whom Amin had expelled in 1972, and more particularly what to do with the property of the expelled non-citizens Asians.

76. The UPC manifesto promised the enactment by Parliament of a law to remove the *"uncertainty"* in the ownership of the Asian properties which Amin had distributed free to his cronies or had nationalised and whose mismanagement contributed greatly to the depressed economy. Museveni condemned the UPC manifesto promise, saying that it aimed at selling the Country to

"foreigners." In 1982 when the UPC government published the Bill on the Asian properties which was enacted, Museveni again virulently attacked the Bill and accused the UPC government of being *"the running dog"* of the British government, and (from the bush) declared that any Asian who returned to Uganda and repossessed his or her property, would be killed. Today the return of some of the Asians, made possible by the vision of the UPC leaders, and part they have played in the recovery of the economy as well as the removal of the human rights blot created by Amin expelling Asians are credited to Museveni and not to the UPC government, which, or to Milton Obote who, instead, are to the Minister, objects of opprobrium.

77. Contrary to the position and belief of the Minister, Museveni on becoming President did not embark on overseeing *"progress towards rebuilding his shattered Country and restoring it to Constitutional government."* His priority was and still remains to implant and entrench his dictatorship by very brutal military means and by removing from Uganda body politics dissenting voices and political organisations and political activities not under the aegis of his National Resistance Movement (NRM). He inherited but rejected, as the Minster knows but does not want to admit, a set of economic policies which IMF, the World Bank and HMG strongly approved and supported and policies which at the time was making the economy to grow at the rate of 6 percent of GDP per annum. He instituted, instead, in 1986 his half-baked policy on barter trade and currency conversion.

78. For purposes of barter trade, regulations required producers of exports crops to sell their produce only to official teams each led by a minister. This meant that producers were to keep crops at home until a team arrived at a designated place and then take their produce there. Because there were often no ready cash, the teams issues to producers chits for quantities of produce received and amounts. To redeem the chits, a day was appointed for the producers to gather at a designated place to which a minister heavily escorted by the army went with cash. Following payments by a minister, armed gangsters (believed to

have been military personnel) frequently attacked the producers either on the way to their homes or at night in their homes and robbed the money. Production and sales of export crops plummeted as a result.

79. The currency conversion, designed to fix and control exchange and interest rates and to control prices in order to show a sharp departure from the policy Museveni inherited, on the other hand, not only wiped out the savings of the farmers, workers and civil servants – an economic avalanche from which they have never recovered – but also for the first time in Uganda, caused all the proceeds from a specific tax to go into private pockets. Two zeroes were stuck off from the shilling so that an amount of less than 100 shillings became of no value and 100 shillings became one shilling. A tax of 30% was imposed as Development Tax on the remaining one shilling. The amount so raised was never published and has never appeared in any budget. No President in a multiparty system would rob the people so easily and so openly, and get away with the robbery.

80. Museveni's economic Policy and military Operations removed an overwhelming majority of the people in the North and North-East from the monetary economy for several years and even now (March 1997), after eleven years, the majority in Kitgum and Gulu Districts are still not in the monetary economy. Half the population of each of the two Districts – around 159,000 each – are in make-shift camps and economic activities are virtually only for subsistence. In 1986 and 1987 because persecutions and military operations, crops were not bought or planted and were, instead, either plundered by the army or destroyed.

81. Except in Towns, the monetary conversion of 1987 was not effected in the North and North East. At a ceremony in Gulu Town in late 1989 where leaders of the rebel army surrendered on signing an agreement with Museveni, he undertook as part of the agreement to arrange for people in Gulu and Kitgum Districts who were still keeping the old (pre 1987) currency to acquire the new currency. A memorandum prepared and submitted to a Uganda Parliamentary Committee in November 1996 by members

of that Parliament from the two Districts stated that one of the reasons for the continued war in the two Districts is because the currency conversion of 1987 has never been effected in the two Districts. Even Museveni's signature on an agreement nor his solemn undertaking have, apparently, been strong enough to rescind the policy of removing the people in the North and North-East from the monetary economy.

82. In 1988/89, Museveni's policy and military operations uprooted millions of people from their homes and farms – thousands and thousands of people (whose numbers and identities were not recorded) were arrested and incarcerated and, just like those who were massacred, were also removed from the monetary economy. The incarcerated crowds of thousands were, while in jails, cynically called Lodgers; they remained in jails for up to a year and the identities or numbers of those amongst them who died or were killed in jails were never given.

83. In light of these considerations on Museveni's economic policy and performance which the Minister so much praises and states (correctly)as having started *"since President Museveni came to power in 1986,"* the Minister appears to be praising policies for the impoverishment of the people of Uganda, for open robbery of public funds, and for genocide and extermination.

84. On purely economic policy, the Minister is wrong in asserting and therefore giving the impression that since 1986, Museveni has pursued a consistent policy *"towards rebuilding his shattered Country ..."* The policy instituted and pursued by Museveni in 1986 and 1987 was not only half-baked, but also in implementation disclosed a strong desire, on his part, not only to control the economy as whole; but also to control even what people should eat and when and where rural people should sell food stuff. It had, for instance, long been as culture in Africa for Towns people to go to homes in rural areas – near and far – and return with much food of various types. Museveni's policy forbade the practice in Uganda. It had also long been the

acceptable economic activity for any licenced trader to go to rural areas and buy from homes food or export crops. Museveni's policy prescribed that all food be taken to designated market and that only official teams headed by his misters were to buy export crops.

85. The IMF, World Bank and donor governments - including HMG, contrary to what the Minister states, found Museveni's 1986/1987 economic policy totally unacceptable to them, and as not deserving their support and funding. That position coupled with the rapidly deteriorating economic situation forced Museveni in 1988 to abandon his own policy instituted in 1986. He turned around to embrace in totality the 1981-85 policy of the UPC government which he had virulently condemned for seven years. He embraced not only the policy of the UPC government, but also the entire programmes and projects which are what he has been implementing for nine years now, since 1988; but not in the North and North-East of Uganda where massacres, devastations and despoliation by his army became his economic policy.

86. Besides massacres, devastations and despoliation, there are equally perturbing aspects of Museveni's economic performance. These other aspects include official acceptance of rampant corruption in high places; increasing and deepening abject poverty in rural areas throughout Uganda; collapsing health and education services with health workers and teachers not being paid, or being paid in arrears after several months - and hospitals, dispensaries and school buildings in dilapidation throughout the country; and despite or in spite of huge annual subventions by donor governments, not a single hospital or secondary school has been built in eleven years.

87. These aspects show that although Museveni adopted in 1988 the entire 198-85 programmes and projects, he also, in implementation, revised them drastically in order to meet his predilection and priorities which were (and are) military rule as opposed to popular support as a basis of rule and therefore to suppress whatever would make his rule accountable to or be

judged by the people. Thus, under Museveni, priority expenditure went to the military and therefore programmes for poverty alleviation, health and education services lost their 1981-85 priority rankings to unleash eleven years of increasing and deepening poverty; collapsing and very costly health and educations services; and dilapidated hospitals, dispensaries and schools where workers therein are paid a pittance and in arrears. Even University lectures have gone on strike three times, and medical doctors all over the Country have also gone on strike, during Museveni's rule: demanding better pay and better conditions of service - something which was previously unknown in Uganda.

88. When Museveni imposed his currency conversation, he wiped out savings and therefore enfeebled the productive capacity of the peasant farmers. When he abandoned his 1986/87 policy, he made no adjustment when the two zeroes which were struck off from the currency returned without their 30% value and accordingly prices, as well as exchange and interest rates increased beyond the capacity of producers of commodities – particularly producers in the rural areas. This someone who, after the conversion, was paying 50 shillings as school fees was suddenly required to pay 5,000 shillings. School enrolment dropped and has continued to drop at an alarming rate. The same is the case in hospitals and dispensaries where a patient has to pay a fee called *"cost sharing."*

89. In situation where the only voice in politics and governance, Museveni is systematically destroying Uganda and nit rebuilding it as the Minister claims. On education, for instance, he has now introduced what he calls universal free primary education for four children per family which is his scheme to destroy quality education in Uganda, not because it is to be free but because it is to be a means to no education for millions for children from now onwards so long as he remains a dictator. Registration of pupils for the universal free primary education began last January (1997). On average, 300 to 400 pupils per class were registered in the available primary schools. No new teachers had

been trained and deployed and no new schools or classes had been built. How poorly paid teachers (often not even paid), without books and equipment can give quality education in a class of 300 to 400 pupils is left by Museveni for people like the Minister to define and to praise.

90. Beside the greater portion of the annual budget to military expenditure as a means as a means to implant and entrench his dictatorship – this depriving poverty alleviation, health and education services of funds, Museveni also introduced and encouraged corruption in his dictatorship as a means to suborn Party politicians to quit their Parties and support him. He was asked about this at a Press Conference in 1989 and the following was his position on corruption:

> "I don't think I have seen somebody who is corrupt and I leave him (sic). But I have got a different way of looking at corruption. For instance, I don't think personally it is good for leaders to get lots of properties. I wouldn't do that myself. But at the same time, I cannot stop others. I have got important things to do, other than battle with corruption. It would cause problems. I have got my ally here Abu Mayanja (minister interjects: I amass it!). I am not going to fight Mayanja over than because I have bigger maters to work on with him like economy, peace, etc."

(Weekly Topic – Weekending Wednesday, 26 July 1989)

91. The position was reaffirmed as recent as December 1996 when Museveni told a Press Conference that fighting corruption was the responsibility of Permanent Secretaries, Police, and the Courts and that his responsibility was to develop the economy and to bring peace. In a multiparty system, no President would take such a cynical and indifferent position on a pervading and rampant corruption in his administration. Museveni's attitude to and position on corruption and he has made corruption a string weapon which he wields to recruit support and to weaken the political Parties. The second reason is that his dictatorship is not responsible and accountable to the electorate and has no

competitors such as political Parties in the politics and governance of Uganda.

92. Hand in hand with corruption, nepotism is also pervading and rampant in Museveni's dictatorship and reasons why it is so are the same as those for corruption. In addition to the army, Museveni had used and uses corruption and nepotism to implant and entrench his dictatorship. He once told the editor of a leading daily that the predominance of people from his Region at all levels in every department was because those people were better educated and better professionally qualified. The Revenue Authority which collects taxes is, for instance, except for a Ghanaian head, manned entirely by people from Museveni's Region.

93. The best example exposes Museveni as the author of corruption and nepotism, and which shows the two evils working hand in hand is the case of Museveni's half-brother (same mother different fathers) who is Major-General in Museveni's army. The Major-General is the biggest supplier of foodstuff to the army. He was "awarded the contract" by the Army High Command of which Museveni is the Chairman. The Major-General's every invoice is paid in full and promptly by the army even when he has not delivered full quantity or not delivered at all.

94. Another example is the case of once leading member of the Uganda Peoples Congress (UPC) who was also *"awarded a contract"* by the Army High Command to supply foodstuff to the army. The award was, seemingly, an aberration in that it was against the policy of Museveni dictatorship not to give business to opposition politicians. It turned out that the *"contract"* was meant to suborn and did suborn the leading UPC member who became a fifth-columnist in the UPC top echelon. When exposed, the erstwhile leading member came out openly and strongly, contrary to UPC stand, to support Article 269 of the Constitution which suppresses the political Parties an Article 271(1) which debars the political Parties from contesting elections. IN addition, the member embarked on a programme to wreck the UPC.

95. The Minister probably does not believe in the existence of the pervading and rampant corruption and nepotism in Museveni's dictatorship just as she does not believe that the dictatorship itself exists. Articles in the Constitution which enfeebles, incapacitate and suppress the political Parties and therefore make Uganda patently a one-Party cum military rules Country are apparently, to the Minister, acceptable dispensation which deserves to be financed and entrenched by the British taxpayers' money. The pervading and rampant corruption and nepotism which even supporters of Museveni's dictatorship have openly condemned and called and for their elimination do not seem to worry the Minister because they are (to her) either good for Uganda or do not exists. Nothing in Uganda therefore seems amiss or worrying to the Minister – not the massacres and the wars still going on; the increasing abject poverty; the collapse of health and education services; the pervading and rampant corruption, or the system and Constitution which establish dictatorship.

96. In the letter from the Minister's office, it asserted that: "although full Party political activity is not permitted under (the) Constitution, there is no outright ban on political pluralism," The Minister's circumlocution on and about the system and the provisions of the Constitution is a dissemblance to disguise the fact that the system and the Constitution have for eleven years, effectively removed the Parties from participating in public affairs including contesting elections and competing for public office or councils. The Minister's belief in the existence of *"political pluralism"* is therefore belief in a chicanery put in the Constitution to enable the dictatorship to grow in strength and entrench itself without competition with the political Parties.

97. The Minister's very strong belief in the chicanery as proof that *"there is no outright ban on political pluralism"* is also expressed approvingly in the letter. The Minister asserts, in the letter, that: *"In the Presidential elections of May this year (1996), several candidates stood for office as individuals"* (and that) *"Although there was no active campaigning by Parties, the*

Party allegiances of the candidates was well-known to the electorates." The assertion is, again dissemblance on then part of the Minister to disguise the fact that Museveni stood as the official candidate of the only constitutionally recognised political Party known as the National Resistance Movement (NRM), the political organisation which has been the sole voice in the politics of Uganda for now eleven years. Candidate Museveni's election slogan was: NO CHANGE, that is to say, no change in the system of rule which he and his army imposed in 1986 which prohibits competition between the NRM and the political Parties in politics and in elections to public office or councils and therefore debars the Parties from having any active or meaningful voice or role in politics, elections or governance. The NRM supporters were free to campaign vigorously and openly for the election of their candidates while the other two (Presidential) candidates each did not have, on account of the constitution and the electoral law, not even a semblance of comparable organisation.

98. To hold, as the Minister does, in the face of the above that "political pluralism" has not been banned or still exists in Uganda is a dissemblance contrived so as to enable others to accept a fraudulent mode of elections which rejects and debars competition amongst the candidates on a level playing field. In the May 1996 fraud, Museveni had the backing of a known political (Party) organisation, with officials and offices – which is heavily and entirely funded by the taxpayers while the other two candidates stood on "personal merit," that is to say, without the support of the campaigning capacity of any political (Party) organisation nit because they wanted to be "independent candidates" but because the Constitution and the electoral law provided that no candidate should compete with the NRM candidate on a level playing field, and that the level playing field should be tilted greatly in favour of the NRM candidate and above all, that the political parties should or must be strictly debarred from fielding a candidate and from supporting and campaigning for the election of any such candidate. The system

therefore, contrary to what the Minister holds, effectively bans "political pluralism" precisely because although there were candidates, the system permitted only one of them to have organisational (political Party) support and banned the political Party organisations which supported or may have supported the other two candidates from participating in the elections.

99. That *"political pluralism"* has effectively been banned was also shown in the case of one of the two candidates who stood against Museveni. He had never been prominent in any political Party and was not known to have been a member of any Party. Had *"political pluralism"* existed and not banned, it is possible that he would have formed a political (Party) organisation rather than mount a campaign without any organisation, particularly as he was of little means; and except for a few friends here and there, he was generally unknown. As his speeches showed, he seemed to have become a candidate not with the hope of winning but to denounce the mode of elections which permitted the candidate(s) of a particular political (Party) organisation to enjoy the freedom of organisational support while denying the other candidates the same freedom.

100. In the case of the second Presidential candidate – the one who had never been a member of any Party – the Minister's assertion that the *"the Party allegiance of the (Presidential) candidates was well-known to the electorate"* is a most callous and uncouth manner of endorsing a largely one-Party elections in which only one candidate, Museveni, was by law, permitted to have the support and the campaigning capacity of a political (Party) organisation with considerable financial and material resources. Museveni, the NRM candidate, was standing on or defending the ten years record of his political (Party) organisation namely, the suppression of all other political (Party) organisation whose supporters had been active in public affairs for ten years. The other candidates, according to the Minister, were not disadvantaged because although the constitution and the electoral law banned their Parties from participating in the elections, their own *"allegiances"* to (or membership of their

party) which was *"well-known to the electorate"* effectively (according to the Minister) matched the campaigning capacity, financial and material resources of Museveni's political (Party) organisation. Even Museveni cannot match the Minister's protection of a fraud and to the Minister, the candidate who never was a member of any Party, still had a *"Party allegiance"* which was *"well-known to the electorate."*

101. Allegiance whether of a candidate to his or her Party, or of member of a Party to their Party can only be of importance in an election if the Party itself is participating in that election and the Party has been active in maintaining that allegiance. In that case of the Museveni's/Minister's model of elections, allegiance to a Party which had been suppressed for ten years, a Party which is banned from participating in the election; and the very Party which is banned from participating in the elections; and the very allegiance which has, in order to destroy it and destroy the Party, been severely battered for ten years is presented and cited as a match to the campaigning capacity, financial and material resources of a political (Party) organisation merely because the "*allegiance....... was well-known to the electorate."* As a cover or a mitigating factor for transparency flawed model of elections, allegiance alone of members of a Party to their Party being *"well-known to the electorate"* actually destroys cover or mitigating factor and expose the model as a vulgar fraud. The case of the third candidate in the May 1996 elections did so.

102. The third candidate, unlike the second, was a member of a political Party of which he was (is) the leader. The Minister's allegiance being "well-known to the electorate" and therefore in favour of the candidature of the third candidate meant and means that the model through it expected him or feared that he would, on account of allegiance, get the votes of members of his Party was also designed to deny him, on account of no allegiance, the votes of the millions of young people who were voting for the first time in 1996 but who were also not members of his or any Party in 1986 when the Museveni dictatorship banned recruitments of new members and therefore had no allegiance to the party of the third candidate or any other Party which was *"well-known to the electorate."*

103. The millions of voters who never were members of a Party therefore not only put the third candidate in the same boat as the second candidate but also destroys the Minister's insinuation that *"the Party allegiance of the candidates"* being *"well-known to the electorate"* was important and presented no undue disadvantage being meted to the second and third candidates precisely because those millions had no Party allegiance. It is absurd to assert or to argue that even the millions of voters who were never members of any Party, nevertheless had Party allegiance which was *"well-known to the electorate."* That would amount, in face of ten years of the ban on Party recruitment and activities, to mind-reading which neither Museveni nor the Minister can claim to have the capacity to do so.

104. It is equally absurd for the Minister to make it appear that in Uganda everybody of voting age (18 years) was in 1985 and 1996 a member of a political Party, had Party allegiance and that the Party allegiance of everyone remained intact and unaffected by Museveni's most aggressive ten years campaign against the existence of the Parties. Although the Minister stated, correctly, that *"there was no active campaigning by Parties"* – including the Party of the third candidate – she also sought to blur or even remove the effect of that fact on at least the third candidate by asserting that: *"the Party allegiances of the candidates was well-known to the electorate."* Prime Minister John Major would most probably consider it, at least, madness and political suicide for the Conservative party; should the Minister advise him that members of the Conservative Party should not campaign, during the next general election, for the Party's candidates because *"the Party allegiances of the candidates (would be) well-known to the electorate."*

105. Minister Baroness Chalker, after defending the indefensible in Uganda for eleven years, now appears to be not

only the chief ideologue of Museveni's dictatorship but also its mother hen in the British Parliament as well as being the dictatorship's Ambassador Extraordinary and Plenipotentiary at large. In her work in the three capacities, the Baroness gives less and less impression that she is a Minister of the Crown responsible to the British Parliament – with the result that she has been bold to mislead MP's and to present them with disbalances in order to protect the dictatorship.

106. The Minister states in her letter that Museveni *"won"* the Presidential election with 72.4% but was too careful, as befits a mother hen, not to state how the Parties reacted to Museveni's victory. Indeed, there is no mention of the position of the Parties on any matter throughout the letter. Museveni's 72.4% was, in fact, within the range of percentages which African dictators used to concoct as margins of their victories in one-Party elections. How Museveni got his 72.4%, made all political Parties to denounce the model of elections and how the Presidential election was conducted. The Parties then resolved that they would continue to struggle to remove the dictatorship from outside the institutions created by the 1995 Constitution – including Parliament – and pronounced that any of their members who would offer his or her candidature for the Parliamentary elections would not have the moral blessing of his or her Party. Legal blessing does not exist because the apex organs of each Party to give it is prohibited to meet under the Constitution.

107. The Minister was therefore not presenting fact when she wrote that in the Parliamentary elections which followed in June 1996, there were *"Candidates representing a variety of Party allegiances."* Since the Parties had publicly pronounced in May that any of their members standing as candidate in the Parliamentary elections would be outlaws, it follows that the outlaws who stood and were elected did not have the Minister's *"Party allegiance."* To the Minister, *"Party allegiance"* was and is so important that even when it did not and could not exists, like in the case of one of the Presidential candidates or the outlaws, the Minister still made it to exists so as to be able to

dissemble that was in fact a gimmick as a very strong factor which was effective and which made the Presidential and Parliamentary elections free and fair.

108. That under the elections model, only Museveni and his NRM could and did produce a manifesto of a national political (Party) organisation and that all the other motley candidates (if they so wished) could produce only personal manifesto and no "Party allegiance" manifesto has not made the Minister to see that the model ensured that even her beloved *"Party allegiance"* was not permitted to be organised or coordinated nationally or nationwide. *"Party allegiance"* was and remains a gimmick and dissemblance to disguise elections which were patently fraudulent so as to legitimise the results.

109. The Minister has entangled herself in a wed that is going to be, at the very least, highly embarrassing to HMG and the British Parliament. While she writes in the letter that she is "confident that we can expect continued improvements," a draft Bill the text of which several newspapers in Uganda have published, points to the opposite direction. The draft Bill stipulates that persons who were elected to Parliament in June last year, not on the ticket of the NRM, are to be made members of the policy and executive organ of the NRM. The Bill is clearly intended to remove from the membership of Parliament every semblance of independent voice just as the referendum will aim at and be conducted in a manner which will ensure the removal of independent voice from Uganda's body politics.

110. The Minister's argument and position that it is "right" to continue to pour millions of British taxpayers' money to a dictatorship which she does not recognise as such for the purpose of improving quality of life in Uganda, is strongly contradicted by Museveni, the Uganda dictator. To Museveni, improvements of the quality of life of the people of Uganda is not his policy. While on a visit to London last January (1997), Museveni stated firmly that his policy is to aid, abet and generate the *"greed"* instinct in human beings and that if, at the end of the day, he made 2 people out of 10 rich, he would consider it a great

success. That is a policy which has practically nothing to do with improving the quality of life in Uganda but a lot to do with officially sanctioning corruption and nepotism.

111. The last point that must be made is that although it is the British Parliament which sanctions British aid to Uganda, there is no comparable institution in Uganda Constitution to debate the policy, deployment, and usage of the aid. The Uganda Parliament, for instance, is elected under a system which does not permit not only at elections times but also at all times the presentation to the electorate of the policies and the ideas of different political (Party) organisations except one. The system therefore not only disfranchises all opposition political (Party) organisations from having any voice in public affairs; but also from having any voice in the deployment, usage, and administration pf the British aid or any other aid.

112. Because of the system of governance imposed by the Military in 1986 and codified in the 1995 Constitution, British aid has been used to finance and facilitate the suppression of the fundamental human rights and freedoms of the individual citizens of Uganda. A referendum and freedoms of the individual citizens of Uganda. A referendum to entrench the system and to make Uganda a fully-fledged one-Party/one-man dictatorship is scheduled for the year 1990 or 2000.

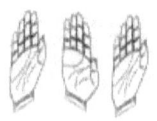

Part V

Dr A.M. Obote's summations.

a. 1963 - Organisation of African Unity (OAU) INUAGRAL SPEECH

His Excellency Milton Obote,
Prime Minister of Uganda

The meaning I attach to this Conference is that we have gathered here to find a basin as to how we can advance the two revolutions which are running together in Africa. There is the revolt against foreign rule and economic and social domination. There is also the revolutionary upsurge which alms at giving Africa a new creed, a new certainty, a new sense of belonging by transforming the mental attitudes and orientation of our peoples and by giving them a political, economic and social standard which would ensure a better life than we have today anywhere in Africa. To me, these goals can only be achieved through a continental and a joint effort by all of us. There seems to be no disagreement that we should collectively work together to achieve these goals.

What appears to me important in this agreement is the quantum and the total effectiveness of the joint effort we are prepared to put to the task. I am in favour of wielding a heavy hammer to give a definite and meaningful shape to the things that we intend to do thus ensuring that our own people and the world at large are left in no doubt whatever as to our intentions. It is, of course, very encouraging that the mere presence of all of us in this city and in this great country is in itself an indication of the beginning of a further step in the continental re-awakening of and desire to unity Africa. This in itself is important is a definite step forward, but I submit that it must be backed with bold decisions and that we must not leave this city with a decision that will be interpreted by the outside world and by our peoples to mean that we have met here only to agree to meet again. I do not say that we must not meet again but the basis of our future meetings must be different from what it is now.

My understanding is that we have met in this Conference so as to explore those areas of agreement which will form the basis of our future discussions and guide our action in such a way that Africa will be able to project her image as a single unit. I do not think it is beyond our ability and powers to establish such a basis. Once this basis is established at this Conference, our future meetings would then take the role of framing what Africa must say and do both within the African continent and in her relations with other countries.

I say all this in full understanding of our history and the effect of that history upon each of us. We have been ruled by other people but the colonial period in Africa which began with Western Europe explorers is rapidly coming to an end. Direct western rule on the Continent of Africa has outlived its historical functions and is now perishing in a fermentation caused by our bid for freedom and independence. We are now developing new ideas and new movements. We are also unleashing new energies in order to give expression to what Africa is. The continent of Africa and her peoples seek a new orientation. Our main difficulty lies in the links we still have with the powers which shattered our culture and exploited our resources human and material. We cannot run away from the fact that the economies of our new states are still dependent on external powers. But our peoples remain sensitive and proud and they look to a day when their leaders will give them full freedom. In my case, the experience is only a few months old and apart from Ethiopia and Liberia, none of us can reckon this sort of experience in terms of decades.

As a heritage from the colonial era, our people are disease ridden and poverty stricken, and this has led to a vicious circle of malnutrition disease and low productivity. A decision at this

Conference to agree to meet again is a decision which does not wage a continent-wide war on the evils that we have inherited. This is a common problem to all of us and its solution calls for joint and bold effort through a machinery which we must establish a certainly not through consultation good though that may be.

There are also new and ominous symptoms of the danger that we face. Unless we are able to establish a strong central machinery, the tendency to stay away from one another and to form groupings against ourselves will grow. The growth of this tendency will help our ex-colonizers and other powers desirous of having a foothold in Africa. And when this becomes a reality the whole basis of our revolt against foreign control will be destroyed.

Our revolution must succeed. This Conference has the task to lay down the foundation for its success. I know that there are great difficulties which we must overcome in order to take a bold step forward. Several centuries of close contact with our ex-colonizers have left deep marks on us. Even in this Conference we can only communicate with one another with the help of the former colonial powers' languages. But we cannot forget or overlook the fact that the labour and products of Africa still lay a decisive part in the national economies of our former colonizers and also the fact that those countries still depend on the raw materials they obtain from their former colonies and on the textiles, machines, and consumer goods which they still sale to such ex-colonies. What we have to decide at this Conference is whether our manners and even our temperament will continue to be dominated by our long association with our ex-rulers. We have also to bear in mind in making that decision the problems of poverty and ignorance of our peoples and the backlog of administrative problems which we individually seem to have accepted as incapable of solution without external aid. I do not say that there is no need for help, nor do I say that we should not welcome any assistance, but I am convinced that any assistance which tends to make us stay away from one another is against Africa and African peoples.

I am one of those who believe that this Conference would be a failure if we are to return to our capitals having only stated principles and having only disclosed, however eloquently, our intentions in respect to the need of African unity. The time for high sounding words, slogans and clichés, and good intentions has come to an end; this is the time for concrete proposals and for action.

I hold the view that however nice one may feel as complete master in one's own house the time has come, indeed almost overdue, for African Independent States to surrender some of their sovereignty in favour of an African Central Legislature and Executive body with specific powers over those subjects where divided control and action would be undesirable. I refer to such subjects as the establishment of an African Common Market, Economic Planning on a continent wide basis, Collective Defense, a Common Foreign Policy, a Common Development Bank and a Common Monetary Zone: The list is by no means exhaustive, and I hope that the Conference will agree to the appointment of a Committee of experts who will investigate the matter of closer economic and political union among African Independent States and report to the Heads of States within a period not exceeding six months.

I also consider that the question of exchange of students both at the Secondary and at the University levels merits far greater consideration than has hitherto been accorded to it. I need not recite the concrete and imponderable benefits that would accrue to the cause of African unity. I may mention the clear advantage that French speaking Secondary School students would derive out of a year's studentship in an English-speaking school and vice versa. We have got to learn each other's language and ways of living and we must catch the future citizens of Africa at the most plastic and most impressionable stage of their lives, and this is one easy and cheap way of going about it.

On no single issue has Africa ever been so solidly united as on the question of apartheid and colonialism and Uganda bows to no one in her determination to see that colonialism in all its form's is liquidated. I would go to the extent of offering Uganda as training ground for the land forces that are necessary for the liberation forces which are needed in the struggle against colonialism. I suggest that Uganda is eminently well suited to serve the three major trouble spots of Angola, Mozambique, South Africa and, if the need should arise, Southern Rhodesia. I suggest that to bring the colonialists to their senses vituperative condemnations have ceased to be effective in the struggle against 20th century colonialism in the context of the cold war. Their pockets should be hurt by the imposition of economic sanction of different for Ms. I venture to suggest that if the white minority of Southern Rhodesia should be permitted to declare themselves independent, the African States should promptly counter this by severing trade and other relations with the United Kingdom and her fellow travelers.

The principle driving force that motivated our ex-colonizers in their colonial adventure was economic and political power. The predominant consideration in their present attempt to maintain their influence in Africa is still the same.

We all know the humiliation suffered by our people under foreign rule and influence. We are not unaware of the battle we still have to fight to free those parts of Africa still under

foreign domination and indignity. Above all, we still have the task of translating political freedom in our states into social and economic freedom. Agreement that we shall meet again and even setting up consultative Committees of Ministers will fall short of the great task. Uganda will support the setting up of a strong political, economic and social machinery to direct our next effort to free Africa, to give African peoples a continental security and to give our continent the pride and dignity she deserves.

ai. Closing Remarks – Vote of Thanks
by His Excellency Milton Obote,

Your Imperial Majesty, Distinguished Presidents, Prime Ministers,

This has been a great and Historic conference. We have, I think, established a basis of a clear mission to carry with us to our various capitals and countries. We have also established a mission which we are leaving here in Addis Ababa with the Provisional Secretariat that we have established in this conference. We have talked here of understanding and cooperation between one another and collectively. We have talked and given and showed great respect to one another. We have done all this in order to erect a strong foundation for the liberation of Africa from foreign domination and influence in order to fulfil our determination and desire for the welfare and advancement of our peoples. In ordinary circumstances I would not have the honour to address this August-Assembly immediately after yourself, Your Imperial Majesty. But I have the opportunity because I am the baby of the Conference. My State, that is the State of Uganda, has been the youngest in this great decision. Uganda, of all the countries of Africa represented here, has been the last to gain her independence, and I take it that my having this opportunity to address this Assembly has a very important and deep meaning and that is that Uganda is not only being initiated into independence that many of us have enjoyed and certainly Your Majesty and your illustrious ancestors and the peoples of Ethiopia have enjoyed for centuries. Uganda has been initiated, but at the same time beginning from Ethiopia running through the United Arab Republic, Liberia and all our countries represented here through the door of Uganda having gained independence only a few months back, we look behind Uganda to see who else is to come through this door and join us in the next Conference.

Africa as a whole has, and is sometime described by our former colonial powers as composed of young countries. This is not because in God's creation the continent of Africa was created last of all continents; this youth refers to the age of coming out of colonial rule. The ex-colonial powers when they speak of this continent as young do not simply see that that very description is in itself a sufficient ground to convict them of acts of humiliation, acts of indignity and piracy committed by them in Africa. We have talked in this Conference and made decisions against colonialism. Being the latest African state to come out of the mouth of that monster we call colonialism Uganda's experience is limited, but within our limited experience we have learned a great deal. We have learned before we came here and we have learned greatly in this Conference. All of us having come out of the mouth of this great monster, lurking everywhere in Africa, we now find that the monster we thought was gone is still with us. Of course, its mouth is now shut, as far as we here are concerned, but its claws are wide open. I take this to be the technique which colonialism uses, if it cannot swallow one alive, it adopts the technique of using its very powerful sharp and poisonous claws to draw the blood out of you. In this Conference, we have agreed with the illustrious President of the United Arab Republic that there must not be any more looting in Africa. We have also agreed with the gallant Prime Minister of Algeria to face realities in a practical way and have resolved to remove the red colour we can still see on that map hanging on the wall. We have resolved that it is our determination that those patches join us in our future conferences. But we went further and here I am proud to say that in future years all of us can go to North and West Africa, feel the air and feel the hospitalities of our peoples living in the great African towns of Casablanca and Monrovia, but forgetting completely any other Charters that had contained the name of Casablanca or Monrovia. We have therefore agreed and firmly resolved to renounce the Casablanca and Monrovia Charters. Instead we have adopted and signed for the first time in the history of Africa one Charter to guide our cause and action. Addressing this august house, the President of Tanganyika told us of the enemies of Africa, he said they were praying, and he said that the African peoples were also praying. Now this is the time of reckoning, we do not know whose prayer has been heard by God. I, of course, cannot put words into the mouths of those enemies of Africa, but I do know that they foresee one thing and that is doom. I know that they will begin to change the tactics and sow seeds of discord amongst us, but I say that Africa is marching ahead to her goal of destiny and honour. Free Africa, for the first time, has met and agreed on what to do. Your Imperial Majesty, this was the deep desire that brought all of us here, and it is indeed of fundamental importance that we should be able to say that at least what we wanted we have found, and we are taking with us.

Your Imperial Majesty and colleagues, it is most grateful that this continental reawakening of Africa should have taken place in this country. The geometrical shape of Africa is that of a question mark. Africa has been putting questions to her sons and daughters and also to colonial powers. It has taken years and ages to answer some of those questions. Let us leave Addis Ababa hoping that we have at long last found some of the answers. And I believe that this Conference will go into history as the first beginning by free Africa to find some of the answers to the questions that Africa as a whole has been asking throughout the ages. During the nineteenth century, European explorers called Africa a dark continent. The explorers who were in any case after Africa's wealth and human resources knew of course of the Ethiopian and Egyptian civilizations to mention only a few but they decided to shut their eyes from these hard facts. They therefore refused deliberately to answer some

of the questions that Africa was putting to them. The consequence of this has been that every year and let us hope that it will soon be every month, they have been sent out of Africa and very often in disgrace.

Your Imperial Majesty and fellow colleagues, the lion feared by many so long is reawakening; we who have been privileged to witness the grand awakening have a bounded duty and obligation to remain true witnesses and I do urge all my colleagues that we regard what we have signed as a declaration of a continental independence and interdependence.

Lastly, Your Imperial Majesty, I wish to thank you and all your subjects. On behalf of my distinguished colleagues, for Your hospitality and Your support and interest You personally gave to the conference. At a time like this and for the problems that are facing us, I cannot imagine a. better host to lead us to the great success we have met with in this conference. Also, on behalf my colleagues, I pay tribute to Your Majesty's Government for the efficient way in which this conference was organized and conducted. Very often reasons are advanced in parts of Africa, not yet independent, that the African is inefficient; I think all of us leave Ethiopia fully convinced that we have seen efficiency at its highest degree. Allow me, Your Majesty also on behalf of my colleagues to express their thanks to the Secretary General of the Conference, the Secretary, the interpreters, all the officials and aids who have made our work easy and very interesting, and to the Ethiopian people who cheered us and kept us happy day and night and we all still remember when we went to plant the trees that they were there in heavy rain. We acknowledge their cheers and we send them all our greetings and well wishes.

Your Majesty, all this made this historic conference the resounding success that it has been. It only remains for me to say, God bless Africa.

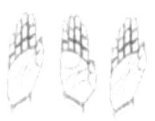

b. THE ROLE OF UPC IN UGANDA'S INDEPENDENCE

PAPER BY A. MILTON OBOTE - 2003

I take this singular and most important occasion to greet all UPC members and to wish every member a HAPPY BIRTHDAY.

The Uganda Peoples Congress (UPC) is today 42 years old and is in shackles. The number one motive for the founding of the UPC was FREEDOM - freedom of the people of Uganda to enjoy and exercise the inalienable, God given human rights in the same way the air is breathed by every human being.

In Uganda today and since 26 January, 1986 the charlatans who now rule the country have nefariously and with great profanity removed the God given human rights and freedoms of every citizen of Uganda from the politics and governance of Uganda.

The Independence of Uganda consisting of the enjoyment and exercise by every citizen of Uganda of his/her human rights and freedoms have, therefore been nullified by the charlatans.

To nullify the God given human rights and freedoms of a people is to declare and to prescribe that the people concerned and not part of the human race.

The UPC, though in shackles and severely gagged now for 16 years, can never join in the blasphemous chorus that the people of Uganda are not part of the human race.

The UPC was a vanguard Party in the struggle for Uganda's Independence. The UPC shall again be a vanguard Party struggling together with the other Parties and multi-partyists in the nullification of the profanity and the blaspheme of the charlatans that the people of Uganda are not part of the human race. The history of our Party on that score is clear and undisputed.

1. It was the Uganda National Congress (UNC), the father of the UPC who made the first call for the Independence of Uganda. The call was a declaration of a political campaign. A political

campaign is like an athletic race and team members who overlap are one. What or the part which the UNC did in the campaign also constitute what the UPC did. The overlapping UNC and UPC members make the campaign which was waged by the UNC and UPC to be one and the same until the finishing line on 9 October, 1962.

2. It was also the UNC and the UPC who waged vigorous and unrelenting Independence struggle until Uganda became Independent.

3. After Independence, the UPC from May 1962 to January, 1971 and again from December, 1980 to July, 1985, acquitted itself most admirably as the son of a great father.

4. It has become politics in Uganda over the years, for impostors to claim the deeds and ideas of the UPC as their own. When they are not claiming the deeds and ideas of the UPC, they are often deriding them. The only political matter belonging to the UPC, because it was the idea of the father of the UPC which impostors have not claimed as their own idea, is the first call for the Independence of Uganda. The charlatans have surpassed all impostors in claiming the ideas of the UPC as their own.

5. When in 1988, for instance, faced with an increasingly depressing economy in a situation where their mentors abroad had suspended their aid to Uganda for absence of acceptable economic policies, the charlatans, as a matter of desperation, plagiarised the Recovery Programme of the UPC first published in 1982 and revised in 1983 and published the entire UPC programme as their own under a new title of Rehabilitation and Development Plan.

6. When the UNC called for the Independence of Uganda, the Party also, at the same time, in 1952 prescribed the Governors and the protectors of the Independent Uganda. The UNC demanded ONE MAN (including woman) ONE VOTE" and 2 SELF GOVERNMENT NOW".

7. In plain language, the father of the UPC prescribed that the fountain of the powers of the Government of Uganda be reposed

always and at all time in the people of Uganda who are to elect, from time to time, for instance, members of Parliament from amongst whom Ministers may be appointed. That is the meaning of One Man or One Citizen, One Vote.

8. The model of public elections such as the elections of members of Parliament which the UNC envisaged and which the UPC supports very strongly, differs greatly from the model which the dictatorship of the charlatans has imposed. In the model which the UPC supports, the voter must be free at all times to form or join associations popularly known as political Parties as vehicles to popularise and sell to all the people his/her broad ideas for the governance of Uganda.

9. At election times, the voters' broad views for the governance of Uganda are articulated in a document normally known as Manifesto or Policy Statement. The Manifesto or Policy statement of every political Party participating in an election must also be submitted to the electorate. It means that every such Party must be free to arrange or convene public meetings or rallies at which it can expose the contents of its elections Manifesto to the electorate.

10. The foremost component in the model of public elections which the UPC strongly supports, is the competition in the public arena of the policies for the governance of Uganda of different political Parties participating in an election.

11. Under the model of elections imposed by the military one-Party dictatorship of the charlatans, policies for the governance of Uganda do not feature and are not presented to the electorate as a whole throughout the country at elections times. The model also debars competition of the policies of different Parties in the public arena between elections. The model, instead, emphasises competition during an election by candidates of its political Party and Independents who are not and must not be supported by any Uganda wide political Party.

12. The elections model imposed by the dictatorship of the charlatans, is a demeaning conspiracy which removes the powers

of the Government of Uganda from being reposed in the people as a whole and places it in the dictatorship.

13. Uganda, like any other Country, is composed of its territory, its land and its people. The territory or land does not belong to the dictatorship; it belongs to the people. To oust the people from governing their territory or being in control of the affairs of the territory is to remove them from being part of the human race and is also a conspiracy which deters the building of the Uganda Nation which can compete with the other Nations in the Global arena.

14. The UNC's call and demand for one man (now one citizen) one vote, and Self-Government Now, was the first Ugandan voice and intent to replace the British Protectorate so as to enable the various Uganda ethnic Nationalities to embark on the task of building the Uganda Nation.

15. The British Protectorate existed without a single Uganda citizen and without a political institution controlled by the people of Uganda but with a hotchpotch of Kingdoms, Districts and ethnic nationalities all controlled from London through a resident Governor.

16. The British Government in London and the resident Governor did not take kindly the demand of the UNC for the Independence of Uganda. Like the charlatans of today, London pronounced and maintained that Uganda or the people of Uganda were not ready for Independence; not ready for democracy and therefore not ready to embark on the task of nation Building.

17. The UNC responded to the London position with a vigorous Uganda wide campaigns programme. The very, very large attendances at UNC rallies, made the Colonial government to seek for ways and means to destroy the UNC. The number one instrument which the Colonialists found for the destruction of the UNC was splits where some leaders without disagreeing with the basic policy or demands of the Party, resigned while propagating that the leadership of the Party was not fit to lead an Independent Uganda.

18. The above ground for splits and resignations became a curse which distracted the attention of the leaders from united efforts to confront the adversary to internecine warfare in the Party for positions in the Party. In the history of political parties in Uganda, the curse has been, perhaps because of their nationalist stands on various national issues, most pronounced in the UNC and UPC.

19. There was a mild split in the UNC in 1955 and a serious one in 1956 and with another serious one in 1957. All the splits occurred during the Annual Delegates Conference each held in Kampala.

20. The Colonial Government became an opportunist scavenger following the split of 1957 and the Buganda Lukiiko also chipped in. The Colonial Government rusticated some leaders of the UNC to various parts of the country; none was charged with any crime. The Lukiiko, without in anyway, supporting the actions of the Colonial Government, passed a resolution which asserted that it had withdrawn its recognition of the Legislative Council (LEGCO) and would only do so after the position of the Kabaka in an Independent Uganda had been made clear.

21. The Resolution of the Lukiiko was to occupy the minds of the UPC leaders from December until September 1962 but the UNC interpreted the Resolution both as positive and negative to its basic demands and campaigns for Independence. The Resolution was regarded as positive because it signaled that the Party's campaigns for Independence which was overwhelmingly supported in Buganda as well as elsewhere in the country, made the Lukiiko to come out with only one matter to be accommodated in the Constitution of Independent Uganda.

22. The UNC interpreted the Lukiiko Resolution as negative because the Lukiiko sought to have the veto power of what national institutions the people of Uganda should have.

23. The veto power which the Lukiiko's Resolution of 1957 sought, was seized by the Colonial Government. While accepting the UNC demands of one man, one vote, the Colonial

Government also undermined it when it enacted in 1958 that elections to the Legislative Council would be held in October of the same year in areas whose Councils want elections. The Buganda Lukiiko promptly rejected the elections and was followed by the District Councils of Ankole and Bugisu.

24. The UNC platform which had been that one man, one vote would empower every man and every woman voter in Uganda to be the repository of the powers of the Government of Uganda, was shattered when the Colonial Government imposed the Buganda Lukiiko and the District Councils to veto the essence of that platform.

25. The October, 1958 elections were held in Busoga - two seats; Bukedi one seat, Teso one seat, Lango one seat, Acholi one seat, West Nile and Madi one seat, Bunyoro one seat, Toro one seat and Kigezi one seat. A total of ten (10) seats. One seat meant the entire District was one Constituency.

26. The UNC won one seat in Busoga, and one each in Bukedi, Teso, Lango and Acholi. A total of 5. The Independents won in Bunyoro, Toro and Kigezi, with the other Busoga seat. A total of 4. DP won in west Nile and Madi, one seat.

27. There was another split in the UNC in November 1958 at the Annual Delegates Conference held for the first time since the Party was formed in 1952 outside Kampala, in Mbale. Very early on the third day of the Conference at about 4 a.m., two Congressmen came to my house at Ntinda in Kampala. They were Paul Ssengendo, the then Personal Assistant to Jolly Joe Kiwanuka, the UNC Chairman and Ndugga Musaazi, a very active Congressman in Luwero. Ndugga had a house in Luwero Town where Congress members from the North used to routinely stop before proceeding to Kampala. I knew both men and they knew me very well.

28. I was not at the Conference but in Kampala because my late father who was to be murdered by the soldiery of the charlatans in 1987 at the age of 89 years and totally blind, was very sick in Mulago Hospital. After visiting my father in Hospital, I decided to

go to Mbale. I had been elected by the Lango District Council in May, 1957 but took my seat in August of the same year. The LegCo was dissolved by the Governor in 1958 to allow for elections in October of 1958. There was no Congress member from the North in that LegCo except myself.

29. We proceeded to Mbale in two vehicles with Ssengendo and Musaazi leading in one vehicle. In Mbale we went to the Elgon Hotel where Jolly Joe was staying. Although I had stayed in the same Hotel a number of times, I had also abandoned it because I did not consider it a suitable place for Nationalist politicians to stay because ordinary people could not go there for a meal or drink. My place in Mbale, therefore, became always Maluku Bar, which served African meals and also had accommodation.

30. On entering Jolly Joe's hotel room, he greeted me jovially with the words: "Good morning Mr. President." I was puzzled and he saw it in my face. He was jovially laughing as he seated me and proceeded to explain the meaning of his curious greeting. Jolly Joe told me that on the evening of the second day, the Conference elected me to be Party President after a full day of debate which began in the afternoon of the first day. At that point, the Secretary General of the Party Dr. B. N. Kununka, entered the room. Of the two Party leaders, I was very close to the Secretary General.

31. After the Secretary General and I had exchanged greetings in Luo (he spoke Luo fluently because after qualifying from Makerere Medical School, he served in Lira Hospital for many years.), Jolly Joe then proceeded to say that he had adjourned the Conference for him and the Secretary General to come to the Hotel, wait for my arrival and then take me to the Conference to deliver my acceptance speech. During the same innocuous exchanges, I asked how they knew that I would come or expected me to accept the election. Jolly Joe answered that Paul Ssengendo had instructions to ring Mbale and report only if I could not go to Mbale; and as for acceptance of the election, he said that the Conference had made a decision, would continue with the remaining business and then stand adjourned sine die

leaving me to wrestle with the problem of whether or not to accept the Conference decision.

32. The fait accompli uttered by Jolly Joe, made me there and then to take a firm decision. I told the Party Chairman and Party Secretary General that unless I meet first my Conference delegation from Lango District and also the Party's founder President, I. K. Musaazi, also the father of Uganda nationalism, I was not going to the Conference and I was not going to make any acceptance speech. Instead, I was returning to Kampala. That made Jolly Joe to send Paul Ssengendo and Ndugga Musaazi to go the Conference place and tell the Lango District delegation to go to Maluku Bar for a meeting with me.

33. When the Conference resumed (I was later told) the leader of the Kigezi District Delegation, moved a motion that the Conference be adjourned to allow for Delegations which wanted to meet me to do so. The motion was seconded by the leader of the Teso District Delegation and carried unanimously. In those days, the UNC Branches except in Buganda were the Districts. In Buganda, each of the 20 counties was a Branch and each Branch sent a Delegation to the Annual Delegates Conference.

34. At Maluku Bar, I met briefly each of the Delegations. I learnt that there was a nasty bad blood between the Party President Musaazi and party Chairman, Jolly Joe Kiwanuka and that the Delegates did not know the cause of the friction between the two men. I also learnt that the Chairman having been a better campaigner and speaker, managed to persuade the Delegates to remove the President from office.

35. I had a lengthy meeting with Musaazi. It was a very sad meeting on both sides. Musaazi told me that Jolly Joe was a thief who was using the Party for personal enrichment and glorification. He explained that the Egyptian Government had donated a sum of money to the Party which Jolly Joe received from the Egyptian Embassy in London and pocketed. The information about the donation, he said was first given to him by the Egyptian Water Engineers in Jinja who were monitoring the

flow of the Nile under the Dam. It was also the same Egyptians who had given Jolly Joe information about the donation.

36. Upon that report, Musaazi said, he went to London and to the Egyptian Embassy. At the Embassy Musaazi told me that he obtained information that Jolly Joe had collected the donation. On return to Uganda, Musaazi said that he asked Jolly Joe to hand over the donation to the Party and that Jolly Joe denied not only receiving the donation but also any knowledge of it. That was, according to Musaazi, the case of the very serious conflict between two of them.

37. Musaazi asked me to accept my election as Party president and also asked me to give what he had told me to the Delegates Conference. He said that the veracity of his story could be seen in the facts that Jolly Joe had refurbished and restocked his White Nile Night Club as Katwe and had also bought new machinery for his newspaper, the Uganda Express. Musaazi emphasised that Jolly Joe never respected nor regarded him as Party leader and that unless I tell the Delegates Conference what he told me, Jolly Joe would treat me as his puppet and would not accept my leadership.

38. Although I never doubted the veracity of what Musaazi had told me, I also felt that I should not begin my leadership of the Party by telling the Delegates Conference of what Musaazi had told me. My acceptance speech which was delivered at about 10 o'clock in the evening, therefore excluded it and concentrated on vigorous campaigns for the realisation of the goals of the Party's programmes of one man one vote and Self-Government Now.

39. On 17 November, 1958, the Governor announced the appointment of a Constitutional Committee with the following terms of reference: -

> "To consider and to recommend to the Governor the form of direct elections on a common roll for representative members of the Legislative Council to be introduced in 1961, the number of representative seats to be filled under the above system, their allocation among the different areas of the Protectorate and the

method of ensuring that there will be adequate representation on the legislative Council for non-Africans."

40. When the Central Executive Committee of the UNC met to consider the appointment of the Committee, particularly its terms of reference and whether or not Party members should serve on the Constitutional Committee, the Party's Central Executive Committee immediately ran into a very serious division of opinion.

41. In the Central Executive Committee, Jolly Joe did not even allow me, as Chairman and leader of the Party to open the debate on the item of the Agenda namely, the Constitutional Committee, its terms of reference and whether or not Party members should serve on the Constitutional Committee. Jolly Joe asked permission to speak first on the Agenda item and I agreed because I knew the breadth of what he was going to say. The thrust of Jolly Joe's argument which was strongly supported by the Party's Secretary General, Dr. B. N. Kununka and a section of the Executive was that the "common roll" was against the interests of the Africans and that there was another way outside the common roll which could accommodate the interests of the non-Africans.

42. Previous to the debate in the Central Executive, whenever Jolly Joe made the same argument I grilled him to share with me that other way outside the common roll. He never did. I therefore formed the opinion that Jolly Joe was purveying Mengo's opinion which turned out to be correct. In the debate, members of the Executive repeatedly asked Jolly Joe to state that other way but never got it. Because the Governor had asked four members of the Party to serve on the Constitutional Committee and because I wanted them to serve with the approval of the Party, I decided to refer the Agenda of the Executive to the National Council.

43. The meeting of the National Council was tricky because Jolly Joe as the Party Chairman, was in the Chair. I had asked him before the meeting to call me, as Party President, to speak first but he refused. He therefore opened the debate on the

Constitutional Committee but I raised a point of order and he yielded and asked me to state the point of order. I told the Council that the meeting was to discuss a national matter referred to the Council by the Central Executive. I went on to say that under the Constitution of the Party, national matters were the responsibilities of the Party President and not of the Party Chairman. Second, I told the Council that under Party Regulations, it was the Chairman of a Committee who reported the deliberations of his/her Committee to next higher organ of the Party. I was the party President and Chairman of the Central Executive Committee and therefore the only person with authority to report to the Council the deliberations of the Central Executive Committee.

44. On the terms of reference of the Constitutional Committee, I tied them to the Party's demands and programmes of one man one vote and Self-Government Now and said that the Colonial Government had accepted one man one vote and that 1961 could be the year of Self-Government Now provided that the people of Uganda accepted the common voters roll or Register. I emphasised to the Council that the name of the Party was "National Congress" which carried no racial connotations and therefore that the Party should not go into Independence carrying a racial luggage. I told the Council that the immediate task of the Party was to get all or many of its organs and individuals to make representations to the Constitutional Committee for one man one vote and for Self-Government Now.

45. The UNC National Council voted overwhelmingly for the Party to give evidence to the Constitutional Committee; for common roll and for the UNC members namely, B. K. Kirya, W. W. Kajumbula-Nadiope, C. J. Obwangor and myself to be members of the Constitutional Committee. Jolly Joe, Dr. B. N. Kununka and a handful of Council member walked out.

46. Soon thereafter, Abu Mayanja, the UNC founder Secretary General, returned to Uganda from Cambridge. He was strongly in support of the UNC giving evidence to the Constitutional Committee. The National Council appointed him to be the

Secretary General in place of Dr. Kununka. From there until the 1962 elections, there existed Obote-Mayanja UNC and Kiwanuka-Kununka UNC. That was so although Mayanja had left Party politics when he became Minister of Education in the Kabaka's Government in 1959.

47. The Obote-Mayanja UNC embarked in earnest to craft the strategic pillars of the evidence which was to be given to the Constitutional Committee.

48. It was considered that the Party's demands for one man one vote and for Self-Government Now, could be met by many Party organs and individuals presenting these demands to the Constitutional Committee. The Party felt it very crucial to devise a system of the distribution of seats in the Legislature in a manner that would be acceptable to all parts of the country. The most difficult aspect of the distribution of seats to all parts of the country on a common formula, was how best to accommodate in a common formula the provision of Article 7 of the Buganda Agreement of 1955 which provided as follows: -

(1) At all times when provision has been made for at least three-fifths of all the representative members of the Legislative Council of the Uganda Protectorate to be Africans and for such number of Africans to be appointed as Nominated Members of the Council as will bring the total number of Africans who are members of the Council up to at least one-half of all the members of the Council, excluding the President of the Council, then Buganda shall be represented in the Legislative Council of the Uganda Protectorate, and for that purpose at least one-quarter of the Representative Members of the Council who are Africans shall be persons who represent Buganda.

(2) The Katikiro shall submit to Her majesty's Representative, that is to say, the Governor, the names of the candidates for appointment as the Representative members of the Legislative Council to represent Buganda, that is to say, the persons who have been elected for that purpose in accordance with the provisions of the Second Schedule to the Agreement.

(3) Notwithstanding the provisions of paragraph (2) of this article a system of direct elections for the Representative members of the legislative Council who represent Buganda shall be introduced in the year 1961 if such system has not been introduced earlier.

(4) Her Majesty's Government shall during the year 1957 arrange for a review by representatives of the Protectorate Government and of the Kabaka's Government of the system of election of Representative members of the Legislative Council who represent Buganda. In such review consideration will be given to any scheme submitted by the Kabaka's Government for the election of such Representative Members based upon the recommendation contained in the Sixth Schedule to this Agreement. Every effort will be made to give effect to the recommendations resulting from such review in time for the election of the representative members of the Legislative Council who represent Buganda when the Legislative Council is generally reconstituted after the general vacation of seats in the Council next following the coming into force of this Agreement.

49. To gauge the position of the Kabaka's Government and the Lukiiko to the potential Constitutional advancement offered by the Constitutional Committee, the Obote-Mayanja UNC floated 130 elected members of the Legislature each representing 50,000 people of which there would be 32 elected members representing Constituencies in Buganda. The float was taken up by other Parties and individuals and became more or less a very common demand. It was however, not the intention of the Obote-Mayanja UNC to have Constituencies demarcated in such an artificial manner. The Party adopted the District (the ethnic base of the people of Uganda) to provide Constituencies and therefore considered the square miles of each District and population density in each District as well as terrain. Detailed considerations of such factors produced a 82 elected members each representing Constituencies ranging from 70,000 to 90,000 people depending on terrain and population density. In the Party's calculations, a constituency was to have a population of 90,000 except in Districts with population density of 50 people per square mile or less were to have constituencies with population of 70,000. The number of elected seats, their

distribution and the basis of their demarcations were presented to the Constitutional Committee by the Central Executive Committee, which the Constitutional Committee accepted. The provision of Article 7 of the Buganda Agreement of 1955 quoted in the above paragraph was met because Buganda was to have 21 of the 82 elected members.

50. On the matter of one man one vote and Self-Government Now, the Obote-Mayanja UNC prepared and sent to its District organs, appropriate demands which each of the District organs presented to the Constitutional Committee.

51. In February, 1959, the suspicion I had in November of the previous year that Jolly Joe was purveying the Mengo position on the Constitutional Committee, was proved to be correct. The Ministers of the Kabaka's Government wrote a letter to the Governor in February after the appointment by the Governor of members of the Constitutional Committee, early in the month. The Governor provided a copy of the letter to each member of the Constitutional Committee. The letter was in the following terms:

> "We have the honour to submit to Your Excellency the views of the Kabaka's Council of Ministers, on the appointment of the Legislative Council Constitutional Committee, the main purpose of which is to assess public opinion on the question of the Common Electoral Roll for Uganda. We would like to refer to our past representations to Your Excellency on this matter. When the introduction of Direct Election was put up for debate in the Legislative Council, its acceptance by Government was conditional to the unqualified acceptance of the idea of a common electoral roll and on giving adequate and effective representation to non-African on the Legislative Council. It should be remembered that all African representative members of the Legislative Council objected to and voted against that motion.
>
> Your Excellency, we still hold the view that as the question of the Common Electoral Roll is tied up with the question of citizenship, and in all fairness, the right time to consider this matter is after the Uganda Africans have attained independence for Uganda, for

this is not a matter which can be decided by the British who are in a position of Trustees to Uganda Africans. We fail to see, Your Excellency, what useful purposes will be served by the appointed Committee. Furthermore, in the recent memorandum from the Lukiiko it was clearly stated how Buganda would deal with such questions as the recent Committee is empowered to discuss. We, therefore, propose to call a Lukiiko Session to look into these matter."

52. While the Constitutional Committee continued with its work outside Buganda, the National Movement was formed in Buganda and it distracted public opinion from the Constitution debate to boycott of Asian owned shops. The National Movement was very violent. Leading politicians in Buganda such as I. K. Musaazi, Eridadi Mulira, the President of the Progressive Party, Godfrey Binaisa and many others became members or supporters of the National Movement. The one politician who took a leading and open opposition to the National Movement, was Jolly Joe Kiwanuka. In the Obote-Mayanja UNC, we regarded the National Movement as a nuisance. The DP leaders seem to have taken the same attitude. In our case, however, the leader of the National Movement Augustine Kamya, sought us and was frequently holding secret meetings with me in the Uganda Club.

53. During 1959, we lost the Secretary General, Abu Mayanja who accepted appointment as minister of Education in the Kabaka's Government. I as President of the UNC made with the approval of the Central Executive Committee, two appointments which were to be of the greatest importance when Uganda became Independent. I appointed John Kale, a brilliant young Congressman from Kinkizi to establish a UNC office in Cairo and to be the Party's liaison officer with the Headquarters of the Afro-Asian Solidarity Committee in Cairo. The Solidarity Committee was very active in the decolonisation campaigns. The second appointment was that of Charles Onyutta, an official of the Party from Nebbi District to be the Party's Ambassador to the Party of Patrice Lumumba. I had met an Alur from Congo who was a member of Lumumba's Party in West Nile in 1957. From that meeting, relations developed between me and Lumumba.

Onyutta was in Leopoldville in 1960 and very close to Prime Minister Lumumba when problems began in that country.

54. The Constitutional Committee (which had taken the name of the Wild Committee after the name of its Chairman), completed its work in October 1959 and its report was submitted to the Governor in early December. In the same month, the Buganda Lukiiko in a resolution, declared Buganda an Independent State. I was due to visit countries in Eastern Europe, the Soviet Union and China on invitations arranged by John Kale.

55. The Central Executive Committee met, discussed the Lukiiko's declaration and decided that I leave the country immediately for the British Government to deal with the declaration of Independence.

56. My journey of less than three weeks, took me to East Germany, Prague, Moscow and Peking. In each country, I asked only for scholarships but I was also given gifts of typewriters, duplicating machines and cameras all of which on reaching Uganda were confiscated by the Government.

57. On return home, I was greeted with the report that the Governor wanted to see me immediately. Two days later, I went to Entebbe to meet the Governor. I suspected and it turned out to be correct, that he was going to take me to task for going to communist countries. The Governor did not mince his words or hide his displeasure when I entered his office. He asked me straight away to explain why I went to communist countries. I pulled out my Passport and gave it to him while I explained that I had gone to Paris to consult with the African members of the French Parliament after which I went to London. The passport showed that I had landed at a Paris airport from Lisbon and that I had left France through a border town to Ostend from where I took the train ferry to Dover and then to London.

58. The entries in the Passport and my explanation ameliorated the Governor and we were soon discussing the declaration of Buganda as an Independent State. I told the Governor that it was my opinion that he should ignore the Lukiiko's resolution and

instead see whether he could convince London to accept the recommendations of the Wild Committee. As we conversed, the lies I had told suddenly overwhelmed me and I began to sweat and fainted. When I recovered, it was with much effort that I did not confess to the Governor about the lies. To a very large extent, the Governor ignored the resolution.

59. In 1959, I had started a project which was very dear to me. It started when the Independent members of the LegCo, elected in October, 1958, together with C. B. Katiti who was elected by Ankole District Council also in October formed a political Party, the Uganda Peoples Union (UPU). I wondered how and why such very capable politicians were not members of the UNC when the UNC was extremely popular in their Districts. I decided to form a small secret Committee to find out. Soon after making that decision and after I had appointed and briefed two members of the secret Committee, a young man I did not know came to see me in the Headquarters of the UNC. He introduced himself and told me that he had been to India where he studied Economics at Delhi University. He greatly impressed me with his nationalism and support for the UNC (Obote wing). He was, however, not a member of the UNC. So, I arranged for him to be a member of the Party, Headquarters Branch. In those days, ten members could form a Branch and we had more than ten members at the Headquarters, all voluntary workers and none was paid. I asked the young man to start work at the Headquarters. He was John Kakonge.

60. I found a third member of the secret Committee and I appointed Kakonge to be the Secretary of the Committee. I gave the Committee one moth in which to submit their Report. After the receipt of that report, I decided I should myself approach each of the Independent members of the LegCo.

61. My objective was not to recruit the Independent members into the UNC but to convince each of them to believe that with the very strong representations the UNC organs were presenting to the Wild Committee for one man one vote which I knew, all of them and particularly their two members on the Wild Committee

were supporting, one man one vote would come in 1961 and Self-Government, soon thereafter. I argued that it was their national duty to promote the Independence of Uganda.

62. I was on a very strong ground because my secret Committee had found that the independents had been members of the UNC and that the majority left the UNC after the split of 1957.

63. The two Independents on the Wild Committee were George Magezi, who was also the Secretary General of the UPU and C. B. Katiti. I concentrated on the two and particularly on George Magezi. My proposal to the Independents was that they consider either to disband their Party or merging it with the UNC.

64. That was the project to which I returned after my visits to Eastern countries. I gave in confidence, an overview of the Independence strategy on which I was working to Serwano Kulubya who was a nominated member of the LegCo and not a Party politician or even a politician. A day or so later Senteza Kajubi visited me at Mengo Social centre where I was staying. I think Kajubi had left the UNC in 1957 and was not in the early months of 1960, a member of the DP, Kajubi asked questions about the Independence Strategy but his interest was whether I would resign from the leadership of the UNC. My answer was in the positive.

A few days later I got an invitation to go in the evening to the house of Yusuf Lule on the outskirts of Kampala. I went and George Magezi was also there. The DP and the Progressive Party leaders were not there. Nothing of substance was discussed and it was agreed to hold another meeting, at the same place, two evenings later.

66. At the second meeting in Lule's house, the DP leader was there alone but not the leader of the Progressive Party. The UPU had the largest attendance followed by the UNC. Before the meeting began, people spoke about a rumour that Apollo Kironde, Mayanja Nkangi and Lamek Lubowa were in the process of forming a Party.

67. Lule opened the meeting with one theme. It was that his reading of the Wild Report, had convinced him that it would be very difficult for the British government to reject the increase in the number of elected members of the Legislative Council from ten to 82. He said he was also of the opinion that the Governor would not nominate a greater number than 82 to the Government side. There was therefore a real possibility of Internal Government by Ugandans in 1961. But, he said, what was lacking, was a strong country wide political Party whose absence the British Government could seize upon to postpone internal Government beyond 1961. Lule proposed either the merger of the existing Parties or their disbandment and formation of a new Party with the leaders of the existing Parties being the founder members.

68. The second speaker, was the leader of the democratic Party. He said that he disagreed with Lule's proposals. The DP leader said that there was already a party which could run the Government of Uganda and it was called DP. He invited everyone to singly join the DP. He ended by saying that there was no necessity for the kind of meeting Lule had convened. After that, the DP leader begged to be excused and then walked out of the meeting.

69. After the departure of the DP leader, someone proposed that instead of discussing mergers or disbandments of Parties, those who had the ears of Mengo, should offer to talk to Mengo because it was more likely that the British Government would seize on Mengo's opposition to the Legislative Council to delay independence than on what Lule had said. The proposal received much support but there was no offer. The meeting lost decorum and direction and was terminated amidst some chaos.

70. From the third week of January, 1960 and throughout February, members of the Central Executive Committee and National Council of the UNC were meeting in Kampala daily in the morning but they all went before the end of February to their Districts and returned to Kampala on or about 5 March. I and a team were also meeting leaders of the UPU daily in the afternoon

and evenings and reporting to the two UNC organs daily in the morning. Accommodation and meals for members of the two UNC organs were paid by the five UNC members of the Legislative Council.

71. After the second meeting in the house of Yusuf Lule, the UPU leaders made very strong representations that the disbandment of the UPU would be counterproductive when elections to the LegCo were due in 1961. There main argument was that disbandment would result in the UNC recruiting UPU members individually and that whatever goodwill, big or small which the UPU had in the Districts which the Independents won in the October, 1958 elections may be lost or may not be gained by the UNC.

72. The two UNC organs discussed the representations of the UPU leaders on the disbandment of their Party. The decision reached was that as a Party, the UPU was more viable at the top and particularly in the Legislative Council but not on the ground. It was further concluded that the UNC would gain more by a merger than by disbandment of the UPU.

73. It was proposed by the UNC and agreed by the UPU that for the merger, each party should bring to Kampala 10 of its members from each District.

74. The two UNC organs decided that for the UNC alone, Branches were by then at sub-county levels be informed that after the merger, the Delegates Conference would be held to approve the merger. When the decision was put to the UPU leaders as a matter of goodwill, they proposed the amendment which was agreed by the UNC that each party would send 5 delegates from each of its sub-county Branches to the Delegates Conference in two months after the merger but to approve the new Constitution of the UNC and not the merger.

75. On 9th March, 10 members of the UNC from each District and 10 members of the UPU from each District, met at the Uganda Club in Kampala and formed the Uganda Peoples Congress (UPC).

76. The first UPC Delegates Conference was held in Kampala at the Indian Women's Association Hall.

77. On the eve of the Conference, I had food poisoning and was admitted in Mulago Hospital. I never attended the Conference but was elected in absentia, President of the party, John Kakonge was elected Secretary General replacing Interim George Magezi.

THE LAST LAP TO INDEPENDENCE.

78. In April, 1960, the Governor announced in the Legislative Council acceptance by the British Government of 82 directly elected members in the Legislative Council. The British Government also rejected a Cabinet (Self-Government) formed by the largest Party in the Council.

79. Some members of the Legislative Council were highly agitated and demanded going to London to argue the case for Self-Government to which I succumbed. My personal opinion however was that so long as the Buganda Lukiiko remained opposed to people in Buganda being represented in the Central Legislature, nothing except nationalism within Uganda will change that opposition.

80. In London, the LegCo delegation obtained the services of a member of the House of Lords to help prepare its case. The delegation had separate meetings with two junior ministers and with the Secretary of State for the Colonies. The case which the delegation presented was that by not accepting the largest Party in the Legislative Council, returned after the 1961 elections, to form a Cabinet, the British Government was effectively giving one part of the country to veto the desires of the rest of the country and was also making the elections to be held in 1961 a lame exercise not designed to meet the desires of the voters. The delegation did not expect a straightforward response and did not get it. The strategy of the delegation was to make the British Government to resolve the dilemma which the Indirect System of Colonial rule had created in favour of the people of Uganda who wanted Independence.

81. The April announcement by the Governor, created much distraction from the campaigns for Independence. Politicians in Toro, Ankole, Bunyoro and Busoga, joined by Town dwellers mostly lawyers left the campaigns and turned their efforts in demanding for the respective status of the Omukama of Bunyoro, Omukama of Toro, Omugabe and the Kyabazinga in Independent Uganda.

82. The Central Executive Committee and the National Council of the UPC adopted, under the generic strategy of increased political activities and campaigns for Independence, two strategic responses on the matter of the status of each of the Traditional Rulers in Independent Uganda. First, was a public Statement which was amended and updated from time to time which stated that the UPC would respect and preserve the position of each of the Traditional Rulers. The second response was the ban on Party leaders at all levels, except the Party leader, not to engage in public debate on the status of the Traditional Rulers.

83. During 1960, the UPC President addressed many meetings at which the matter of the status of the Traditional Rulers was raised. At each meeting, the Party President emphasised the paramountcy of the voice of all parts of the country being in the Central Legislature, as the surest guarantor of the status, dignity and position of each Traditional Ruler.

84. The matter of the status of the Traditional Rulers was a distraction which strengthened the stand of the Lukiiko and the Kabaka's Government but to which some politicians and some lawyers were dragging the other Kingdoms into at a time when, unlike the Lukiiko and the Kabaka's Government, the other Kingdoms had already lost due to nationalist campaigns since 1952, the power of vetoing the march of the people to Independence.

85. The loss of the power of veto became very clear in June, 1960, when the Legislative Council passed an Ordinance for holding direct elections to the Legislative Council in the year 1961 in 82 Constituencies. The ordinance did not make any

provision, like in 1958, that a Kingdom Legislature could elect representatives to the Central Legislature. The ordinance also gave Notice to the Lukiiko and the Kabaka's Government - the outcome of the representations by the LegCo delegation in London - that their veto power was temporary.

86. June and July, 1960 were glorious months for the UPC because one man one vote had been accepted not only by the people of Uganda, but also by the Colonial power - Britain and had become the law of the land.

87. When the registration of voters began, the UPC leaders and members went full blast to get many people and particularly known members of the Party to register. The number of people who registered as voters outside Buganda was 1,300,433. In Buganda, due to intimidations caused by the opposition of the Lukiiko and the Kabaka's Government, only 36,006 people registered as voters.

88. At the May, 1960 Delegates Conference because the UNC had had no Regulations (because there were no elections) for adopting the Party's parliamentary candidates, the Conference, by resolution, authorised the District Executives to adopt candidates for the 1961 elections. The decision caused some problems for the UPC. In one District, two good and strong Party members stood against each other in one Constituency which also had a DP candidate. In another District, a candidate adopted by the District Executive was also adopted by two other Parties and on Nomination Day, he was returned unopposed. In another District, three candidates adopted by their District Executive did not turn up for nomination.

89. The 1961 elections to the Legislative Council, was contested by five political Parties namely:-

Democratic Party (DP)

Uganda African Union (UAU)

Uganda Hereditary Chieftainship Party (UHCP)

Uganda National Congress (UNC) - Jolly Joe and Dr. Kununka

Uganda Peoples Congress (UPC)

90. In the latter months of 1960, the Central Executive Committee and National Council of the UPC discussed and approved the party's election Policy Statement (Manifesto). The printing of posters for each candidate was also approved. After the candidates had been adopted, each submitted to Headquarters details of his poster. There was, however a very serious disagreement on distributing in each Constituency the photograph and Message from the party President.

91. It soon came to light that the above disagreement was rooted in a clandestine campaign by the DP in Western Uganda that the UPC President was a communist. The Party candidates in the West, therefore, refused to have in their Constituencies the photograph and Message from the Party President. However, when those candidates found that the electorate wanted some message from the Party President, they rushed to the Party Headquarters and took to their Constituencies the posters in Luo with the photograph of the Party President for his Constituency in Lango North.

92. A photograph of the UPC President with the Bishops in East Germany was distributed in western Uganda by the DP. The dirty campaign, if it did, helped the DP to win 9 out of 18 seats in the West.

93. The UPC Party President was returned unopposed in his Constituency. He was therefore in the Party headquarters in the evening when the elections results were being broadcast by Radio Uganda. The DP was winning seat after seat in Buganda but the UPC was also doing the same in the East and North.

94. About midnight, a telephone call was received in the UPC Headquarters. It was from Lincoln Ndawula the brother of the Kabaka who also was a friend of the UPC President. Lincoln told the Party President that the Kabaka wanted a word with him. The conversation between the Kabaka and the UPC President was very short. The Kabaka asked the Party President to defeat the DP. The short answer was; "We are waiting for the results." Soon thereafter, food arrived at the UPC Headquarters from Mengo Palace.

95. The full 1961 elections results of the seats were as follows: -

DP 44

UPC 35

UNC 1 (Jolly Joe and Dr. Kununka)

Independents 2

96. The DP won 20 out of 21 seats in Buganda and lost only one to the UPC. In the East, North and West, where in today's parlance, the elections were free and fair, the UPC won 34 to 24 won by the DP.

97. The boycott of the elections in Buganda, made the entire exercise in Buganda a farce. In Bugerere Constituency, for instance, 133 voters elected a legislator with a majority of 11, whereas in Busoga West 22,923 voters elected the UPC Vice-President with a majority of 21,295. That majority in only one Constituency in Busoga was even more than all the people who voted in Buganda in 21 Constituencies which was 13,297.

98. The Central Executive Committee and the National Council of the UPC met and considered the elections results. It was decided that the majority of seats in the Legislative Council won by the DP and the very effective boycott of the elections in Buganda, were very serious factors which would work to dampen unimpeded march to Independence and despite the boycott, the UPC should accept the results of the elections which was done. It was resolved that on the strength of the popular votes which showed the UPC to have the confidence of the electorate more than any other Party, programmes for the march to independence be deepened and updated. The popular votes were as follows: -

UPC 494,959

DP 415,718

UNC 31,712

UAU 1,172

UHCP 6,559

INDEPENDENTS 48,457

99. There was a provision for the Legislative Council to elect 9 specially elected members. One of 3 members specially elected by the UPC members of the Council, was Miss Joyce Masembe (Later Mrs. Mpanga) and when she went to America for studies, the UPC elected in her place Mrs. Eseza Makumbi. This was the first time any Party had introduced women into high politics and elected them to the Legislature.

100. An old issue arose with a vengeance after the 1961 elections. The issue was called "Lost Counties". The Kingdom of Bunyoro waged a vigorous campaign in the Districts in the West, East and North and sought the support of the political Parties for the return, before Independence, of its Counties which the British ceded to the Buganda Kingdom in or before the year 1900. The Bunyoro campaign had been going on intermittently for decades but this time, it had elements which impacted adversely on a united country marching towards Independence.

101. The UPC issued Statements which called for the issue of the Lost Counties to be resolved through a Referendum. Nothing was done.

102. The UPC campaigns for Independence was invigorated by public rallies and also representations to the Governor by the Central Executive Committee for the British Government to resolve Buganda Lukiiko's opposition to the Legislative Council. The Central Executive Committee proposed elections to the Legislative Council in which the Colonial Government would provide sufficient security to the people in Buganda to register as voters and to cast their votes.

103. Alternatively, the Central Executive Committee proposed (to the Governor) that since under the Buganda Agreement 1955, it was provided that Buganda was always to be represented in the Legislative Council, the Lukiiko and the Kabaka's Government had broken that Agreement and should, therefore not be recognised by the British Government.

104. The UPC campaigns, made the British Government to appoint what was called Relations Commission. When a

Committee of members of the Legislative Council (including the UPC President) met the Commission, the Commission's Chairman asked the question which contained what was to be Mengo's flagship for an honourable climb down. The question was: What would be the stand of the LegCo members if Buganda's representatives in the LegCo were elected by the Lukiiko and not direct elections? There was no answer because the matter had not been considered.

105. It turned soon thereafter that the Commission had already discussed with Mengo the matter it put to the LegCo members and that Mengo had agreed to the Lukiiko electing Buganda's representatives. The Commission was in Uganda at a time when the UPC, DP, the Kingdoms and the District Councils were busy preparing themselves for the Constitutional Conference which was to begin in London at the end of September.

106. Out of the blue, the UPC President was invited to meet the Kabaka and the invitation was accepted. Nothing of substance was discussed but the Kabaka said that he and his Government and the Lukiiko were not against Independence and suggested that if the Party President met the Katikiro, Michael Kintu, he would find the truth.

107. There was no immediate reaction to what the Kabaka had said. Instead, an urgent meeting of the Central Executive Committee was called. The predominant opinion at the meeting was against any meeting with the Katikiro. It was argued very strongly that any meeting with the Katikiro would be leaked to the Press and would be relished with outrageous claims such that the UPC had agreed to the Kabaka being the Head of State at Independence which, if made would damage the UPC throughout the country because every Traditional Ruler wanted to be the Head of State at Independence whereas the Districts did not want any Traditional Ruler to be the Head of State at Independence. I did, however, manage to get the meeting to agree to my meeting the Katikiro.

108. The first meeting with the Katikiro, turned into a series of meetings. In the series, the Ministers in the Kabaka's

Government disclosed that they had discussed with the Relations Commission the British proposal that the Lukiiko should elect Buganda's representatives in the Legislative Council and that they liked the proposal. I argued most strongly that since representatives from the other Kingdoms and from the Districts had been elected directly, Buganda's representatives would bear the stigma of puppets of the Lukiiko, if elected by the Lukiiko. The Ministers told me that the Lukiiko would support indirect election because the Lukiiko of 1955 supported it when they approved the Handcock Report under which the British Government restored the Kabaka to his throne.

109. When I reported the Handcock Report provisions on Buganda's representatives to the Central Executive Committee, the exchange of views led to the discovery that both the Lukiiko of 1955 and 1961 were not elected bodies. The Central Executive Committee felt very strongly that the position of unelected bodies should not be allowed to "pollute" the LegCo which had an overwhelming number of directly elected members. It was decided that since the indirect election was a British proposal, a letter be written to the Governor. The letter was written, and the response was that the Secretary of State for the Colonies would put further proposals to the Kabaka's Government.

110. Before the UPC delegation left for the Constitutional Conference, the Central Executive Committee and National Council gave the delegation two very firm objectives. They were:-

(i) Date of Independence to be announced during or at the end of the Conference.

(ii) Another election to the Central Legislature before Independence.

111. In London, the UPC delegation engaged the District and Kingdom delegations in discussing the two UPC objectives. A general agreement was obtained from all those delegations to support the two objectives.

112. The British Government singled out the UPC, Buganda and DP delegations as difficult delegations and decided to hold side meetings with their leaders.

113. The first to go to the side meeting was the Kabaka. His delegation had two matters namely, Federal agreements for Buganda and the Lukiiko to elect Buganda's representatives to the LegCo. The British Government rejected the first saying that it could only be discussed when an Independence Constitution was being considered which was not the task of this Conference. On the second matter, the British Government proposed that provided the Lukiiko was directly elected, they would undertake to get the UPC and DP to agree to indirect elections.

114. The second delegation leader to go to the side meeting was the DP leader. He had only one matter namely, that instead of Uganda having a Chief minister, the British order in Council be amended for Uganda to have a Prime Minister. The request was accepted. He rejected the indirect election for the Buganda representatives when it was put to him.

115. The UPC leader was the last to go to the side meeting. He had two matters as given in para 110 above. The first point put to him was the indirect elections. The Secretary of State thanked the UPC for its letter to the Governor which opposed the unelected Lukiiko to elect Buganda's representatives and thereby pollute the LegCo. The Secretary of State said that he had put to the Kabaka who agreed that indirect elections be decided by a Lukiiko elected on the same suffrage as members of the LegCo and asked for the position of the UPC. The UPC leader responded that provided many people registered as voters without intimidation and the Lukiiko election was free and fair, the UPC would reluctantly support indirect elections.

116. On the first UPC matter, the Secretary of State said that the British Government needed time to consider Uganda's performance after the Conference before they considered the date for Independence. The UPC leader responded that his two points (which had been sent to the Secretary of State) were intimately related and wanted the two discussed together. He

went on to argue that had the March 1961 general elections not been seriously flawed by an effective boycott in one province, he would have expected this very Conference to write the Constitution of Independent Uganda. Since the Conference was not going to write that Constitution, the UPC leaders argued, he was proposing the next logical step which, in his view, was announcement of the date of Independence followed by another election and another Conference to write the Constitution of Independent Uganda. The Secretary of State responded that the argument was powerful, but Independence was a matter for the British Government to decide and not the Conference. The response of the UPC leader was that delegations from Uganda were in London and so was the British Government.

117. As the UPC leader was leaving the room, the Secretary of State said that the other two leaders also did not get everything they wanted, and everyone should be happy because no one got everything he wanted. The UPC leader responded that he had got nothing, but the Secretary of State said, "that is not true".

118. On the last day of the Conference (9 October 1961) the Secretary of State announced what he called decisions he had made. He announced that the Federal arrangements which Buganda wanted would be discussed in detail at a future Constitutional Conference which would write the Constitution of Independent Uganda.

119. The secretary of State then announced that the Buganda delegation had agreed to Buganda being represented in the LegCo; the elections of the Buganda representatives would be by the Lukiiko after the Lukiiko itself had been directly elected. This announcement made the DP delegation to walk out and the Conference was adjourned.

120. The third announcement after resumption was that Uganda was to have a Prime Minister in March of the following year. It was the matter which the DP delegation sought the most and which made them to return to the Conference.

121. As the Secretary of State prepared to close the Conference, the UPC leader raised a point of order and made a speech demanding another general election in the following year and also demanded the date of Independence to be announced. The District delegations applauded loudly and five of them spoke in support of the two UPC demands.

122. The Secretary of State adjourned the Conference arguing that Independence date was a matter for the British Government and not the Conference to decide. After the third adjournment and as he began to argue in the same vein as twice before, the UPC leader on a point of order said: *"Mr. Secretary Sir, if that is the only reason for delaying the people of Uganda's natural request, then do not close the Conference; instead, let us all discuss the request for another fortnight."* There was much applause by the District Delegations.

123. After the fourth adjournment, the Secretary of State said that he had consulted the Prime Minister and was pleased to announce that "Uganda shall be Independent on 9 October 1962 provided all arrangements can be made in time." He said nothing about another general election, but it was clear that another general elections was part of the arrangements to be made in time.

124. The Congress got the Independence date and was determined not to allow another Party to get the Instruments of independence just as the DP had in March 1961 "stolen" the fruits of the Congress campaigns for one man one vote.

125. At the end of the Constitutional Conference, the Buganda delegation sent a Team of 3 to return home that same night of 9 October. They arrived home on the morning of 10 October and immediately reported to the Lukiiko which was in session that Buganda had got all that was in demand. That afternoon, a public Rally was organised at Katwe where Kabaka Yekka was formed.

126. On return home, the UPC delegation reported to the Central Executive Committee and National Council. The meeting

resolved without knowing if or whether or when a general election would be held, to start work for it without delay.

127. The elections to the Lukiiko was discussed. The meeting reaffirmed the earlier decision taken which the party president had put to the secretary of State. On the matter of the UPC contesting the Lukiiko elections, the meeting decided that Buganda's voters-face on representation in the Central Legislature was not complete so long as there was the option of indirect elections to which the Party was opposed. It was decided therefore that the party would not contest elections to the Lukiiko.

128. When the Uganda (Electoral Provisions) Order in Council 1961 of the British Government was published in early November, the strategy of the UPC for an election in early part of 1962 was already in place. The Order dealt mainly with elections to the Lukiiko. According to the Order, the Legislative Council was to be known as the "National Assembly". By the end of December, all UPC preparations, except Policy Statement (Manifesto) were in place. The manifesto was awaiting the outcome of the Lukiiko elections and whether or not the elected members of the Lukiiko would opt for direct or indirect elections to the National Assembly.

129. Registrations of voters in Buganda including Kampala Municipality began on 27 November 1961. Unlike in 1960, there were no intimidations and large numbers of people turned up everywhere to be registered; 805,647 registered as voters.

130. Buganda was divided into 68 Lukiiko Constituencies, the DP contested all the 68 seats and won 1 (returned unopposed in the Lost counties). On 22 February 1962, elections were held in 67 of the Constituencies (one Constituency had returned a candidate unopposed).

131. On 17 March 1962, the 68 elected members of the Lukiiko, 6 Kabaka's Ministers and 6 nominees of the Kabaka met and decided on Buganda being represented in the National Assembly

through indirect elections. Three days later, the UPC published its elections Policy Statement (Manifesto).

132. 2 April 1962 was Nomination Day in the 61 National Assembly Constituencies outside Buganda. The elections were contested by five political Parties and 10 (ten) independents as follows: -

Bataka Party of Busoga

Democratic Party

Uganda African Union

Uganda National Congress

Uganda Peoples Congress

133. During the campaign, the UPC leaders and candidates sought for a copy or copies of the DP elections Manifesto but never succeeded to get one. The fear that the DP which had been in Government for a year would produce a startling manifesto, evaporated into thin air.

134. The results of the 1962 elections held on 25 April 1962 gave the UPC not only increased popular votes from 494,959 in 1961 to 537,598 in 1962 but also increased the number of seats in the Central Legislature from 35 in 1961 to 37 in 1962. Outside Buganda the increase was from 34 to 37.

135. Except for the amorphous KY which existed only in Buganda, the 1962 elections erased fringe Parties from Uganda's body politic. The Party which suffered the greatest loss in the 1962 elections was the DP. Whereas the DP won 44 seats to the LegCo in 1961 (20 of them in Buganda), the Party won only 22 seats to the National Assembly in 1962 and even lost 2 seats it won in 1961 outside Buganda.

136. Since 1962 the rationale of the DP for its 1962 great loss, has been that the indirect elections for Buganda's representatives was a conspiracy by the British Government and the UPC to remove the DP Government. The rationale carry the undemocratic meaning that the DP accepted and accept as a very good event the impact of the 1961 boycott of elections in Buganda caused by much intimidations which enabled less than

14,000 voters to elect 21 members to the Central Legislature. To accept intimidations and election boycotts caused by intimidations as good or even very good events is to assassinate democracy.

137. The UPC election Manifesto of 1962 dealt with the DP rationale. I quote at length what the Manifesto said:

> "Without foresight, drive and leadership of the U.P.C. the bulk of the people in Buganda would still be opposed to the Central Authority covering the whole country. There is no doubt that in such a situation no one today would be speaking of celebrating Independence Day on 9th October 1962. Apart from this important achievement there is the pride which is now being expressed openly throughout the country of belonging to Uganda. This again has become possible through the activities of this dynamic party.
>
> The opposition which has been directed against us in our activities to unite the country is centered on the mode of electing Buganda members of the National Assembly. The whole country knows that Buganda boycotted the elections held in March 1961 and that government by consent is an essential characteristic of a democratic government. The government set up after the last elections was to Buganda with 21 seats in the National Assembly not a government by consent and therefore not a democratic government. The U.P.C. believes in elections which are real and do show the mandate of the people. The March elections were not real and did not show the mandate of the people in Buganda because the majority of the people registered against it an effective opposition. The whole of Buganda has now had an election on universal adult franchise to elect the Buganda Lukiiko members. The results of this Lukiiko elections has proved to all that those 21 members who were elected from Buganda constituencies in March 1961 had no support and mandate from the people who live in Buganda. The best policy would be for our opponents to accept with grace the voice of the people. The people in Buganda have spoken and spoken for indirect elections to the National Assembly, and that should end the dispute as it is completely democratic to accept the decision of the majority."

138. On 26 April as I was preparing to leave Lira for Kampala, a convoy of KY members arrived at my house. We travelled to Soroti, Mbale, Tororo, Iganga and Jinja and addressed huge meetings in each Town. We arrived in Kampala when it was already dark. I did not therefore address a meeting the UPC had organised at Clock Tower.

139. The UPC and KY had agreed during the elections campaign to form a coalition Government after the 25 April elections to the National Assembly. The basis of the agreement was the acceptance by KY of matters in the UPC Manifesto. There were no other conditions by either Party. I therefore went to meet the Kabaka who was the behind the scene leader of the KY, in the morning, on 27 April to tell him that the Governor had asked me to form a Government. The Kabaka gave me a free hand to decide on which KY member should be in the Government.

140. After the elections on 25 April, the UPC Government deliberately took office on 1 May, Labour Day, 1962. The UPC Government embarked immediately to implement the Manifesto promises and to produce a 5-year Development Plan. The UPC Government also wasted no time in researching and analysing matters which were to be considered in the second Constitutional conference in London.

141. The second Constitutional Conference which began in late August, was essentially to write the Constitution of Independent Uganda. Kingdoms, and District delegations were at the Conference. The UPC delegation at the Conference was also the Government of Uganda. The research and analyses which the UPC Government had done, helped greatly to speed up the deliberations of the Conference.

142. Although the Lukiiko and the Kabaka's Government had been demanding, for years, for Federal arrangements, it turned out at the Conference that the demand had no meat and bones on it. Because the UPC had formed a coalition Government with KY, the UPC delegation (in London) provided meat and bones in the Buganda demand on the basis of the research and analyses

done by the Central Executive Committee and National Council before the Conference.

143. The issue of the Lost Counties was on the Agenda and the kingdom of Bunyoro was greatly being supported by the other Kingdoms and the Districts on its demand that the Counties be returned before Independence. The UPC delegation, that is, Uganda Government proposed to the secretary of State that with only weeks remaining before Independence day, the Government could not even implement the UPC proposal for a referendum and therefore that the Secretary of State, Bunyoro and Buganda should discuss the issue in a side meeting.

144. Side meetings were held whose outcome was that the British government, Bunyoro and Buganda delegations agreed that it be written in the Constitution of Uganda that a referendum be held two years after Independence for the people in four Counties to decide being part of Buganda or part of Bunyoro or form new Districts.

145. The federal arrangements for Bunyoro, Toro, Ankole and Busoga were also dealt with inside meetings between their respective delegations and the Prime Minister of Uganda (also UPC leader). Complete agreements were reached with each of them.

146. The second Constitutional Conference ended in a most harmonious and euphoric spirit. The delegations returned to Uganda to be witnesses to the achievement of the Congress call in 1952 for one man one vote and Self-Government Now. It took 10 years.

147. I very nearly missed Uganda's Independence. I went to the Dam in Jinja on 8 October to receive Prime Minister Jomo Kenyatta. While on the bridge, a lorry heavily loaded with goods travelling from Jinja direction, nearly crashed into me.

148. On 9 October, the Duke of Kent representing his cousin, Her Majesty Queen Elizabeth II, handed the Instruments of Independence to me - the UPC President.

149. Our Congress led the people of Uganda to do what the people of Uganda must never be called upon again to do; to remove foreign rule from the soil of Uganda.

150. The rule of the charlatans which has already heavily mortgaged the country and sold the peoples' heirlooms at giveaway prices, may again bring the humiliation of being ruled by foreigners.

151. I pay humble Tribute to the nationalists who sacrificed their lives for the people of Uganda to be free. I call upon the Youth to pick up the baton and to continue with the struggle until every citizen of Uganda is free to enjoy and exercise his/her inalienable, God given, human rights and freedom.

I have written and now present this Paper in the spirit of our National Motto:

FOR GOD AND MY COUNTRY.

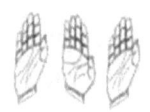

Epilogue

1. My Last Words

It has been difficult out of the 1961/2 Lancaster House Conferences held in London to pave way for the independence of Uganda from British colonialism to have duly set in place processes to resolve the outstanding national question in Uganda. These conferences suffered inadequacies of necessary and fuller representation of the country's diversities and multiplicities.

One such area among the many of deficient representation was the multinational district of Bukedi in Eastern Uganda.

I must be upfront with the readers that I collated the records for this book as they were collatable and were interesting to me. I have intentionally steered clear of making any interpretations on the texts or the messages apart from offering guiding introductory remarks to the salient epochs of the selected history, where Dr A.M. Obote's presence was felt in both his own words and those of others who observed and / or were tracking his political presence.

I have compiled and sequenced these documents with the preceding disclaimer that it was for no other purpose, but belief in sharing enabling information for making better decisions.

I have assumed, may be as Columbus did, that I have hit or pressed all the right buttons and, if not, you will accept that my intentions were honest and driven more for the memories of Dr Apollo Milton Obote and of the founding members of UPC in Bukedi, namely Israel Ochwo Alecho, Balaki Keba Kirya, Joseph Wasukulu and Yacobo Maloba.

All the above named, have been or were recalled by the ancestors, at later stages.

I am associating the later four with Dr Obote for two significant political events. First, in June 1961 on Entebbe Road, they were involved in a road accident which ended the life of Israel Ochwo Alecho at the young age of 36 years; an outcome which thrust into Milton Obote's Palm, aged 34 years, an unexpected and unplanned for family of seven. The other is that this was the UPC leadership of Bukedi and the Bukedi delegation to the 1961 Lancaster House Conference was to discuss Uganda's Independence. Technically nationalities habiting Bukedi district were not represented by those who sat at the decision-making table in that said Conference; by fiat, colonial records show that one 'Kirya' attended as representative of Bukedi District, namely, of the nationalities of Itesot, Jopadhola, Gweri, Nyole, Samia, Samia-gwe. A 'Kirya', (possibly of Gweri nationality, or of Soga origin) was not a delegated person by the 'Bakedi' i.e. did not represent the nationalities of Bukedi district as it then was. It may be safe to assume that Milton Obote who represented the UPC as a fact, represented Bukedi by default. I say so because he was the only one of high political standing who knew the weight of the empty Bukedi chair at the 1961 Lancaster Conference.

There are issues swirling around the Afrika habitat of Uganda called LOST counties which publicly, is limited to Buganda (Southern Region). This has been and will be attended to elsewhere in another publication. However, in the interim, this issue has attracted a lot of emotions with the potential to fracture the habitat of Uganda. It remains, according to interested parties, an unresolved matter; but it was, at least, tabled at the decision-making table during the 1961 Marlborough Conference, and briefly touched on in the 1962 Lancaster Conference on the political independence of Uganda. The question I raise here and will be raised elsewhere is about the inclusion of Bukedi in Uganda without the consent of attendant nationalities, namely Gweri, Jopadhola, Nyole, Samia and Iteso; and by subterfuge by Her Majesty's Government, that convened the conference, sponsored the travels to and from London, and was a party to the notarised document that bestowed political self-government to the nationalities in the habitat of Uganda.

I contend that in the scheme of things, Bukedi is a 'lost district of five counties, namely, Bugweri, Bunyole, Samia, Bukedia and Padhola as they were neither represented at the decision-making table in Lancaster Independence Conference nor have benefited from any consultation, as to what they like or dislike about being in Uganda – to be addressed in details elsewhere in another publication. Subsequent Kampala-based political rulerships have assumed that Bukedi is some backyard and the attendant nationalities do not merit being consulted on the matter of what they like or dislike.

Bukedi will wake up, and should wake up, and make the demand or assert the right to be consulted on what they like as an integral part of the political governance of Uganda. It will not be enough to offer or collect crumbs falling from the political decision-making table located elsewhere and which location was never even accented to by the 'Bakedi'.

The papering over of this gap has gone on for far too long and will likely function in perpetuity unless a stop is put to it. The 'Bakedi' for lack of better word or description are entitled to negotiate their participation in the habitat called Uganda, with nothing assumed to be on or off the table.

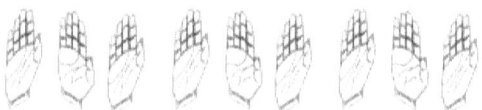

Subject Index

1

1960, 4, 12, 14, 19-21, 23, 27, 33, 273, 276-278, 280, 281, 290
1961, 11, 24, 27, 33, 78, 267, 269, 270, 275-277, 279-283, 286-292, 296, 297
1962, 4, 10, 25, 27, 35, 38, 39, 42, 44, 48, 49, 53, 55, 56, 77, 104, 110, 132, 209, 260, 263, 269, 289-292, 297

A

A.C. Duffield, 90, 108
Abraham Lincoln, 30
Abu Mayanja, 10, 11, 25, 26, 151, 240, 269, 273
Acholi, 16, 264
Addis Ababa, 58, 73, 255, 257
Adoko Nekyon, 80, 149
Africa, 4, 8, 12, 15, 18, 25, 28, 29, 38, 43, 44, 45, 51-54, 57-59, 61, 62, 66-73, 76, 77, 102, 104, 106, 117, 119, 120, 122, 138, 150, 157, 172, 173, 208, 216, 237, 250-255, 257, 258
Africa Report, 25, 35, 193
African Socialism, 90
African Unity, 5, 6, 51, 64, 67, 73, 143, 180, 250
Akena Adoko, 14
Akena p'Ojok, 148
Akokoro, 116
Alabama, 93
Ali Picho, 109
Amit Bhaduri, 7
Amnesty International, 127, 164, 165, 166, 167
AMO Conference, 74
Andrew Cohen, 161
Anil Clerk, 12
Ankole, 204, 264, 275, 279, 294
Anyoti, 16, 108, 170, 194, 195
Apac, 152, 221, 225, 226
Archbishop Janan Luwum, 115
Archbishop of Canterbury, 182, 183, 185
Arthur Bamber, 111
Arua, 152
Asian, 36, 235, 273
Atartuk, 123

B

B.B.C, 60, 74, 77, 121, 199
Babiiha, 83
Baganda, 27, 28, 29, 30, 33, 35, 36, 93, 94, 100, 161-163, 177, 204
Bakedi, 297, 298
Balaki Keba Kirya, 3, 12, 296
Bank of Uganda, 135
Banyoro, 27
Barlev, 121
Baroness Chalker, 246
Barrie Penrose, 172
Bataka Party, 290
BATARINGAYA, 83
Ben Kiwanuka, 91
Benedicto Kiwanuka, 161
Benon Ogwal, 220
Berkshire, 172
Besimesi Nyafwono, 3, 12, 308
Blacknell, 172
Bombo, 187, 197
Bosco Sebulindee, 186
Boston, 32
Brian Sedgemere, 209
Britain, 14, 31, 40, 45, 47, 50, 56, 61, 104, 111, 117, 145, 156, 187, 195, 199, 208, 211, 215, 280
British Colonial Empire, 38
British Parliament, 207, 215, 246, 248
British rule, 8

Buganda, 26-30, 33, 35-37, 47, 77, 78, 84, 85, 89, 93-102, 161-163, 176-178, 187, 197, 202, 204-206, 263, 264, 266, 270-274, 279, 280, 282-291, 293, 297
Bukedi, 11, 264, 296, 297, 298
Bukedia, 298
Bunyoro, 162, 264, 279, 283, 293, 294
Busoga, 23, 25, 264, 279, 283, 290, 294
Busoga College, 23, 25

C

C-130, 174
Cairo, 273
Cardinal Emannuel Nsubuga, 150
Casablanca, 256
Catch-22, 212, 214, 216
Catholic, 27, 168, 169, 183, 185, 186, 194, 220
CCM, 140
Central Executive Committee, 267-269, 271, 273, 274, 277, 279, 281-286, 289, 293
Central Legislature, 253, 279, 280, 286, 289, 291
Charles Grassley, 194
Charles I, 55
Chartham House, 161
Chester Crocker, 150
China, 104, 274
Chinese, 61, 104
Christine Tolofina Awino, 12
Chui Battalion, 129
Civil Service, 82
Clare Short, 207
Clyde Sanger, 29, 56
Coffee, 29
Colin Legum, 161, 176, 180
Colin MacLean, 187
Colonel Amin, 80
Colonial Office, 38, 47
Colonial Secretary, 57

Columbus, 296
Common Man, 90
Common Market, 45, 47, 253
Commonwealth, 4, 23, 40, 43-45, 47, 61, 63, 78, 80, 121, 142, 143, 145, 179, 208
Congo, 67, 80, 273
Constance Tolofina Awino, 12
Constitution, 4, 41, 49, 78, 81-83, 94, 97, 99, 102, 109, 208, 210-215, 219, 241-243, 247-249, 263, 268, 273, 278, 286, 287, 288, 293
Constitutional Committee, 267, 268, 269, 270, 271, 272, 273
Corner Kilak, 218, 219, 221, 222, 224
Cotton, 29
Coup, 5, 84
Cyprus, 121, 122

D

Daily Telegraph, 84, 182, 189, 194, 197, 202
Dar es Salaam, 56, 57, 116, 120, 124, 126, 133
Delhi University, 275
Democratic Party, 6, 27, 30, 33, 35, 36, 69, 144, 161-163, 189, 206, 281, 290
Dr 'Biz', 115
Duke and Duchess of Kent, 52
Duke of Kent, 294
DUKE OF KENT, 49

E

East Africa, 47, 49, 53, 55, 63, 93
East African Common Market, 47
East African Community, 109, 122
East African Federation, 28, 54, 64, 78
East African Standard, 58

Edward Mutesa, 79, 84, 85, 93, 97-99, 102
Egypt, 121, 123
England, 26, 55, 115
Engur, 26
Entebbe, 47, 52, 58, 97, 101, 136, 169, 172-174, 274, 297
Eric Downtown, 84
Eric Wells, 187
Eseza Makumbi, 283
Ethiopia, 58, 93, 117, 251, 255, 258
Europe, 36, 45, 47, 69, 72, 104, 251, 274
European, 47, 52, 96, 121, 257
European Common Market, 47, 52
Evaristo Nyanzi, 160

F

Falcon Star, 173
Felix Onama, 80
FOR GOD AND MY COUNTRY, 294
Francis Butagyira, 152
Frank Kalimuzo, 109
Fred Rwigyema, 217
Fredrick Forsyth, 172
Fredrick Mutesa, 89, 97
FRELIMO, 203
French, 45, 193, 253, 274

G

Galukande, 108
Ganda, 9, 10, 11, 115
Godfrey Binaisa, 16, 109, 172, 177, 200, 273
Governor, 20, 21, 32, 39, 117, 262, 264, 267, 268, 270, 272, 273, 274, 276, 278, 279, 284, 286, 287, 292
Gowon, 123, 139
GREGORY JAYNES, 159
Gulu, 25, 129, 221-225, 228, 236
Guwedeko, 123
Gweri, 297

H

Handcock Report, 285, 286
Henry Kalema, 180
Henry Kyemba, 109
High Court, 100
Hitler, 227
HMG, 143, 207, 210, 211, 215, 216, 228-232, 235, 238, 248
Human Rights, 164, 166, 167

I

Ian Raitt, 142
Ibingira, 86, 110
Iganga, 151, 152, 292
India, 17, 36, 275
International Herald Tribune, 158, 159, 180
International Security Agency, 172
Israel Ochwo Alecho, 3, 11, 296, 297, 308
Iteso, 297
Itesot, 297
Ivory Coast, 47

J

Jack S Alecho-oita, 13
Jaffer Nimeiry, 139
Jamaica, 121
James II, 55
Jennifer Nantume Senkatuka, 308
Jeroham Stephen Alecho, 12
Jesse Stephen Alecho, 12
Jinja, 94, 266, 292, 294
Jomo Kenyatta, 26, 56, 294
Jopadhola, 297, 308
Joseph Kiwanuka, 24, 26
Joseph Ssebayiga, 196
Joseph Wasukulu, 296
Joyce Masembe, 283
Julius Nyerere, 29, 56, 143, 157
Junta, 114, 219, 220-223, 225, 227
Justice Sheridan, 100

Justine Stephen Alecho, 12

K

Kabaka, 4, 27, 30, 33, 35-37, 55, 78, 84, 85, 93-97, 99-102, 106, 161, 162, 263, 269-273, 280-282, 284-287, 289, 290, 292, 293
Kabaka Yekka, 4, 30, 35, 36, 37, 55, 78, 162, 289
Kabarole, 154
Kaboha, 154
Kakoge, 182, 183
Kakonge, 57, 275, 278
Kakungulu Primary School, 308
Kalema, 83
Kalule-Settala, 83
Kampala, 11, 25, 49, 52, 54, 57, 79, 80, 84, 93-96, 100, 101, 116, 117, 121, 136, 151, 152, 158-160, 165, 168, 170, 173, 174, 176, 182, 183, 185, 187, 188, 192-194, 197, 200-202, 205, 263, 264, 266, 276-278, 290, 292, 298
Kapeka, 197, 205
Karamojong, 227
Katikiro, 94, 98, 285
Katongole, 109
Kawanga Ssemwogerere, 154, 206
Kayira, 177
Kenya, 4, 21, 26, 31, 32, 34, 36, 47, 51, 54, 56, 62, 77, 93, 101, 104, 105, 117, 119, 135, 140, 177, 178, 308
Kenya African Union, 26, 32, 56, 77, 104
Kenya Polytechnic, 308
Kibisi, 198
Kigezi, 11, 264, 266
Kigozi, 84
Kirya, 86, 177, 269, 297
Kisoko Junior School, 308
Kitaka Gawera, 165
Kitgum, 16, 217, 218, 221, 223, 224, 225, 228, 236, 237

Kitgum Militia, 16
Korea, 172
Kumi, 226, 228
Kununka, 265, 268, 269, 281, 282
Kutesa, 154
Kyabazinga, 279

L

Labour Government, 111
Lakidi, 110
Lancaster Conference, 297
Lango, 16, 23, 25, 26, 30-32, 77, 144, 226, 264, 266, 282
Legislative Council, 6, 24, 26, 27, 30-33, 51, 78, 104, 263, 267, 270-272, 276-281, 283-285, 290
Liberia, 251, 255
Libya, 47, 119, 177, 180
Lincoln's Inn, 174
Lira, 25, 221, 223, 224, 225, 226, 228, 265, 292
London, 2, 10, 13, 14, 27, 32, 38, 45, 46-48, 54, 63, 74, 93, 101, 107, 109, 115, 127, 142, 148, 156, 167, 172-174, 176, 192, 200, 229, 248, 262, 266, 274, 279, 280, 285, 286, 288, 293, 296, 297, 308
London Conference, 47
London GUARDIAN, 29, 56, 156
London Times, 32, 47, 86, 89, 116
Lord Salisbury, 57
lost counties, 48, 99
Lubega, 148
Lubiri, 170, 180
Lubiri barracks, 170
Lubowa, 83, 110, 276
Lukiiko, 30, 35, 36, 97, 98, 99, 101, 102, 263, 264, 271-274, 279-281, 284-290, 292, 293
Lumu, 86
Lusaka, 17
Luwero, 189, 190, 196-198, 201-206, 264

Luwuliza-Kirunda, 151
Luyimbazi-Zake, 83
Lwamafa, 83

M

Madam Christina, 176
Magezi, 86, 152, 276, 278
Makerere University, 9, 23, 25, 104
Malaya, 172
Malcom Rifkind, 234
Malire Barracks, 168
Maluku Bar, 265, 266
Manifesto, 261, 281, 290-293
Manjasi High School, 308
Mao, 114
Marlborough Conference, 297
Martin Lowenkopf, 25
Martyrs, 194
Mau Mau, 31, 77, 104
Maudling, 57
Mbale, 152, 264, 265, 292, 308
Mbarara, 128, 129, 130, 154
McILROY, 182
Mengo, 55, 93-97, 99, 102, 106, 162, 163, 268, 272, 276, 277, 282, 284
Mengo Hill, 93, 95, 106
Michael Kintu, 285
Military Commission, 143, 144
Minister of Education, 27, 83, 109, 127, 269
Moammar al-Gaddafi, 119
Mogadishu Agreement, 139
Mogadishu Treaty, 119, 120
Monrovia, 256
Morocco, 47
Moscow, 45, 109, 274
Moses Ali, 177
Movement for the Struggle of Political Rights, 156
Mowlem, 26
Mozambique, 54, 68, 157, 203, 254
Mpigi, 151, 152, 189, 193, 201
Mubende, 151, 189, 201

Mudende, 176, 177, 178
Muduuma, 183, 185
Mulungushi Club, 17
Musaazi, 264, 265, 266, 267, 273
Museveni, 11, 74, 156-160, 177, 178, 189, 192, 197, 200, 203-213, 215-248
Mustafa, 121, 123
Mwiri, 23, 25

N

Nairobi, 21, 23, 26, 58, 89, 95, 100, 119, 156, 158, 159, 202, 218, 308
Nakazzi, 198
Namirembe, 169, 187
Namugongo, 194, 195, 196
Nathan Karema, 190, 198
National Assembly, 36, 39, 40, 81, 209, 290-292
National Consultative Conference, 16
National Movement, 273
National Resistance Army, 189, 192, 197, 200, 212
National Resistance Movement, 202, 208, 213, 235, 243
Ndugga Musaazi, 266
Nebbi, 228, 273
Neil Smith, 172
New York, 45, 46, 53, 102, 159
Ngobi, 86
Nile, 144, 228, 264, 266, 267
Nilotics, 161
Nkrumah, 23
Nkwanga, 177
Northern Uganda, 16, 23, 129, 217
Nusur Jogojogo, 198
Nyankole, 204
Nyarwanda, 204
Nyole, 297

O

O.A.U, 73
Obote, 1-5, 7-12, 14-21, 23-27, 29, 30, 32-34, 37, 42, 44-48, 50, 52-54, 56-60, 62, 63, 74-80, 84-86, 89-93, 95, 102, 104, 108, 113-117, 119, 126, 142-151, 156-163, 172-174, 176-178, 180, 181, 187-190, 194, 198, 200, 202-204, 207, 209, 212, 233, 235, 250, 255, 269-275, 296, 297, 308
Obwangor, 83
Obyara Anyoti, 16
Ochieng, 3, 85, 86
October 9, 27, 39, 40
Ocwet, 207
Odaka, 83
Ojera, 83
Olcott Deming, 57
Oluoch, 108
Omugabe, 279
Omukama of Bunyoro, 279
Omukama of Toro, 279
ONAMA, 83
Oosting, 164
Opiote, 17
Opobo, 115
Opon-Achak, 195
Owako, 21
Oyite Ojok, 159

P

Pakistani, 36
Pakwach, 228
Palm, 8, 9, 12, 18, 297
Pan African Freedom Movement of East, 28
Paradise Lost, 91
Paris, 183, 274
Paul Ssengendo, 264, 265, 266
Peking, 45, 274
Personal Merit, 8, 243
Peter Otai, 170, 187, 201

Portugal, 45, 51, 68
Posner, 164
Prime Minister, 25, 44
Prof Ali Mazrui, 9
Professor Geoffrey Till, 7
Professor H. Butterfield, 7
Protestant, 25, 168, 169, 190, 220
Public Prosecutions, 166

Q

Queen, 49, 94, 294
Queen Elizabeth II, 294

R

Raymond Ingram, 172
Recovery Programme, 260
Red Cross, 95, 190, 193, 197, 198
Refugees, 5, 100
Rehabilitation and Development Plan, 260
Resty Kegabane, 186
Reuter, 121, 122
Rev. F.B. Welbourn, 55
Rev. Godfrey Bazira, 196
Rev. Sserwada, 196
Rhodesia, 49, 51, 53, 55, 63, 68, 93, 122, 254
Ronald Ngala, 56
Rubaga, 168, 169, 170
Rubongi Primary School, 308
Runchie, 5, 182, 183
Rwanda, 45, 140, 217, 219
Rwot Adwong, 26

S

Sahara, 45
Sam-7, 177
Samia, 297, 298
Samia-gwe, 297
Samson Kiseka, 204
Sandy, 57
SAS, 179

Saudi Arabia, 119, 180
Save Uganda Movement, 16, 21
Saza Chiefs, 99
Scotland Yard, 172
Sebalu, 154
Sebana-Kizito, 152
Second World War, 38, 72
Secretary General, 164, 258, 265, 266, 268, 269, 273, 276, 278
Secretary-General, 97, 99, 102
Seewoogur Ramgoolam, 139
Self-Government, 262, 267, 269, 270, 272, 275, 279, 294
Sempa, 102
Senator Allan Ellender, 57
Senteza Kajubi, 36, 276
Serwano Kulubya, 276
Sese Seko Kuku Ngbendu Wa Za Banga, 8
Seyyid Jamshi Abdullah, 119
Shafique Arrain, 12
Siad Barre, 139
Sibo, 109
Sir Ferdinand Cavendish-Bentinck, 57
Sir Roy Wellensky, 51
Socialist International Information, 69
Soldier of Fortune, 172
Soroti, 226, 292
Southbank University, 308
Southhall College of Technology, 308
Soviet, 104, 274
Standard Vacuum Oil Company, 26
State Research, 129
Sudan, 140, 144, 220, 221, 224, 225
Suez Canal, 121
Sunday Times, 172
Sword of Damocles, 210

T

T.S. Eliot, 7
Tanganyika, 28, 29, 33, 36, 47, 54, 56, 58, 256
Tanzania, 62, 94, 116, 117, 119-122, 124, 126-131, 135, 136, 138-140, 142, 143, 156, 180
Ted Heath, 111
Teso, 226, 264, 266
The New Vision, 223
The Party, 4, 8, 11, 147, 270, 271, 281, 291
Thomas Hammarberge, 164
Thucydides, 140
Timothy Raison, 184, 188
Tito Okello, 202, 203
Tom Mboya, 23, 26
Toro, 264, 279, 294
Tory Party, 111
Turkey, 121, 122, 123
Tutsi, 217, 219

U

Uganda, 1-6, 8, 10-12, 14, 16, 17, 19, 21, 23-34, 36-45, 47, 49-63, 67-71, 74, 77-79, 81, 82, 84, 86, 88-90, 93, 95-98, 101-106, 107-109, 111, 113-117, 119, 121-123, 126-144, 146-151, 153-156, 158-162, 164-167, 169, 172-178, 180-185, 187-190, 194-197, 199, 200, 202, 204, 206-221, 223, 224, 226-243, 246, 248-253, 254-256, 259-264, 266, 267, 269-275, 277-282, 285, 287-291, 293, 294, 296-298, 308
Uganda African Union, 6, 281, 290
Uganda Development Bank, 187
Uganda Freedom Army, 176, 180
Uganda Government, 32, 50, 51, 57, 93, 96-98, 184, 194, 199, 293
Uganda Hereditary Chieftainship Party, 6, 281
Uganda National Congress, 6, 24, 26, 32, 259, 281, 290

Uganda Patriotic Movement, 159, 177, 180
Uganda Peoples Congress, 6, 8, 29, 33, 55, 78, 142, 151, 156, 159, 219, 234, 241, 259, 278, 281, 290
Uganda Peoples Union, 6, 275
Uganda People's Union, 27
Umar Bongo, 139
UN National Human Development, 233
United Arab Republic, 255, 256
United Nations, 43, 45, 52, 56, 71, 95, 97, 102, 104, 156
University of East London, 308
USA, 35, 93, 122, 149, 150

V

Vietnam, 104

W

Wabusana, 197

Waligo, 154, 155
Wanda, 21
Wanume Kibedi, 127
Weekly Topic, 240
West Africa, 68, 123, 256
West Nile, 144, 228, 264, 273
Whitehall, 21
Wild Committee, 24, 27, 273, 274, 275, 276
William Nadiope, 89
William Woolf, 101
World Bank, 183, 235, 238

Y

Yacobo Maloba, 296
Yona Okoth, 187
Yusuf Lule, 172, 177, 200, 276, 277

Z

Zaire, 140, 144, 173, 174, 189, 197
Zambia, 17

Author's Profile

Jack Stevens Alecho-Oita is the author of: African Historical Presence: Reminiscences of Dr A.M. Obote of Uganda.

Profession: Aeronautic Engineer

Life: Born in 1949 in Tororo, Uganda – of Jopadhola parentage, Israel Ochwo Alecho and Besimesi Nyafwono; with 3 brothers and 2 sisters; married Jennifer Nantume Senkatuka; and has 5 children and 2 grandsons.

Studied: Rubongi Primary School – Tororo; Kakungulu Primary School – Mbale; Mulanda Primary School – Tororo; Nabuyoga Primary School – Tororo; Kisoko Junior School – Tororo; Manjasi High School – Tororo; Kenya Polytechnic – Nairobi, Kenya; Southhall College of Technology – London, United Kingdom; University of East London – London, United Kingdom; Southbank University – London, United Kingdom.

Jack Stevens Alecho-Oita is a retired Aeronautic Engineer (AMSLAET) and Social Worker with vast work experiences, widely travelled in the world, and with interest in politics and publishing.

www.ingramcontent.com/pod-product-compliance
Lightning Source LLC
Chambersburg PA
CBHW030103170426
43198CB00009B/471